TEACH III

Enhancing Knowledge, Intelligence and Lifelong Learning

Dr. BCMR

Dedication

To the students who taught me how to teach

Table of contents

CHAPTER 9: PLANNING THE LESSON PLANS 221

CHAPTER 10: TEACHING IN THE LABORATORY 271

CHAPTER 11: EVALUATION METHODS 292

Preface

In the contemporary educational landscape, the imperative to enhance knowledge, intelligence, and lifelong learning resonates more profoundly than ever. This series, encompassing TEACH I, TEACH II, and TEACH III, is designed to empower educators and students alike. TEACH I: Cultivating Persona and Building Characters focuses on identifying and nurturing essential qualities in both teachers and students. TEACH II: Motivating Minds and Enhancing Productivity emphasizes the importance of motivation, resilience, and intellectual growth in driving development. Finally, TEACH III: Enhancing Knowledge, Intelligence, and Lifelong Learning delves into strategies for fostering a love of learning and equipping individuals with the skills needed for lifelong success. Together, these volumes provide a comprehensive framework for transformative education.

"TEACH III: Enhancing Knowledge, Intelligence, and Lifelong Learning" is crafted not merely as a guide for educators but as a thoughtful exploration of the intricate dynamics of teaching and learning in a rapidly evolving world. It seeks to illuminate the pathways that empower both educators and students to thrive within the complexities of modern education.

Education is inherently paradoxical, encompassing the dual imperatives of conformity and liberty. Conformity is vital for fostering productivity and establishing a structured environment that lays the groundwork for foundational skills. Yet, liberty—the freedom to explore, question, and innovate—is essential for nurturing creativity and critical thinking. In this book, I grapple with the challenge of balancing these seemingly opposing forces, offering insights into how educators can create classrooms that honor both the need for structure and the importance of creative freedom.

Drawing from my experiences and reflections, I have endeavored to weave together philosophical inquiries, psychological principles, and practical strategies to guide educators in their quest to cultivate independent, lifelong learners. The notion of "teaching intelligence" extends beyond mere knowledge transmission; it embodies the commitment to nurturing students' abilities to think critically, engage deeply with content, and embrace challenges as opportunities for growth and self-discovery.

The chapters of "TEACH III" invite educators to reflect on their pedagogical practices, encouraging them to prioritize inquiry, exploration, and meaningful dialogue in the classroom. By fostering a culture of curiosity and intellectual engagement, we can create learning environments that not only value knowledge but also inspire a genuine love for the process of learning itself. This book advocates for a transformative shift in education—a move toward empowering students to take ownership of their learning journeys and develop skills that will serve them well beyond the confines of formal education.

As educators, we hold the profound responsibility of shaping the minds and hearts of the next generation. We possess the ability to ignite passion, cultivate curiosity, and instill a lifelong love of learning. "TEACH III" serves as both an invitation and a challenge to embrace this responsibility fully. It encourages us to reflect on the impact we have on our students' lives and to recognize the potential we possess to facilitate meaningful change in their educational experiences.

In embarking on this journey, I encourage you to engage with the content of this book as a living document—one that invites reflection, adaptation, and growth. May it inspire you to rethink traditional approaches to teaching, embrace innovative strategies, and commit to fostering a dynamic, engaging, and supportive learning environment. Together, let us strive to enhance knowledge, intelligence, and lifelong learning—transforming the educational landscape for generations to come.

As you navigate the pages of "TEACH III," may you find not only practical insights but also inspiration to embrace the art and science of teaching, ultimately shaping a brighter future for your students and the communities they will impact.

Author name: Dr. BCMR (Bhaskar Chandra Mohan Ramisetty)
Date: October, 2024.

Disclaimer

In the creation of this book, I utilized artificial intelligence tools for proofreading, refining, and improving the clarity and flow of the content. The use of AI was intended to enhance readability and coherence, without altering the integrity of the work. All interpretations, perspectives, and reflections are grounded in my personal experience and understanding. **This whole book was edited using ChatGPT.**

Author name: Dr. BCMR (Bhaskar Chandra Mohan Ramisetty)
Date: October, 2024.

Chapter 1: The Vision of a Socially Useful and Productive Citizen

Vision:

"To create Socially Useful and Productive Citizens (SUPC)"

The ultimate goal of education should be to create Socially Useful and Productive Citizens (SUPC) who contribute meaningfully to their communities and the world at large. This begins with instilling a sense of responsibility, empathy, and collaboration in students, equipping them with academic knowledge, a moral compass, and the practical skills necessary to navigate life. Socially useful citizens are those who recognize the interconnectedness of society and the impact of their actions on others. They are problem-solvers, innovators, and compassionate leaders working for the greater good.

To achieve this, educators must go beyond rote learning, fostering critical thinking, creativity, and emotional intelligence in their students. Encouraging active participation in community service, teamwork, and ethical decision-making helps students understand the importance of contributing positively to society. They should be taught to value diversity, fairness, and inclusivity, becoming adaptable individuals who can work towards solving social, environmental, and economic challenges.

In shaping productive citizens, education empowers students with the tools to continuously learn and grow, enabling them to be agents of change. By creating such individuals, we build a future where societies thrive on cooperation, compassion, and shared progress, ultimately advancing humanity.

This book series—TEACH I, TEACH II, and TEACH III (this book)—is dedicated to understanding the diverse dimensions of the modern educational landscape, particularly from the perspective of developing nations, underprivileged students and substandard institutions. These books empower teachers with invaluable skills within their hands to maximize the learning outcomes and teacher's impact.

TEACH I: Cultivating Persona and Building Characters explores the educational setup through evolutionary, psychological, and philosophical lenses, considering the diversity of students, teachers, and classrooms. It encourages self-reflection on the role of the teacher while also exploring new possibilities in education. *TEACH I* is more about developing a teacher's personality. *TEACH II: Motivating Minds and Cultivating Productivity* centers on the personality development of students, emphasizing the importance of motivation, integrity, and productivity and how educators could impart these personality traits.

In this book, *TEACH III: Enhancing Knowledge, Intelligence, and Lifelong Learning*, the focus shifts to training the mind with cognitive skills, fostering a deep enthusiasm for lifelong learning, and preparing students to acquire knowledge and intelligence independently throughout their lives. A few redundancies will be encountered in this book due to contextual needs and interconnected topics.

Philosophy and Psychology in Educational Institutions

As emphasized in the previous books, *TEACH I* and *TEACH II*, philosophy and psychology are the most important pillars of a true education. I believe an institution cannot truly be considered an educational establishment if it lacks departments dedicated to philosophy and psychology. Education is fundamentally incomplete without these essential disciplines. Unfortunately, we are witnessing the gradual disappearance of these departments as the focus increasingly shifts toward more mechanistic outcomes. In ancient times, universities prioritized philosophy, acknowledging its foundational role in learning. No educational institution should exist without a philosophy and psychology department because these subjects are not merely ancillary; they are at the heart of education itself. Philosophy helps articulate the nature and purpose of education, while psychology sheds light on the methods and processes employed to deliver that education. The intricate interplay between these two fields establishes a solid foundation for a holistic educational experience, one that fosters intellectual growth as well as personal and social development.

The Nature of Education: Philosophy

Philosophy serves as the cornerstone of any educational institution. It prompts critical inquiry into fundamental questions regarding knowledge, existence, ethics, and the very purpose of education itself. What is the nature of knowledge? What role should an educator play? How can students best be educated? These are not mere rhetorical questions; they are essential for understanding the fabric of education. Engaging in philosophical discourse enables both educators and students to reflect on their beliefs, values, and assumptions. This reflective practice cultivates a culture of inquiry that is crucial for developing critical thinking skills.

Moreover, philosophy encourages dialogue about the ethical dimensions of education. In an era marked by rapid technological advancements, ethical considerations surrounding data privacy, equity, and access to education have become paramount. The philosophical framework provides essential tools for critically assessing these ethical dilemmas, thereby fostering responsible citizenship among students. By embedding philosophical inquiry into the curriculum, institutions can help cultivate a generation of thoughtful individuals equipped to navigate complex moral landscapes.

The Way of Education: Psychology

While philosophy provides the foundational principles, psychology offers valuable insights into the cognitive, emotional, and social dimensions of learning. Understanding how students learn, what motivates them, and how they develop is essential for effective teaching. Psychology enlightens educators about the diverse learning styles and needs of students, enabling differentiated instruction that accommodates individual differences. This is particularly relevant in today's diverse classrooms, where students hail from various cultural and socio-economic backgrounds.

Furthermore, psychology illuminates the emotional aspects of learning. Emotional intelligence, resilience, and mental health are crucial components of a successful educational experience. An educational institution that integrates psychology into its framework is better equipped to support the holistic well-being of its students. By recognizing the interplay between emotional and cognitive development, educators can cultivate a supportive environment that fosters both academic success and personal growth.

Interconnectedness of Philosophy, Psychology and Pedagogy

The relationship between philosophy and psychology is not one of separation; rather, it forms an interwoven tapestry that enriches the educational experience. In my view, all departments should be connected with the departments of philosophy and psychology. For instance, discussions on pedagogical approaches inherently draw upon philosophical perspectives. The choice between constructivist and traditional teaching methods, for example, is rooted in differing philosophical views about the nature of knowledge and the role of the learner.

Moreover, psychology contributes to philosophical inquiries by providing empirical evidence that informs our understanding of human behavior and cognition. Philosophical debates about free will and determinism, for example, resonate in psychological research on decision-making processes and behavioral influences. Fostering dialogue between these disciplines is essential for a comprehensive understanding of education.

Pedagogy, as the art and science of education, is intricately linked with both philosophy and psychology. Philosophy defines the purpose, values, and ethical foundations of education, addressing questions about what should be taught and the role of the teacher. Psychology offers practical insights into how students learn, think, and develop emotionally and cognitively. By combining philosophical inquiry with psychological understanding, pedagogy creates a holistic educational approach. This approach encourages not only knowledge acquisition but also the development of critical thinking, emotional intelligence, and personal growth. Pedagogy thus serves as a bridge, applying both philosophical and psychological principles to foster well-rounded, intellectually capable learners.

Freedom and Encouragement for Dialogue

To create an enriching educational environment, institutions must promote freedom and encourage dialogue, discussion, and debate at philosophical levels. This exchange should not be confined to faculty; it must also extend to students. Encouraging students to engage in philosophical discussions cultivates critical thinking, self-reflection, and a deeper understanding of their own beliefs. Students learn to articulate their thoughts, consider alternative perspectives, and engage respectfully with differing viewpoints.

Furthermore, institutional policies should reflect a commitment to interdisciplinary collaboration. Philosophy and psychology departments must actively engage with other academic disciplines, fostering a culture of inquiry that transcends traditional boundaries. This engagement can manifest in various forms, such as interdisciplinary courses, joint seminars, or collaborative research projects. Such initiatives not only enrich the educational experience but also embody the interconnected nature of knowledge in our increasingly complex world.

Consequences of Exclusion

Excluding philosophy and psychology from educational institutions can lead to serious repercussions. Without a philosophical foundation, education risks becoming a mechanistic process focused solely on rote memorization and standardized testing. As a result, students may emerge from the educational system equipped with knowledge but lacking critical thinking skills, ethical grounding, and the ability to engage in meaningful discourse.

Similarly, neglecting psychology can result in a failure to address the diverse needs of students. Educational practices may become rigid and unresponsive, ignoring the emotional and social dimensions of learning. Consequently, students may feel alienated, disengaged, or unsupported in their educational journeys.

A Vision for the Future

Incorporating departments of philosophy and psychology into educational institutions is essential for the holistic development of students. Philosophy provides a conceptual framework for understanding the deeper purpose of education, while psychology offers critical insights into the processes of learning and human behavior. These disciplines, deeply intertwined, enhance the educational experience by nurturing critical thinking, ethical reasoning, and emotional well-being.

Institutions must foster an environment that encourages open dialogue across disciplinary boundaries, cultivating not only intellectual growth but also emotional and ethical resilience. Through such interdisciplinary engagement, students become capable of navigating life's complexities with wisdom, empathy, and fortitude. Therefore, the integration of philosophy and psychology stands as a cornerstone for meaningful education in an evolving world where developing thinkers, innovators, and compassionate individuals is a necessity, not an option.

To realize this vision, institutions should embed these subjects into their curricula, promote interdisciplinary collaboration, and create spaces for thoughtful dialogue. Additionally, providing psychological support services and mentorship underscores the value of these principles in everyday life. Only then can education fulfill its true purpose: to empower individuals to think critically, act ethically, and contribute meaningfully to society.

The Path of Immediate Reward and Least Work

Humans, by nature, tend to operate along the shortest route to reward or gratification. This inclination can be traced back to an evolutionary survival mechanism: seeking immediate rewards provided essential resources—food, safety, and social connections—that were vital for survival. Psychologically, our brains are wired to respond favorably to immediate rewards through a complex interplay of neurotransmitters, primarily dopamine. When we engage in behaviors that lead to gratification, dopamine is released, reinforcing those behaviors and creating a positive feedback loop. Consequently, if an easier path exists to achieve a desired outcome, individuals often gravitate toward it.

The Shortest Route to Gratification

Similar to the "path of least resistance," the path of least work suggests that when presented with multiple options, individuals naturally select the one requiring the least effort. Take, for example, studying for an exam. A student might choose to skim through their notes or read summaries online instead of engaging in comprehensive study sessions that demand deeper cognitive effort. The immediate reward of feeling prepared is often more appealing when achieved with less effort, even if it compromises long-term understanding and retention of knowledge. This behavior exemplifies the neurological wiring of the brain, where the anticipation of rewards frequently overshadows the benefits of delayed gratification.

The Trade-off of Short-term vs. Long-term Gratification

The structure of modern civilization challenges this instinctual tendency. While our natural inclination is toward immediate rewards, much of what we undertake today is aimed at achieving long-term goals. For instance, students spend 16 to 20 years in formal education not merely for immediate satisfaction but to secure better futures. Similarly, adults often endure long work hours over decades to provide for their families and ensure a comfortable retirement. This paradox creates a complex tension between immediate gratification and long-term reward, necessitating a shift in mindset and behavior.

The neurological underpinnings of this conflict reside in the concept of temporal discounting, which posits that the perceived value of future rewards diminishes over time. Research suggests that the farther away a reward is, the less likely individuals are to feel motivated by it. People tend to prefer smaller, immediate rewards over larger and delayed ones, which significantly influences decision-making processes across various contexts, including education and career choices.

The Challenge of Motivation

Motivation is a spectrum of obsession and desperation, which are two extremes. The challenge lies in motivating individuals to engage in activities that may not yield immediate rewards yet are vital for long-term success. The sheer breadth, depth, and complexity of knowledge required in modern society can feel overwhelming. For instance, think about a medical student who must memorize an extensive array of information and apply that knowledge in clinical settings. The immediate gratification of passing an exam is overshadowed by the extensive preparation required, often leading to feelings of burnout and discouragement.

The ability to prioritize long-term goals over short-term satisfaction significantly impacts personal development. Research has shown that children trained to delay gratification tend to perform better academically and display improved social skills as they grow.

Training the Mind for Long-term Gratification

While the human brain is naturally inclined toward immediate rewards, it can adapt to embracing longer-term goals. This adaptability can be fostered through a systematic approach to education and personal development. Employing techniques such as goal-setting, mindfulness, and cognitive restructuring can help individuals reframe their perception of effort and reward.

Goal-setting is a practical tool for navigating the complexities of long-term objectives. By breaking larger goals into smaller, manageable tasks, individuals can create a sense of immediate accomplishment, fueling their motivation to continue working toward their ultimate aims. For example, a graduate student tackling a thesis can establish daily writing targets that foster a sense of progress rather than feeling overwhelmed by the enormity of the entire project.

Cognitive restructuring involves altering the way we perceive challenges and rewards. For instance, by viewing studying not as a chore but as an opportunity for personal growth and development, one can shift motivation from a negative experience to a positive one.

The Role of Education and Training

The balance between immediate gratification and long-term rewards is a critical aspect of modern education. Educators play a fundamental role in creating environments that promote perseverance and dedication. By incorporating strategies that underscore the importance of long-term goals—such as project-based learning, collaborative tasks, and reflective practices—teachers can assist students in recognizing the true value of their efforts.

Incorporating real-life applications into learning can significantly boost motivation. For instance, a teacher might illustrate the importance of scientific research by discussing its impact on societal advancement, thereby creating a meaningful connection between academic efforts and tangible outcomes. This relevance has the potential to spark students' intrinsic motivation, encouraging them to commit time and energy to their education in pursuit of future rewards.

The Challenges of Studying STEM

I dreaded mathematics as a school student. Other than geometry, most of the math just flew over my head. I progressively steered away from math by choosing biology. Still, math continued to bother me in the form of calculations in the laboratory and biostatistics. I manage the level of math required for my profession. However, when it comes to complex equations or new symbols beyond +, -, ×, ÷, %, (,), and =, I am immediately lost. I wish I had been better at math as a school student, but I cannot go back and learn it all now. Therefore, stemming from this inferiority, I have an instant fear and instinctual respect for math teachers and students! I teach Molecular Biology, Genetic Engineering, and Stem Cell Biology to students pursuing bioengineering and biotechnology. In the back of my mind, the feeling of inferiority lingers, knowing that these are the students who are proficient in the math I fear and respect.
Studying Science, Technology, Engineering, and Mathematics (STEM) disciplines often presents unique challenges compared to other academic fields. These difficulties arise from various psychological, neurological, and trainability factors, all of which influence how students engage with the complex concepts and problem-solving processes inherent to STEM learning.

Most knowledge is conveyed through words or numbers—language and mathematics, are often intertwined. Words provide a means of describing knowledge, while numbers offer dimensions to that knowledge. Modern-day intelligence, therefore, often involves the manipulative use of words and numbers. Abstract numbers are used to describe and predict the world around us. Mathematics serves as the language of data and change, guiding our understanding of the mechanisms of the universe. However, not everyone can instantly grasp its abstract nature. It takes time, training, and effort to develop the necessary skills to think in these terms.

In STEM fields, subjectivity has no place. One must not only know and understand the material but also reproduce it exactly as it is intended. This demands significant mental conformity—it is what it is, not what one prefers it to be. In this realm, there is often a gap between what can be seen and what must be believed. Understanding complex concepts in science and mathematics requires the discipline to trust the frameworks provided, even when immediate comprehension eludes us. It is this rigorous and objective approach that defines the intellectual rigor of STEM.

The significant psychological challenge in STEM education is the cognitive load that these subjects impose. The students have to learn the whole legacy of intelligence since the origins of humans. We have to learn specific vocabulary, rules, principles, theories, and so many other facts. Often, one has to work with all these in imagination and numbers. In STEM fields, students are frequently required to integrate abstract concepts, mathematical reasoning, and complex problem-solving strategies. This demanding combination can easily overwhelm their cognitive resources. As a result, students may experience feelings of frustration, anxiety, and a lack of self-efficacy, particularly when grappling with intricate theories and applications.

Hierarchical cognitive emergence in STEM

Hierarchical cognitive emergence is a critical concept in STEM education, representing the layered, stepwise development of cognitive skills required to master complex subjects within science, technology, engineering, and mathematics. This process is distinctly structured and sequential, meaning that knowledge must be acquired in a specific order, where foundational concepts are learned before progressing to more advanced, abstract thinking. This cognitive progression is essential because it builds a framework upon which increasingly complex information and reasoning skills are anchored, allowing learners to solve problems and innovate effectively.

This hierarchy differs markedly from many other fields, where learning paths are often more flexible and do not require such stringent adherence to a sequence. In STEM, however, each level of understanding builds directly on previous knowledge, creating a unique challenge for both educators and students. Educators are tasked with constructing curricula that support this structured development, while students must engage in the patient, disciplined work of mastering each level before moving on.

The Building Blocks of Hierarchical Cognitive Emergence

In STEM, hierarchical cognitive emergence starts with basic knowledge acquisition and proceeds through more complex stages of comprehension, application, analysis, synthesis, and, ultimately, evaluation. Each stage introduces new cognitive challenges and requires a deeper integration of knowledge and skills. For instance, a student studying mathematics may begin with arithmetic, which forms the basis for algebraic thinking. Without a solid grounding in arithmetic, understanding algebra becomes significantly more difficult. Similarly, mastering algebra is essential for calculus, which involves abstract concepts and higher-order operations.

This cumulative approach is vital in all areas of STEM. In biology, for example, a student needs to understand cellular structures before they can grasp genetics and biochemistry, which require knowledge of how molecular processes influence cellular functions. In physics, understanding the basic principles of motion and force is necessary before tackling complex topics like thermodynamics or quantum mechanics. This hierarchy enforces a methodical and disciplined approach to learning, as each new concept relies on and integrates previous knowledge, forming a web of understanding that allows for sophisticated problem-solving.

The Necessity of Sequential Learning in STEM

Sequential learning in STEM is essential because of the logical structure of the knowledge in these fields. Concepts are often interdependent; a comprehensive understanding of a single topic may require mastery over multiple related concepts. For example, engineering requires knowledge of mathematics, physics, and materials science. Each of these subjects has its own internal hierarchy, but together, they converge to enable problem-solving in engineering contexts. A student cannot design a bridge, for example, without an understanding of forces (physics), materials' tensile strength (materials science), and structural calculations (mathematics).

The process is more than a simple accumulation of facts—it is an intellectual journey that shapes how students think, analyze, and apply knowledge. Sequential learning allows students to gradually increase the complexity of their cognitive abilities, which is vital for their eventual ability to handle STEM's inherent challenges. This progressive learning also builds the mental resilience required to tackle difficult concepts as students become accustomed to disciplined study and intellectual rigor.

Hierarchical Cognitive Emergence and Skills Development

As students advance through the hierarchical structure of STEM knowledge, they are not only learning facts but also developing critical cognitive skills that are essential for innovation and advanced reasoning. These include:

1. Problem-Solving: STEM fields are, by nature, focused on solving real-world problems. The hierarchical learning model teaches students to break down complex problems into manageable parts, a skill that is invaluable both within and outside of academic contexts.

2. Analytical Reasoning: Each stage in the hierarchy of knowledge in STEM builds on the last, requiring students to synthesize information from multiple levels of understanding. This integration promotes strong analytical skills, enabling students to assess situations, identify relevant information, and develop logical solutions.

3. Logical Deduction: The cumulative nature of STEM learning fosters the ability to make logical connections. A student who understands basic chemistry concepts will, for instance, be able to deduce the outcomes of reactions, predict molecular behaviors, and apply this understanding in various scientific and practical contexts.

4. Abstract Thinking: Higher levels in the cognitive hierarchy require abstract reasoning, a skill that is highly emphasized in subjects like mathematics and physics. Abstract thinking allows students to conceptualize beyond the tangible, which is critical for theoretical research and innovation.

5. Creativity within Structure: Though often overlooked, STEM also fosters creativity, albeit within a structured environment. Creativity emerges as students acquire the tools to explore new concepts, test hypotheses, and innovate within the constraints of logical frameworks.

These skills are developed through consistent engagement with the subject matter, and each layer of knowledge reinforces the last, producing a progressively more robust cognitive framework.

Comparing Hierarchical Cognitive Emergence in STEM with Other Fields

While STEM's hierarchical structure is well-defined, other fields, such as the humanities or social sciences, often allow for greater flexibility in the learning process. In literature, for instance, a student may analyze complex texts without needing to have mastered all foundational texts beforehand. Critical thinking and interpretation in such fields can often begin at more advanced levels, with students drawing on personal insights, cultural knowledge, or emotional understanding.

The hierarchical nature of STEM learning presents unique challenges. The constant requirement for sequential mastery can feel overwhelming, especially for students unaccustomed to this level of rigor. Unlike fields where personal interpretation is valued, STEM disciplines demand precision, leaving little room for subjective perspectives. This structure requires students to engage in extensive rote learning, practice, and problem-solving, often leading to cognitive fatigue.

Hierarchical Cognitive Emergence: Implications for Teaching in STEM

Educators have a significant role in facilitating students' journey through the cognitive hierarchy. Effective teaching strategies must be designed to respect the sequential nature of learning in STEM while also encouraging intellectual curiosity and creativity. Here are some approaches that educators can take:

1. Building Strong Foundations: In the early stages, teachers should focus on ensuring that students thoroughly understand foundational concepts, as these will serve as the building blocks for all future learning. This may involve repeated practice, formative assessments, and revisiting key ideas to reinforce understanding.

2. Gradual Increase in Complexity: Teachers should gradually introduce more complex concepts, helping students make connections between different levels of knowledge. Scaffolding assignments that progressively build on each other can help students navigate this learning hierarchy without feeling overwhelmed.

3. Encouraging Critical Thinking and Synthesis: While STEM learning often emphasizes rote learning initially, teachers should foster opportunities for critical thinking as students progress. Encouraging students to synthesize information from different domains and apply it creatively can enhance their understanding and engagement.

4. Fostering Resilience and Intellectual Discipline: Teachers can help students develop resilience by normalizing the challenges associated with STEM learning. By acknowledging the difficulty of mastering these subjects and celebrating incremental achievements, educators can help students build confidence and perseverance.

5. Incorporating Collaborative Learning: Working in groups allows students to learn from one another and approach problems from multiple perspectives. This approach can alleviate some of the psychological stress associated with STEM's hierarchical structure, as students can pool their collective knowledge to overcome obstacles.

Neurological Considerations

From a neurological perspective, the way the brain processes mathematical and scientific concepts differs significantly from its processing of language-based or artistic subjects. Research indicates that engaging with STEM content activates specific brain regions associated with analytical thinking and problem-solving, such as the prefrontal cortex. Challenges arise when students struggle to activate these areas effectively. This can lead to a phenomenon known as "math anxiety," which I experience very well!

Math anxiety interferes with working memory and negatively impacts test results because the stress response triggered by anxiety can disrupt cognitive functions. In contrast, subjects that do not heavily rely on quantitative reasoning tend to evoke fewer neurological stress responses. This allows students to focus more effectively on the material without experiencing the cognitive overload that often accompanies STEM disciplines.

STEM: No Shortcuts, Just Steady Growth

While STEM disciplines can be incredibly rewarding and lead to lucrative career paths, the initial hurdles may deter students who struggle with the psychological and neurological demands of these fields. **The fundamental challenge in STEM education lies in its demand for the gradual acquisition of knowledge and skills across multiple disciplines, starting from early childhood.** There are no shortcuts in this process; every individual must begin from a foundational level. Once a gap in learning emerges, it becomes increasingly difficult to bridge, and catching up often feels overwhelming.

For instance, consider a student who struggles with foundational mathematics during their early years. As STEM subjects become more complex, especially in fields like engineering or physics, the lack of mathematical fluency hinders progress. Concepts in calculus, for example, build directly on earlier knowledge of algebra and geometry. Without a solid grasp of these basics, the student faces significant barriers to understanding advanced topics. This cumulative nature of STEM subjects means that falling behind early creates a compounding effect, making it increasingly difficult to regain lost ground.

Trainability plays a crucial role in shaping how students approach STEM subjects. The skills required in these fields—such as critical thinking, analytical reasoning, and quantitative literacy—are often more challenging to develop than those needed in many other disciplines. While trainability can enhance students' abilities over time, the initial steep learning curve in STEM can be discouraging. However, with sufficient motivation and a high degree of trainability, one can effectively grasp STEM disciplines.

The Problems of the Institution

The best educational programs and models are well-known and widely adopted, yet learning outcomes can vary significantly from one institution to another. Only a select few institutions manage to achieve the ideal outcomes that these models promise. Most underperforming schools, despite their good intentions, face several key challenges. The quality of students, often influenced more by external pressures than by intrinsic motivation, plays a significant role in this struggle. Similarly, the quality of teachers is crucial; without skilled and passionate educators, even the most effective curriculum falls short. Infrastructure limitations also hinder the learning environment, while the gap between planning and implementation remains a major obstacle in the pursuit of true educational excellence.

No plan is good unless it is well implemented.

The Teacher Problem

Two major challenges persist: underprepared or unmotivated students and teachers. When students lack proper preparation or motivation, and teachers are either insufficiently trained or disengaged, the entire learning process suffers. This weak foundation impacts the educational system, leading to suboptimal outcomes and stifling the potential for genuine intellectual growth. When I began teaching, I had no formal training for the first two years. I had never studied any course or program in education. It is a common and unfortunate assumption that anyone can teach. Surprisingly, some individuals manage to succeed despite a lack of training. They must be natural! It wasn't until I started my teaching career at SASTRA Deemed University that I received my first real professional training, earning a certification in "High Impact Teaching Skills" through a program conducted by Wipro Mission 10X and Dale Carnegie Training in 2010. This experience marked a pivotal moment in my development as an educator, where I learned about lesson planning, Bloom's taxonomy, and other essential aspects of teaching. From that initiation, my process of improvisation began and continues to this day. I believe every teacher should receive some form of training, mentoring, and initiation early in their career. Countless teaching resources are available in print and video formats, yet ultimately, the key to improvement lies in the teacher's motivation to evolve and refine their craft. This series of books is dedicated to that very pursuit, focusing on enhancing teaching through philosophical and psychological foundations. It aims to inspire young educators to not just absorb methods and techniques but to internalize the deeper purpose of education, fostering growth in both themselves and their students.

The Student Problem

The training of the mind is indeed a continuous and intricate process, beginning from birth and evolving with every experience. The mind takes shape as it navigates through various stages of life, influenced by both external factors and internal needs. While the brain is naturally equipped with basic cognitive skills to respond to immediate situations—where thought and action yield quick results—human beings have advanced far beyond this simplicity. In modern life, the gap between thought, action, and outcome is often extended. We read, learn, and observe today, yet the actions we take might only materialize next week, with results that may not become evident until months or even years later. **This embodies the true essence of "the training of the mind"—to cultivate the ability to think deeply, plan long-term, and execute actions with patience.** Such foresight and capacity for delayed gratification are not instinctive; they require years of disciplined mental training. This process shapes our cognitive abilities, sharpening our capacity to engage in complex problem-solving, strategic planning, and profound reflection. This mental training instills in us the strength to think far beyond immediate needs and short-term results, guiding us toward richer intellectual and personal growth.

Undertraining in Prior Educational Programs

Most formal education occurs at the intersection where the obligation to teach meets the obligation to learn. However, not every educational setting progresses at the intended pace, nor does it consistently achieve the desired quantity and quality of learning outcomes. Especially in the rural setting, not all students have access to quality schools, supportive parenting, mentors, or adequate resources. As a result, many students enter college with gaps in their training or lack the motivation necessary for higher-level learning, which poses significant challenges to their educational journey and overall development. Undertraining in earlier educational programs is a pervasive issue that can have far-reaching consequences, particularly in higher education. I teach both undergraduate and postgraduate students; I encounter this challenge regularly. Each cohort of students brings a remarkable diversity in motivation, cognitive skills, and prerequisite knowledge. While some degree of heterogeneity is expected, the disparity in foundational knowledge among students is often alarmingly wide. In this context, we focus primarily on cognitive skills, specifically the fundamental knowledge that should have been acquired in previous schooling but has not been fully developed.

Underperforming students typically fall short either in their communication skills or their knowledge base—or, in many cases, both. This deficit often stems from inadequate teaching methods or flawed learning environments in their earlier educational experiences. Compounding the problem, many of these students have faced poorly designed or poorly implemented assessments that fail to accurately measure their understanding or skills. ***Often, the whole education system fails because of the teachers' complacent or sympathetic approach to implementing the assessment.*** This creates a vicious cycle: students who lack the necessary foundational knowledge slip through the huge cracks of faulty assessments and arrive at higher education institutions ill-prepared for the rigors of advanced study. For these students, the transition can be overwhelming, and they begin to struggle significantly in both comprehension and application.

This gap in preparation not only affects the students themselves but also places teachers in a difficult position. Educators often face a moral and pedagogical dilemma: should they lower the rigor of their assessments to accommodate underprepared students, or should they push these students toward higher expectations, knowing they may lack the foundational skills needed for success? The temptation to adopt a humanistic approach—where teachers tone down the assessments or assist students in passing—is strong. However, this approach ultimately undermines the very essence of education. It leads to the production of graduates who are not equipped with the necessary skills and knowledge to function effectively in their fields. Thus, the undertraining of students in earlier stages of education becomes not just a student issue but an institutional failure that devalues the entire educational process.

The real solution lies in strengthening the bridge between prior educational levels and higher education, ensuring that both teaching and assessment are aligned with the desired outcomes. This would involve more stringent entry requirements, targeted remedial programs, and a focus on building both cognitive and communication skills before students move to advanced levels. Failing to address this foundational issue risks perpetuating a system that graduates students who are not fully prepared for the demands of their careers or further academic pursuits. We cannot and should not give up on these undertrained students.

Effective Measures to Empower Undertrained Students.

Recognizing, acknowledging, and addressing students' lack of prerequisite knowledge and cognitive skills can often drain my enthusiasm. It is disheartening to watch them struggle with the material while hesitating to ask for help, leaving me to wonder at times if they truly care. No matter how much optimism and energy we, as educators, bring to the classroom, we face a persistent dilemma: should we teach effectively to a select few or deliver superficial understanding to the entire group? Having encountered both scenarios, I believe you would agree that neither outcome is genuinely satisfying. Addressing the issue of underprepared students in higher education demands a compassionate yet principled approach—one that bridges gaps in foundational knowledge, communication skills, and cognitive abilities without compromising academic standards or diluting the essence of education.

Below are five key measures that could be implemented to ethically support undertrained students while preserving educational rigor and fairness.

1. Implementing Diagnostic Assessments for Early Identification

One of the most ethical and practical solutions is to administer comprehensive diagnostic assessments at the beginning of a course or program. These assessments would identify the specific areas where students lack prerequisite knowledge or skills. By doing this, educators can develop tailored remedial plans for individual students rather than treating the entire cohort uniformly. The results from these assessments would provide valuable insights into each student's readiness and pinpoint where additional support is necessary. Diagnostic assessments not only benefit the teacher but also give students a clearer understanding of their own learning needs, thus fostering self-awareness and accountability.

2. Offering Bridge Programs or Remedial Courses

Ethically, it is essential to provide structured and targeted support to undertrained students. Bridge programs or remedial courses that focus on reinforcing foundational knowledge and skills present an effective measure. These courses could be conducted before or in parallel with the start of the main academic program, ensuring no stigma is attached to participation. By dedicating resources to these programs, institutions can equip students with the basic cognitive skills needed to succeed in their advanced studies. Such initiatives reinforce the educational mission without lowering academic expectations for regular coursework.

3. Personalized Mentorship and Tutoring

One of the most humane and ethical ways to support undertrained students is through personalized mentorship and tutoring. These students benefit greatly from one-on-one guidance that specifically addresses their unique struggles. By pairing students with mentors—who may be more experienced students or faculty members—we foster a culture of peer support while also offering the personalized attention they need. Tutoring services that focus on both cognitive skills, such as comprehension and critical thinking, and personality development, including confidence and communication, provide a more holistic intervention. This approach enables students to bridge gaps more effectively and sustainably.

4. Reforming Assessment Methods to Promote Learning

Revisiting assessment methods is crucial in addressing the needs of undertrained students without compromising learning outcomes. Ethical education demands assessments that not only test recall or basic understanding but also encourage deeper learning. Incorporating formative assessments that focus on continuous feedback rather than high-stakes summative assessments provides students with opportunities to learn from their mistakes. This method reduces anxiety and allows students to gradually improve without the pressure of a single exam determining their fate. However, it is vital that the assessments maintain high standards, ensuring that students genuinely acquire the requisite knowledge and skills.

5. Establishing a Growth-Mindset Culture within the Classroom

Perhaps the most ethical approach is to cultivate an environment where students are encouraged to develop a growth mindset. Teachers should emphasize effort, persistence, and improvement rather than innate intelligence. By fostering a culture in which failure is viewed as part of the learning process rather than a mark of incapability, students can gain the confidence to engage more fully with the material. This environment encourages students to take ownership of their learning journey and reduces the stigma associated with seeking help. Additionally, it upholds the principle that every student has the potential to improve with the right support, discipline, and persistence.

An effective strategy for chaperoning

Conformity drives productivity by providing structure and consistency, while liberty fuels creativity by allowing freedom of thought and exploration. Yet, the paradox emerges: to achieve true progress, both must coexist—productivity demands order, but creativity requires freedom. Balancing the two becomes the art of fostering innovation and efficiency together. Chaperoning involves guiding students along the structured path of learning while fostering a sense of freedom, which is challenging for any teacher. The teacher must skillfully "play" with these dynamics, ensuring students feel supported yet unrestrained.

One approach I have consciously adopted is to initially demand conformity and gradually reduce this requirement as the learning progresses, eventually leading to full autonomy. This mirrors the progression of a student's academic journey—primary education is characterized by strict conformity, while postgraduate studies offer more liberty. A teacher could begin with stringency to ensure students have a firm foundation, gradually easing restrictions as they gain confidence, allowing them to spread their wings and eventually fly independently. The same principle can be applied across various levels of education. For a program, conformity may be demanded early and relaxed as students advance, allowing for more freedom. In a single course, this approach can unfold similarly—beginning with structured expectations and progressively loosening them. Even in a single class, starting with clear boundaries and ending with greater liberty encourages both productivity and creativity. This gradual shift helps students develop critical thinking and independence while maintaining the necessary discipline for meaningful learning early on.

Exploiting gratification for increased motivation

Gratification comes through consumption and production.

It is natural for students to feel under-motivated in academic activities that involve a high cognitive load. Some may not have been consistently trained to delay gratification, a skill crucial for academic success. Gratification, a positive feeling we all seek from childhood to adulthood, can be broadly categorized into two types: consumption and production. Consumption involves activities like eating, listening to music, playing, reading stories, or socializing, which offer instant gratification with minimal cognitive effort. On the other hand, production, such as writing a book, composing a poem, increasing knowledge, learning new skills, or achieving good grades, requires effort and is often delayed, yet it is essential for personal advancement. In both cases, comparison with peers can amplify the sense of gratification. Gratification through consumption is easier, less cognitively demanding, and immediate, which is why we naturally gravitate towards it. By contrast, gratification through production demands effort, patience, and persistence, making it less immediately attractive but more rewarding in the long term. In the end, each of us is ultimately valued by our ability to produce and the contributions we make to society. This is why it is essential to train ourselves to find gratification through production rather than relying solely on consumption for satisfaction. Developing the mindset to derive fulfillment from creation, effort, and achievement not only fosters personal growth but also leads to more meaningful and lasting rewards. By learning to appreciate the process of producing something valuable—whether it is knowledge, skills, or tangible outcomes—we build resilience and cultivate a deeper sense of purpose in our lives.

Consumption-Based Gratification in Education

Consumption-based gratification is driven primarily by the dopamine system, which is responsible for the pleasure we derive from immediate rewards, such as praise, tangible rewards, or quick feedback. In the classroom, this form of gratification can manifest through:

- Short-term rewards: Giving students immediate incentives, such as verbal praise, points, or prizes like chocolates or pens, taps into this system. These rewards create a direct connection between task completion and positive feedback, boosting engagement in the moment.
- Gamification: Integrating elements of game design, such as badges or level-ups, where students receive quick rewards for their efforts, capitalizes on this dopamine-driven motivation.
- Instant feedback: Providing prompt feedback on quizzes, assignments, or participation reinforces student effort and promotes the continuation of desirable behaviors.

While consumption-based gratification is effective in motivating students in the short term, it must be used strategically to avoid over-reliance on external rewards. Over time, students may become dependent on these incentives, reducing their intrinsic motivation to learn. Therefore, teachers should combine this approach with strategies that foster long-term engagement. ***The first goal of teaching is to train the students for delayed gratification.***

Personal Advancement-Based Gratification in Education

Personal advancement-based gratification is driven by serotonin and oxytocin, hormones associated with social recognition, belonging, and long-term satisfaction. This form of gratification occurs when students achieve personal or academic goals, gain recognition, or feel a sense of accomplishment within a group setting. In the classroom, it can be fostered through:
- Goal setting and achievement: Encouraging students to set personal goals and giving them opportunities to achieve these goals fosters a sense of accomplishment. When students receive recognition for their progress, whether through praise, grades, or public acknowledgment, they experience the gratification of advancement.
- Group work and collaboration: Assigning collaborative projects where students can succeed as a team taps into oxytocin's role in fostering belonging and connection. Recognizing group achievements can enhance students' motivation to contribute and succeed within the group.
- Long-term recognition: Acknowledging sustained effort or improvement over time—such as giving awards for "most improved" students—promotes a sense of growth and personal advancement. This recognition provides deep satisfaction, especially when students feel their hard work is noticed and valued.

Using Gratification to Induce Productivity

To maximize productivity, teachers should blend short-term gratification with long-term satisfaction. Here are strategies that can help:
1. Balanced Rewards: Use immediate rewards for smaller tasks or initial engagement but gradually shift toward promoting intrinsic

rewards through the satisfaction of mastering complex subjects or overcoming challenges.

2. Recognition of Effort and Progress: Focus on recognizing individual and collective progress rather than just outcomes. This fosters a sense of achievement and personal growth, which sustains motivation.

3. Peer Recognition and Social Learning: Encourage students to recognize and appreciate each other's work. This taps into the social gratification system (serotonin and oxytocin), creating an environment where personal and group advancement feels rewarding.

4. Feedback Loops: Provide both instant feedback (dopamine-based) and long-term feedback on personal growth and learning (serotonin-based), ensuring students feel gratified by their efforts in both the immediate and future contexts.

By strategically combining dopamine-driven short-term gratification with serotonin and oxytocin-driven long-term recognition, teachers can motivate students to engage deeply, persist in their learning, and develop intrinsic motivation that extends beyond the classroom.

Chapter 2: Building Skills: Input, Processing and Output

I like to think of most contemporary education as the learning of facts—encompassing principles and ideas—and the refinement of the methods we use to acquire and apply these facts. However, in a typical academic setting, the practical applications of this knowledge, especially in comparison to real-life or industry situations, are often limited. It is unrealistic to expect that students can be taught every real-life or professional scenario they may face in the future while in college. Instead, we should aim to equip students with the skills necessary to navigate uncertainties and solve problems independently.

To handle problems effectively, it is essential to recognize that each situation presents data that requires interpretation—whether it involves a faulty machine, a buggy algorithm, a failed protocol, or a theoretical dilemma that needs resolution. Identifying the key problem is the primary objective, necessitating a thorough analysis of all available data. This process demands that students possess the ability to study, dissect, and comprehend the issue at hand.

Once they have grasped the nature of the problem, students must then process the information to determine what might be wrong or what adjustments need to be made. The output stage follows, which may involve several iterations of testing and refinement to arrive at an effective solution. These problem-solving skills can be categorized into three essential components: input, processing, and output. By cultivating these skills, students become adept at navigating complex challenges and applying their knowledge in practical contexts.

Input: Critical Observation

The first component of this educational framework is the skill of inputting information, which hinges on critical observation. In an age inundated with information, the ability to discern credible sources and recognize relevant data is paramount. This begins with fostering an environment where students learn to observe not just with their eyes but with their minds and hearts. Encouraging curiosity, prompting questions, and instilling the discipline to seek deeper truths are vital. For instance, a student studying biology should not merely memorize the parts of a cell; they should engage with the intricacies of cellular functions, observe them in real-world contexts, and understand their significance in the broader scope of life sciences.

Critical observation enables students to sift through the noise and identify what truly matters. It transforms information gathering from a mechanical process into an intellectual exercise that lays the groundwork for meaningful learning.

Processing: Critical Thinking

Next, education must prioritize the skills of processing information, prominently through critical thinking. This is where students synthesize the facts they have gathered, analyze their implications, and develop informed opinions. Critical thinking is not merely a skill; it is a mindset that encourages inquiry, skepticism, and open-mindedness. It prompts students to ask, "Why?" and "How?" as they grapple with complex ideas and navigate multifaceted problems.

For example, when studying historical events, students should not only recount dates and facts but also engage in analyzing the causes and consequences of those events. They should evaluate differing perspectives and recognize biases, ultimately forming their own reasoned conclusions. This analytical approach prepares them for the complexities of real-world decision-making, where problems are rarely black and white.

Output: Diverse Forms of Expression

The final dimension of this educational paradigm is the output of knowledge, which can take diverse forms. Education should encourage students to articulate their understanding creatively and effectively. This could manifest in traditional formats, such as essays and presentations, but also in innovative avenues like multimedia projects, debates, and collaborative problem-solving exercises. The emphasis here is on adaptability—the ability to convey ideas in a manner that resonates with different audiences and contexts.

For instance, a student might choose to present their findings on climate change through a visual art piece, a digital campaign, or a formal research paper. By offering various means of expression, educators empower students to harness their unique strengths and foster their creative potential.

I believe that education must be a multifaceted endeavor that emphasizes the learning of facts while honing the skills necessary for their acquisition and application. By instilling critical observation as a means of input, fostering critical thinking for processing information, and encouraging diverse forms of output, we equip students not only to navigate the complexities of their academic pursuits but also to thrive in an ever-evolving world. This holistic approach to education cultivates informed, engaged, and adaptable individuals who are prepared to contribute meaningfully to society.

Skills of Input:

The skills of input in education encompass the abilities and processes involved in acquiring information, knowledge, and experiences. These skills form the foundation upon which further learning and cognitive development are built. Key skills of input include:

1. Active Listening

Active listening involves fully concentrating, understanding, and responding to what is being said. It requires giving undivided attention to the speaker and interpreting both verbal and non-verbal cues. This skill enhances comprehension and retention, allowing students to grasp and process information more effectively.

2. Reading Comprehension (language skills)

Reading comprehension is the ability to understand, interpret, and draw meaning from written text. It involves recognizing vocabulary, understanding context, and critically analyzing the material. Strong reading comprehension skills enable students to absorb knowledge from textbooks, articles, and other resources, forming the basis for deeper learning. Reading is education as it requires motivation and cognitive efforts.

There are those who cannot read but wish to, and there are those who can read but do not. Blessed are those who can read and do read.

3. Note-taking

Note-taking involves recording important information from lectures, discussions, or reading materials in an organized manner. Effective note-taking captures key ideas and concepts while encouraging students to process and summarize information. This skill serves as a valuable reference tool for future study and reinforces learning through active engagement. Notes should be in the form of phrases, doodles and maps, never in full sentences. Revisiting the notes on the same day or the next is important. Students should be encouraged to practice recollection of the entire story upon looking at the phrases or maps.

4. Questioning
The ability to ask relevant and thoughtful questions stimulates deeper exploration and understanding of a subject. Questioning encourages curiosity and clarifies areas of confusion, allowing students to engage more actively in the learning process. It also fosters critical thinking, helping students identify gaps in their knowledge. I believe that all education should start with questions, a lot of them!

5. Focus and Concentration
Focus and concentration involve maintaining sustained attention on a task without distractions. It requires mental discipline and the ability to filter out irrelevant stimuli. Strong concentration enhances learning efficiency, allowing students to absorb information more effectively in shorter periods of time. Focus is an effortful and purposeful habit that is prone to fading unless upheld by discipline.

6. Critical Observation
Observation is the skill of noticing details, patterns, and relationships in data or phenomena. It enables students to make connections between what they learn and the real world. Sharp observational skills are particularly valuable in scientific experiments, problem-solving, and understanding complex systems.

7. Memory Retention
Memory retention refers to the ability to store and recall information over time. It involves both short-term and long-term

memory processes, which are strengthened through active engagement and repetition. Effective retention enables students to build on prior knowledge and apply what they have learned in new contexts.

8. Information Filtering

Information filtering is the process of identifying and selecting relevant information from a vast pool of data. It requires critical thinking and the ability to distinguish between essential facts and extraneous details. This skill is crucial for managing the overwhelming amount of information available in today's digital age.

9. Time Management

Time management involves organizing and prioritizing tasks to make the most efficient use of available time. It requires planning, setting goals, and balancing study sessions with other responsibilities. Effective time management helps students avoid last-minute cramming and fosters a steady, productive learning routine.

10. Digital Literacy

Digital literacy is the ability to effectively use technology to access, evaluate, and engage with information. It encompasses navigating online platforms, using educational software, and critically assessing digital sources. This skill is essential for students in the modern age, where much of learning and research happens online.

Skills of Memorization:

The skills of memorization focus on techniques and strategies for retaining and recalling information effectively. While memorization is just one aspect of learning, it is important for building foundational knowledge and understanding. Key skills of memorization include:

1. Repetition and Practice: Regular repetition and practice help reinforce memory pathways, making it easier to recall information when needed. Techniques such as spaced repetition and active recall can enhance long-term retention.

2. Visualization: Creating mental images or visual representations of information can aid in memorization. Visual learners often benefit from diagrams, charts, mind maps, and other visual aids to organize and remember complex concepts.

3. Association: Making connections between new information and existing knowledge helps in encoding and storing memories. Mnemonic devices, acronyms, and memory hooks are examples of associative techniques that facilitate recall.

4. Chunking: Breaking down large amounts of information into smaller, manageable chunks can improve memory retention. Organizing information into meaningful groups or categories enhances comprehension and recall.

Skills of processing

Processing skills are the ability of the student to process information based on constraints, context, or needs. The efficiency of processing is one of the greatest cognitive skills, including the knowledge base, that humans have developed over millions of years. Each of these skills enables students to process information meaningfully, ensuring not just the acquisition but also the utilization and adaptation of knowledge in diverse contexts.

1. Critical Thinking

Critical thinking is the ability to evaluate information, arguments, and evidence to make reasoned judgments. It involves questioning assumptions, identifying biases, and assessing the reliability of sources. This skill is vital for students to discern between relevant and irrelevant information in the learning process.

2. Problem-Solving

Problem-solving entails identifying a problem, analyzing possible solutions, and selecting the most effective approach. It requires creativity, logic, and persistence to find workable solutions to challenges. Students need this skill to apply theoretical knowledge to practical situations, enhancing real-world learning.

3. Synthesis of Information

Synthesis is the ability to combine different ideas and information into a cohesive whole. It involves drawing connections between diverse concepts to form new insights or perspectives. This skill enables students to integrate knowledge from various disciplines and see the bigger picture in their learning.

4. Application of Knowledge

Application of knowledge refers to using learned concepts and principles in new or unfamiliar situations. It involves transferring theoretical knowledge into practical contexts, such as solving real-world problems. This skill ensures that students can not only understand the material but also utilize it effectively in life.

5. Analysis and Evaluation

Analysis is the process of breaking down information into its constituent parts to understand it better. Evaluation involves assessing the validity, significance, or worth of information based on criteria. These skills help students critique material, identify key components, and make informed judgments about its relevance or quality.

6. Logical Reasoning

Logical reasoning involves thinking systematically and using deductive and inductive reasoning to draw conclusions. It requires following a coherent line of thought and applying rules of logic to ensure that conclusions are sound. This skill is essential for students to construct valid arguments and solve problems rationally.

7. Conceptual Understanding

Conceptual understanding goes beyond memorization, involving a deep grasp of underlying principles and relationships between concepts. Students need to understand how different ideas interrelate and how these connections affect their understanding of a subject. This skill is crucial for long-term learning, ensuring that knowledge is retained and applicable.

8. Creativity and Innovation

Creativity involves thinking outside the box and coming up with original ideas or approaches. Innovation takes creativity further by applying these ideas to create new methods, solutions, or products. For students, this skill fosters an ability to approach learning in novel ways, helping them solve problems uniquely.

9. Reflective Thinking

Reflective thinking involves examining past experiences and learning from them to improve future actions or decisions. It requires self-awareness and the ability to critically evaluate one's own performance. Students with this skill can adapt their learning strategies, ensuring continual personal and academic growth.

10. Decision-Making

Decision-making is the process of choosing the best course of action among various alternatives. It involves weighing evidence, considering consequences, and making informed choices. This skill empowers students to take responsibility for their learning and to make thoughtful, reasoned decisions in their academic and personal lives.

Skills of output:

Output skills include delivering processed information in the most effective and timely manner. There is huge scope for articulation and talent in the skills of output. It is intertwined with soft skills because the output is received by somebody else. As a professional in the future, a candidate will need a lot of skills, including certain personality traits, for likability and productivity. Here is a limited list of output skills that a student must have for effective communication and productivity, including technical and professional competencies:

1. Verbal Communication
The ability to clearly articulate thoughts, ideas, and concepts through spoken language is essential. It involves conveying information effectively in conversations, discussions, and presentations. Verbal communication also includes active engagement in discussions and the capacity to adjust tone and language based on the audience.

2. Written Communication
Writing skills are critical for academic success and professional life. Effective written communication involves clarity, coherence, and proper grammar. Whether it is writing reports, essays, or emails, students must be able to present their thoughts in a structured and logical manner.

3. Presentation Skills
Presenting information to a group is a key output skill that requires confidence, clarity, and the ability to engage an audience. Students

should be able to use visual aids, such as slides, and explain
complex concepts in an understandable way.

4. Collaboration and Teamwork

Working effectively in groups is fundamental in both academic
and professional settings. Students should be able to contribute
ideas, respect differing opinions, and work toward a common goal.
This involves communication, compromise, and the capacity to
work harmoniously with others.

5. Time Management

Efficiently managing time is crucial for meeting deadlines and
balancing multiple responsibilities. Students should develop
strategies to prioritize tasks, set goals, and allocate appropriate
time to complete work while maintaining high productivity.

6. Public Speaking

The ability to speak confidently in front of an audience is an
important skill. Public speaking requires clear articulation,
persuasive techniques, and a strong presence. Students must learn
to handle anxiety and communicate ideas effectively in formal
settings.

7. Active Listening

Active listening involves fully focusing, understanding, and
responding to the speaker. It is key to participating in discussions
and collaborations effectively. This skill also involves interpreting
non-verbal cues and asking clarifying questions when needed.

8. Creativity and Expression

Being able to think creatively and express ideas innovatively is an
important output skill. It involves using imagination to generate
new ideas, solve problems, and create work that stands out in its
originality.

9. Adaptability and Flexibility

The ability to adjust to new situations and respond to unexpected challenges is crucial. Students should be flexible in their approach and willing to change strategies when necessary. Adaptability also involves openness to new ideas and evolving circumstances.

10. Self-expression and Emotional Intelligence

Students need to express their emotions and understand the emotions of others. Emotional intelligence includes empathy, self-awareness, and the ability to manage one's emotions in stressful or challenging situations, enhancing interpersonal relations.

11. Touch Typing

Invariably, all professions and inevitably all professionals will work with a laptop or a computer. Apart from using various software, learning to type at the rate of thought is an invaluable skill that allows the flow of words from the mind to the computer smoothly. Therefore, proficiency in touch typing enhances productivity by allowing students to write quickly and efficiently without looking at the keyboard. This skill is vital for modern academic and professional tasks, ensuring faster and more accurate document creation.

12. Specific Skills in Professional Tools

Mastery of tools like Microsoft Office, Google Workspace, or specific software related to one's field (e.g., MATLAB, Photoshop) is essential for professional productivity. Competence in these tools allows students to work effectively on academic or professional projects and deliver quality results.

13. Digital Literacy and Technological Savvy

In a digital age, students must be proficient in navigating digital platforms and tools. Understanding how to use online resources, manage digital files, and communicate effectively through digital means (e.g., email and social media) is crucial for productivity.

These output skills are essential for students not only to demonstrate their learning but also to thrive in collaborative, professional, and technological environments. While the aforementioned skills of input, processing, and output are discussed in the context of students, they are equally important for teachers. Specifically, output skills refer to how we deliver, conduct, and teach a class. While we explored several strategies and methods in TEACH I and TEACH II, we will delve more in TEACH III. Two key aspects of output skills in teaching are the language of words and the language of the body. How can educators best use these languages to enhance their delivery?

Rhetoric in teaching

In general, students are focused on marks and clearing the examinations comfortably. To obtain such objectives, knowledge, however volatile, is sufficient. However, ideally, students should develop habits of learning in such a way that they can deal with new knowledge or uncertainties independently in the future. Teaching these intricate skills of input, processing, and output requires constant coaching of the learners in order to build skills and make them practice. Therefore, teachers should employ the skills of a coach, a salesman and a parent at the same time. One of the powerful methods of instructing is Rhetoric.

Rhetoric, the art of persuasive communication, has always been a powerful tool, not just in public speaking but in teaching. Rhetoric, in a way, stimulates the mind to respond rather than passively absorb information. It excites the recipient's mind, urging it to feel, perceive, and remain alert. Through well-crafted sentences, rhetoric can have a profound influence, as if one mind is speaking and interacting with another. This engagement fosters an active dialogue between minds, creating a dynamic exchange that encourages deeper reflection and makes the communication more impactful and resonant.

I was often too shy to express myself freely like an orator; doing so seemed more suited to a political rally than a classroom. Yet, this hesitation can cause us to lose students' attention and engagement. While rhetoric cannot be heavily applied in subjects like mathematics or other technical fields, it remains a powerful tool to inspire and motivate students, enhancing their productivity. A teacher, much like an orator, must use language effectively to instruct, engage, and inspire. When used skillfully, rhetoric transforms a lecture into a captivating experience, drawing students deeper into the subject matter. In teaching, rhetoric—through ethos, pathos, and logos—helps connect with students intellectually, emotionally, and ethically, making learning more impactful and memorable.

One way rhetoric enhances teaching is through the establishment of ethos—the credibility of the teacher. By demonstrating mastery of the subject matter, a teacher gains the trust and respect of students, making them more receptive to the content. Ethos is not merely about expertise but also involves the teacher's character, integrity, and passion for the subject. When students sense the teacher's dedication and sincerity, they are more likely to engage deeply because they trust that the information provided is both valuable and reliable. Establishing this credibility fosters a learning environment where students are willing to explore complex topics without reservation.

Pathos, or the appeal to emotion, is another critical aspect of rhetoric that can be seamlessly integrated into teaching. While facts and logic are essential, appealing to the emotions of students can ignite interest and motivation. Through storytelling, vivid examples, or even humor, teachers can make lessons more relatable and less abstract. Pathos, when used appropriately, humanizes the material, bridging the gap between dry theory and students' lived experiences. For instance, in a biology class, a teacher might not merely describe cellular processes but might also connect them to real-world applications, like medicine or environmental issues, sparking a sense of relevance and urgency in students.

Logos, the logical appeal, is at the heart of all academic instruction. Teachers must structure their arguments and lessons coherently, providing clear explanations and logical sequences of thought. Using logos involves more than just presenting information—it requires guiding students through reasoning processes, encouraging them to see connections, question assumptions, and arrive at conclusions. Teachers can use rhetorical questions, analogies, and structured debates to sharpen students' critical thinking skills. By making the logic of a subject transparent, teachers help students develop intellectual independence, empowering them to analyze and synthesize knowledge rather than passively absorb it.

In addition, rhetoric aids in the art of persuasion, which is integral to motivating students to think critically and engage with the material. A teacher must often persuade students to embrace a topic they might initially find uninteresting or difficult. This is where rhetoric excels—by framing challenges as opportunities and by showing the value of mastering the content, teachers can influence attitudes and inspire effort. The use of rhetorical techniques such as repetition, emphasis, and contrast can highlight key points, ensuring they resonate with students long after the class ends.

The Rhetorical Classroom: A Collaborative Learning Environment

One of the most powerful aspects of rhetoric in teaching is its ability to create a collaborative learning environment. Through rhetorical strategies, teachers can encourage dialogue and debate, allowing students to engage with one another and explore different perspectives. This collaborative approach not only enhances cognitive skills but also helps develop important social and communication skills. Rhetoric fosters a classroom culture where ideas are shared, questioned, and refined, promoting a deeper understanding of the material.

For instance, in a classroom discussion, a teacher might use rhetoric to frame a provocative question that encourages debate. As students articulate their ideas, challenge their peers' viewpoints, and defend their own positions, they engage in critical thinking and problem-solving. The teacher, by guiding this discourse, helps students not only develop their cognitive skills but also learn the art of persuasion, negotiation, and respectful disagreement.

This collaborative learning environment also improves productivity. When students are actively engaged in dialogue, they are more likely to take ownership of their learning. Instead of passively receiving information, they become active participants in the educational process, contributing to a more dynamic and productive classroom experience.

Limitations and Responsible Use of Rhetoric

While rhetoric is a powerful tool for enhancing cognition and productivity, it must be used responsibly. There is a risk that rhetoric, if not carefully employed, can become manipulative or superficial. A teacher might use emotional appeals to persuade students without providing sufficient logical reasoning, leading to shallow understanding. Similarly, a focus on ethos without a genuine foundation of knowledge can lead to a loss of trust if students eventually perceive the teacher as lacking true expertise.

Therefore, rhetoric in teaching must always be grounded in truth and used in the service of genuine learning. Teachers must strike a balance between appealing to emotion and reason, ensuring that their rhetorical strategies foster critical thinking rather than mere persuasion. Whether through structured argumentation, emotional appeal, or the establishment of credibility, rhetoric transforms the classroom into a space where students are not only informed but also inspired, motivated, and prepared to apply their knowledge in meaningful ways. However, the responsible use of rhetoric is key, ensuring that the ultimate goal remains the development of critical thinking and deeper understanding.

Here are a few examples of sentences used in educational settings, illustrating the difference between rhetorical and straightforward expressions:

1. With Rhetoric: "How can we expect our students to become critical thinkers if we do not encourage them to question the status quo?"
 Without Rhetoric: "We need to encourage students to question the status quo."

2. With Rhetoric: "Is it not our duty as educators to ignite a passion for learning in our students and help them realize their full potential?"
 Without Rhetoric: "Educators should help students realize their full potential."

3. With Rhetoric: "When we close our doors to collaboration, are we not shutting our students off from invaluable learning experiences?"
 Without Rhetoric: "Collaboration provides valuable learning experiences for students."

4. With Rhetoric: "In today's rapidly changing world, how can we prepare our students to face the future if we stick to outdated teaching methods?"
 Without Rhetoric: "We need to update our teaching methods to prepare students for the future."

5. With Rhetoric: "Are we not responsible for creating a safe and inclusive environment where every student feels empowered to express their ideas?"
 Without Rhetoric: "We should create a safe and inclusive environment for all students."

6. With Rhetoric: "If we truly believe in fostering a love for learning, how can we ignore the importance of integrating creativity into our curriculum?"
 Without Rhetoric: "We should integrate creativity into our curriculum to foster a love for learning."

7. With Rhetoric: "Is it not disheartening to think that some students may never discover their unique talents if we do not offer diverse learning opportunities?"
 Without Rhetoric: "We need to offer diverse learning opportunities for students to discover their talents."

8. With Rhetoric: "In an era where information is at our fingertips, how can we expect our students to be discerning consumers of knowledge without teaching them critical evaluation skills?"

Without Rhetoric: "We need to teach students critical evaluation skills to help them discern information."

9. With Rhetoric: "Do we not owe it to our students to challenge them, to push them beyond their comfort zones, and to help them grow?"
 Without Rhetoric: "We should challenge our students to help them grow."

10. With Rhetoric: "How can we claim to prepare our students for the future if we do not equip them with the skills to navigate complex, real-world problems?"
 Without Rhetoric: "We need to equip students with skills to navigate real-world problems."

Confucian and Aristotelian Body Language

Body language, often an unspoken language, reflects not only individual temperament but also deep cultural and philosophical roots. The body is a canvas, communicating ideas, emotions, and values without uttering a word. For over a decade, I grappled with restricted body language, feeling trapped in my own expressions. Observing Western professors in Denmark or on YouTube, I felt their animated gestures exaggerated, a stark contrast to my own subtlety. To use 'excess' body language felt like a show-off. Striving for change, I began incorporating small movements and more eye contact into my interactions. This ongoing journey has fostered genuine connections with my students, enhancing their engagement and my own confidence. While I am still evolving, I have discovered the power of authenticity in expression, allowing me to convey ideas more vividly and resonate with my audience on a deeper level.

When examined through the lenses of Confucian and Aristotelian philosophies, body language reveals two vastly different worlds—one steeped in reverence for tradition, hierarchy, and social harmony and the other in pursuit of persuasion, expression, and intellectual dominance.

Confucian Body Language: The Subtlety of Social Harmony

Confucianism, rooted in the teachings of Confucius, is a philosophy that values social order, respect for hierarchy, and harmonious relationships. It emphasizes the individual's role in a collective society, where one's behavior should always reflect respect and humility. Confucian body language is, therefore, subtle, restrained, and understated. Movements are controlled and purposeful, reflecting self-discipline and an awareness of one's place within the social structure. There is a deliberate minimization of ego in every gesture.

Psychologically, this restraint aligns with a collective mindset. In cultures influenced by Confucianism, social conformity is valued over individual expression. The limited use of eye contact, for instance, reflects humility and respect for authority or elders. Direct eye contact in such contexts could be interpreted as aggressive or confrontational, so averting one's gaze demonstrates reverence. The body assumes a neutral posture, one that neither asserts dominance nor draws unnecessary attention. Subtle bowing or nodding serves as an acknowledgment of the other person's status or contributions without the need for elaborate verbal expression.

This reserved approach extends to emotional expression as well. Emotional outbursts or exaggerated gestures are avoided, as they disrupt the social harmony that is central to Confucian thought. The self is secondary to the community, and body language, therefore, aims to reflect stability and peace rather than individuality. This reflects a deep psychological alignment with the collective consciousness, where each person sees themselves as part of a larger whole. The suppression of overt emotion in body language ensures that relationships maintain their balance without generating discord or discomfort.

Aristotelian Body Language: The Art of Persuasion

In stark contrast, Aristotelian body language is more dynamic and expressive, reflective of Aristotle's emphasis on logic, reason, and rhetoric. Grounded in Western philosophy, Aristotelian thought celebrates the individual's ability to reason, debate, and persuade. The body, in this context, becomes an essential tool for communication and expression, amplifying speech and argument with deliberate gestures, confident posture, and direct eye contact.

From a psychological perspective, Aristotelian body language promotes individual expression and persuasion. A confident stance, with open arms or pronounced gestures, invites the audience to engage with the speaker's ideas. Direct eye contact here serves as a tool to establish a connection and assert authority. While Confucian body language seeks to maintain social order through humility, Aristotelian body language seeks to convince, to sway, and to dominate the conversation through logic and emotional appeal.

Aristotle's belief in rhetoric as an art of persuasion reflects this bodily confidence. To persuade, one must embody the argument, literally and figuratively. Gestures that accompany speech—such as an open hand to invite trust or a firm posture to project certainty—are critical to the effectiveness of communication. These movements appeal not only to the intellect but also to the emotions of the audience, engaging them in a way that goes beyond words.

In terms of emotional expression, Aristotelian body language is much more open. It is not afraid of intensity or passion. Anger, joy, frustration—all are allowed to surface as long as they serve the purpose of enhancing the persuasive power of the argument. Where Confucianism teaches restraint to preserve harmony, Aristotelian thought permits expression to heighten impact.

Psychological Implications: Two Worlds of Identity and Social Interaction

The psychological underpinnings of Confucian and Aristotelian body language highlight two distinct approaches to identity and social interaction. Confucianism leans toward a collectivist mindset, where the self is minimized in favor of group harmony. This results in subdued body language, with limited emotional display, because personal expression is less important than maintaining societal order. The individual, psychologically, is often more attuned to the needs and expectations of others, making modesty in body language a reflection of inner discipline and deference.

Aristotelian body language, on the other hand, reflects an individualistic and rational worldview, where personal expression is key to effective communication. The body becomes an instrument to project confidence, persuade, and assert one's position in discourse. Psychologically, individuals in such cultures are more focused on standing out, expressing their ideas, and influencing others through logic, emotion, and appeal. This emphasis on persuasion manifests in more active and assertive body language, symbolizing the intellectual and emotional engagement that Aristotle valued.

Teachers can significantly enhance the teaching-learning process by harnessing the power of body language expressions to create a more engaging and dynamic classroom environment. By employing deliberate gestures, varied facial expressions, and purposeful movements, educators can effectively convey enthusiasm and passion for the subject matter, capturing students' attention and fostering a deeper connection to the material. For instance, utilizing open postures and maintaining eye contact can promote a sense of trust and inclusivity, encouraging students to participate actively in discussions. Additionally, integrating body language cues—such as nodding in affirmation or using hand signals to emphasize key points—can reinforce verbal communication, making complex concepts more accessible and memorable. Ultimately, by being mindful of their own body language, teachers can create a stimulating atmosphere that not only promotes learning but also nurtures students' emotional and social development.

Chapter 3: Knowledge

The Instinct to Know

The greatest unique human instinct is undeniably the drive to know more, to explore further, to dig deeper into the mysteries of existence and improved living. This fundamental impulse to seek knowledge has propelled humanity to the forefront of life on Earth, transforming our species into one of the most successful. It is this insatiable curiosity and desire to understand the world that has not only shaped our civilization but also continuously pushed us toward greater achievements over time.

From ancient times, humanity's quest for knowledge has been evident in the great strides made in understanding the universe, nature, and the self. The early humans, in their primitive state, relied on curiosity as a survival tool. Learning how to make fire, create tools, and hunt animals were more than just innovations for survival—they marked the beginning of our journey toward knowing more and knowing better. As we discovered fire, we didn't stop at its practical uses but began to wonder: What is fire? What fuels it? This very wondering, this desire to know deeper, led to the foundations of science and math.

Ancient civilizations made significant contributions to knowledge, each shaping culture and intellect uniquely. Egypt focused on spirituality, reflected in monumental pyramids and burial practices. Mesopotamia pioneered early records in astronomy, mathematics, and governance. Greece, with figures like Pythagoras, Socrates, and Aristotle, laid the foundations for philosophy, ethics, and science. In India, scholars such as Aryabhata and Brahmagupta advanced mathematics with innovations like zero and the decimal system, while Vedanta and Ayurveda enriched philosophy and medicine. China, through Confucianism, Taoism, and technological innovations like papermaking, significantly impacted global knowledge, as did Mesoamerican civilizations in astronomy, architecture, and calendars.

The exchange of ideas through trade routes like the Silk Road allowed these ancient contributions to merge, creating a rich amalgam of knowledge. Collectively, the contributions of these diverse civilizations formed the foundation of modern intellectual progress, illustrating humanity's universal quest for understanding and discovery. Each civilization played a pivotal role in advancing knowledge, demonstrating the interconnectedness of human innovation across time and space.

This journey toward knowledge did not stop in the ancient world but continued with greater fervor throughout history. During the Renaissance, a period aptly described as a rebirth of knowledge, humanity turned its gaze both backward to the wisdom of ancient scholars and forward toward new frontiers. Artists, scientists, and thinkers like Leonardo da Vinci and Galileo embodied this quest for deeper knowledge. Leonardo, often called the "Renaissance man," sought to understand the human body, the mechanics of flight, and the natural world in ways no one had before. Galileo, driven by the desire to know far beyond what the eye could see, turned his telescope toward the heavens and forever changed our understanding of the universe.

In modern times, this instinct to know more has taken us even further, both literally and metaphorically. We have delved into the subatomic world through quantum mechanics, explored the depths of space through powerful telescopes, and decoded the human genome to understand the very blueprint of life. The technological revolutions of the 20th and 21st centuries, including the invention of computers, space exploration, and the rise of artificial intelligence, have all been driven by humanity's desire to know better and know deeper.

One of the most inspiring examples of this pursuit is our journey into space. The Apollo moon landings were not merely an achievement of engineering but a profound statement of our desire to know farther—to reach beyond the bounds of Earth and understand our place in the cosmos. Today, with missions to Mars and deep space exploration, we continue to push the boundaries of knowledge, fueled by the same ancient instinct that drove early humans to explore new territories.

We continue to seek answers to profound questions: What is the meaning of life? What is the nature of consciousness? What does the future hold for humanity? Our desire to know the past and the future, to understand where we come from and where we are headed, defines us as a species.

The greatest human instinct is to know more, to know better, to know deeper, and to know farther—both to the past and into the future. This relentless desire to acquire knowledge has established humans as the superspecies. It is this instinct for the continuous pursuit of understanding that distinguishes us from all other species. Our aspiration to know more has transformed us from mere survivors into thinkers, innovators, and explorers. This powerful instinct has given rise to civilizations, shaped cultures, and will persist as a driving force propelling us into the future. Thus, humanity thrives on the boundless power of knowledge, affirming our status as a superspecies in the grand tapestry of life.

The major shift in knowing that transformed the world of knowledge lies in the transition from applied sciences to basic sciences. For centuries, the pursuit of knowledge was driven by its immediate survival benefits—knowing how to use something to sustain life. However, the shift towards understanding the nature of things without immediate utility revolutionized human existence. This transition taught us to explore knowledge for its own sake, leading to profound breakthroughs in science and technology. By seeking to understand and manipulate the workings of nature, humanity unlocked unprecedented advancements, shaping the course of modern civilization. Basic science propelled applied science.

In today's world, the rate at which we acquire knowledge is accelerating at an unprecedented pace, reshaping our understanding of reality and our place within it. Each passing second brings forth new discoveries, insights, and advancements that collectively expand the vast reservoir of human knowledge. This phenomenon, driven by technological innovation and the interconnectedness of global communication, is a testament to the human spirit's insatiable curiosity.

Consider the remarkable advancements in various fields, from medicine to artificial intelligence. Just a decade ago, concepts like CRISPR gene editing and artificial neural networks were in their infancy. Today, they are transforming industries and offering solutions to complex challenges. This rapid evolution exemplifies how knowledge is no longer a linear journey; it is an exponential explosion. Information once painstakingly gathered over the years is now accessible at our fingertips, enabling us to learn and grow in ways that were unimaginable to previous generations. Each discovery serves as a stepping stone, allowing us to delve deeper and think more critically about our world. The journey of knowing is not just a personal endeavor; it is a collective mission that propels humanity forward.

To know is eternal

The question of whether knowledge is permanent delves into the very nature of what we consider knowledge to be. Knowledge, as traditionally understood, is the accumulation of facts, principles, and truths about the world. However, the permanence of this knowledge has always been a matter of debate. While some forms of knowledge remain relatively stable, others undergo significant transformations over time. Knowledge is dynamic and context-dependent, shifting in response to new discoveries, technologies, and perspectives. This philosophical examination of knowledge reveals that it is, in fact, not permanent but evolves continuously, shaped by the cultural, social, and intellectual environments in which it exists.

Over millennia, human knowledge has undergone profound transformations, exemplified by the shift from the geocentric to the heliocentric model of the universe, which revolutionized our understanding of astronomy. Over a century, our grasp of physics changed dramatically with Einstein's theory of relativity and quantum mechanics, replacing Newton's classical mechanics. In the last 50 years, advancements in genetics and molecular biology, from recombinant DNA technology to the Human Genome Project, have redefined our understanding of heredity. Over the past decade, our knowledge of climate change has evolved significantly, emphasizing its immediacy. In just five years, artificial intelligence has transformed technology, reshaping human-machine interaction. Even in a single year, like during the COVID-19 pandemic, our understanding of viral transmission and treatment rapidly advanced, highlighting the dynamic nature of knowledge.

Knowledge is not a static or permanent entity. It is subject to change, influenced by new discoveries, cultural shifts, and technological advancements. What was considered certain knowledge millennia ago has been completely overturned, and even knowledge acquired within a single year can be transformed by new evidence or insights. From the cosmos to the genome, from the physical laws that govern the universe to the ethical challenges posed by new technologies, the evolution of knowledge is a testament to the dynamic nature of human understanding. Therefore, knowledge should not be viewed as a permanent fixture but as an evolving process, one that continuously adapts to the ever-changing world we live in.

In the rapidly evolving landscape of knowledge and technology, the imperative to educate students takes on a heightened significance. The changing nature of knowledge, influenced by advancements in technology and the constant flow of information, necessitates that students develop not only a solid foundation of facts and concepts but also an openness to new ideas and an adaptable mindset. This adaptability becomes the cornerstone of navigating the complexities of modern life, empowering individuals to respond effectively to the challenges and opportunities that arise in an ever-shifting world.

Education should cultivate an environment where students are encouraged to question, explore, and embrace diverse perspectives. In this context, fostering an open-minded approach is essential. When students are taught to engage with differing viewpoints and challenge their own assumptions, they become better equipped to grapple with the nuances of knowledge. This is particularly relevant in today's society, where information is abundant, yet discerning what is credible and relevant can be a daunting task.

Moreover, as knowledge evolves, the necessity for adaptability becomes paramount. The skills and information that may have been relevant yesterday could become obsolete tomorrow.

Therefore, it is crucial to instill a sense of adaptability in students. This can be achieved by teaching them not just the "what" of knowledge but the "how." How to learn, how to adapt, and how to apply knowledge in different contexts are vital skills that students must acquire. For instance, in fields such as technology and science, breakthroughs occur at a rapid pace. Students must be prepared to pivot their understanding and embrace new information as it emerges. This flexibility in thinking allows them to thrive in an unpredictable world.

Importantly, the concept of lifelong learning emerges as a key theme in this discourse. Knowledge is not a finite entity to be mastered and then set aside; it is a continuous journey of growth and discovery. Educating students, as well as the self, about the need for lifelong learning encourages them to view education as an ongoing process that extends beyond formal schooling. This perspective nurtures a growth mindset, wherein individuals recognize that their abilities and intelligence can be developed through dedication and effort. As they move through life, they will encounter new ideas and challenges that require them to adapt and learn continuously. Embracing the changing nature of knowledge equips them with the tools to become informed citizens, innovative thinkers, and resilient individuals who can contribute meaningfully to society.

Types of Knowledge: Facts, Principles, Logic, and More

Knowledge, the foundation for intellectual growth and problem-solving, can be classified into various types that serve distinct functions in learning and decision-making. Each type of knowledge plays a crucial role in understanding the world and applying information effectively. Below are key types of knowledge with examples:

Knowledge, in its many forms, represents the external world as perceived and processed by the human mind. Philosophically, the types of knowledge can be understood as different pathways through which we access, engage with, and expand our understanding of reality.

1. Factual Knowledge: This is the most basic form of knowledge, consisting of objective truths about the world. It is rooted in empiricism, where knowledge is obtained through observation and experience. Example: Knowing that water boils at 100°C under standard pressure reflects the empiricist view of knowledge acquisition through sensory experience.

2. Conceptual Knowledge: This involves understanding the relationships between facts and weaving them into a coherent system. It aligns with rationalism, where knowledge is derived from intellectual and logical structures. Example: Grasping the concept of democracy requires not just knowing individual facts about elections or governance but seeing how they relate to a broader system of political thought.

3. Principles: These are fundamental truths that govern phenomena, often reflecting a deeper order in the universe. They are linked to the philosophical pursuit of universal truths, echoing the metaphysical quest for understanding the underlying laws of reality. Example: Newton's First Law of Motion represents a principle that governs physical behavior, pointing to an inherent structure in the natural world.

4. Procedural Knowledge: This form is rooted in pragmatism, emphasizing the practical application of knowledge through action. It is the "how-to" of tasks, emphasizing process over content. Example: The steps involved in conducting a scientific experiment embody procedural knowledge, where action leads to discovery.

5. Tacit Knowledge: Tacit knowledge aligns with phenomenology, where knowledge is deeply personal and experiential, often beyond words. It is the wisdom embedded in practice, shaped by lived experience. Example: A skilled artist's ability to create intuitively, without explicit instructions, illustrates tacit knowledge gained through immersion in the craft.

Breadth of Knowledge and Depth of Knowledge

The breadth of knowledge refers to the wide range of topics, subjects, or disciplines an individual is familiar with. It encompasses surface-level understanding across various areas, offering a general grasp of multiple fields. For example, a student with broad knowledge might understand basic principles of biology, history, mathematics, and literature without specializing in any one area. Breadth allows individuals to connect ideas across domains, fostering interdisciplinary thinking and adaptability. It equips learners with the flexibility to tackle diverse problems and engage in broader discussions.

Depth of knowledge, on the other hand, signifies a thorough and detailed understanding of a specific area. It involves a deeper exploration of a single subject, allowing individuals to master complex concepts and specialized skills. For example, a scientist with deep knowledge of genetics can analyze intricate DNA sequences and understand molecular interactions. Depth allows for expertise, enabling individuals to innovate or lead within their chosen field.

If knowledge is categorized based on hierarchical cognitive emergence, we could divide it into two distinct categories:

1. Sequential Knowledge – This category includes disciplines or areas of knowledge that rely on hierarchical cognitive emergence. In these fields, learning follows a structured, sequential progression where foundational concepts are prerequisites for more advanced understanding. Examples include STEM subjects (like mathematics, physics, and chemistry), where each level of knowledge builds upon prior concepts, forming a structured intellectual hierarchy.

2. Non-sequential Knowledge – In contrast, this category encompasses areas of knowledge that are more flexible and less rigidly hierarchical. Here, learning does not necessarily require a strict progression, allowing for more interpretive, experiential, or associative understanding. Fields such as literature, history, and the arts often fall into this category, where concepts can be learned and applied in a variety of ways without following a strictly cumulative structure.

Both breadth and depth are essential in education and intellectual development. Breadth provides context and a broad perspective, while depth allows for specialization and advanced problem-solving. Striking a balance between the two ensures well-rounded intellectual growth, enabling individuals to navigate both general and complex issues effectively.

The various types of knowledge—factual, conceptual, principles, procedural, logical, strategic, declarative, and tacit—each play a significant role in understanding and navigating the world. Together, they form the basis of intelligence and problem-solving, equipping individuals with the capacity to analyze, reason, and act effectively across different domains. By recognizing and cultivating these diverse forms of knowledge, one can engage more deeply with both simple and complex challenges.

Types of knowledge based on validity

The landscape of knowledge is a multifaceted terrain that can be categorized into several types, each playing a significant role in our understanding of the world around us. This classification not only enriches our comprehension of knowledge but also highlights the importance of discerning between different types. Among these categories are eternal facts, time-specific facts, opinions, models, subjectivity, objectivity, and beliefs.

Eternal Facts represent the bedrock of knowledge. These are truths that remain constant, regardless of context or time. For instance, the fundamental principles of mathematics, such as the Pythagorean theorem, hold true irrespective of advancements in technology or shifts in cultural paradigms. Eternal facts provide a stable foundation upon which further knowledge can be built, serving as universal truths that guide reasoning and understanding.

Facts for the Time, in contrast, are contingent upon the current context and can change with new discoveries or societal shifts. Historical events serve as prime examples; the interpretation of a specific event can evolve as new evidence comes to light or as perspectives change over time. For example, the understanding of significant events like wars or revolutions may shift as historical scholarship advances, revealing previously overlooked details or biases in earlier narratives. Recognizing facts for the time is crucial for developing a nuanced understanding of our history and society. Opinions occupy another vital space in the knowledge landscape. Unlike eternal facts, opinions are subjective interpretations shaped by personal experiences, cultural background, and individual beliefs. They reflect an individual's perspective on a matter and can vary widely from person to person. While opinions can foster rich discussions and debates, they must be approached with caution. It is essential to differentiate between opinion and fact, as opinions, while valid, do not carry the same weight as verifiable truths.

Models serve as frameworks that help us understand complex phenomena. In science, for instance, models simplify intricate processes, allowing us to make predictions and draw conclusions based on limited data. The atomic model, which illustrates the structure of atoms, is a prime example. While models provide valuable insights, they are not infallible; they are approximations that can evolve as new information emerges. Hence, we must remain open to revising our models in light of fresh evidence.

Subjectivity and objectivity represent two contrasting approaches to knowledge. Subjectivity emphasizes personal perspectives and emotional experiences, which can enrich our understanding of human behavior and culture. However, it also introduces potential biases that can cloud judgment. Objectivity, on the other hand, seeks to eliminate bias and personal influence, striving for a neutral and factual representation of reality. In scientific research, objectivity is paramount; rigorous methodologies are employed to ensure that findings are based on empirical evidence rather than subjective interpretation.

Lastly, beliefs play a significant role in shaping our understanding of the world. Beliefs can stem from cultural, religious, or personal convictions and often provide individuals with a sense of identity and purpose. However, beliefs can also be resistant to change, even in the face of contradictory evidence. This highlights the tension between belief and knowledge; while beliefs can motivate and inspire, they must be examined critically to ensure they do not obstruct our pursuit of truth. Each type of knowledge plays a unique role in our lives, guiding us as we navigate the intricacies of existence.

Misinformation and Validation of Knowledge.

As humans, we are often puzzled and troubled by the inexplicable—magic, unexpected experiences, ambushes, and so-called 'miracles.' These events unsettle us, prompting our innate instinct to seek understanding. We instinctively search for reasons or explanations for what has occurred. Typically, the knowledge we seek in such unsettling circumstances originates from external sources or is fabricated by our minds in an attempt to alleviate the uncertainty. However, we must ask ourselves: Is that knowledge true or false? Can we truly test it? Often, we find that it is not possible to ascertain its validity. The likelihood of such knowledge being misinformation is alarmingly high, marking the genesis of misinformation itself.

Moreover, certain individuals deliberately generate and propagate misinformation for personal or collective gain. The longer we hold a belief to be true, the more challenging it becomes to relinquish it, even in the face of compelling evidence to the contrary. How, then, can we discern true information from misinformation, whether it stems from external sources or our own minds?

In a world brimming with information, an overwhelming portion is composed of misinformation, creating a complex landscape for those seeking knowledge and truth. Misinformation can arise from various sources, including traditional practices that persist despite being disproven by modern understanding. Ego often plays a significant role in this resistance to change, preventing individuals from discarding "ancestral" knowledge. This reluctance to adapt may be deeply intertwined with cultural identity, causing individuals to cling to outdated beliefs, even when confronted with compelling evidence to the contrary.

Additionally, misinformation is frequently propagated by those with strong beliefs who seek to assert them as truths. These individuals can become ardent advocates for their perspectives, often at the expense of critical thinking and evidence-based reasoning. In such instances, the dissemination of misinformation transforms into a form of self-affirmation, where the need to validate one's beliefs eclipses the pursuit of objective truth. The consequences of this can be far-reaching, as persuasive rhetoric influences others, leading to widespread acceptance of erroneous information.

Deliberate fabrication of misinformation for motives such as financial gain or the pursuit of power further complicates this issue. Individuals and organizations may craft false narratives or manipulate data to further their agendas, targeting specific groups or communities. Such manipulation reinforces existing biases and stereotypes, fostering division and mistrust within society. Here, misinformation becomes a tool of exploitation, as those in positions of influence leverage it to achieve their goals, often at the expense of the broader community.

The rise of social media exacerbates this problem, as the rapid dissemination of information can lead to the virality of misinformation. The ease with which individuals share content often circumvents critical evaluation, allowing unverified claims to spread uncontrollably. The challenge lies not only in discerning truth from falsehood but also in fostering a culture that values critical inquiry and skepticism toward unverified information. The saddest part of modern education is that we do not teach children how to truly know or how to validate knowledge. I was never taught any philosophy or psychology during my schooling— nothing that I can recall included these topics. There was one teacher, during my eighth standard or so, who mentioned Socrates and questioning as a way of knowing. I understand that it can be challenging for children to grasp, and equally difficult for educators to teach, the process of validating information and deducing knowledge. Ideally, these critical thinking methods should have been introduced in high school. Imagine how remarkable our society would be if misinformation disappeared as quickly as it appeared. How peaceful it would be if everyone valued truth and opposed falsehoods. What a wondrous place it would be if each person recognized their own biases and understood the foundation of their knowledge preferences. How thoughtful society could become if we all spoke the language of truth. I often wonder why we do not teach more philosophy and psychology in high schools.

We would not have to engage in this constant, perpetual struggle against misinformation if critical thinking and validation of knowledge were integral parts of education. Teaching children how to evaluate information from an early age could drastically reduce the spread of falsehoods. If society were grounded in truth and understanding, the battle against misinformation would not be so relentless. Instead, we would foster a culture where knowledge is critically assessed, and individuals are equipped to effortlessly discern fact from fiction. The fight would not feel eternal if everyone knew how to question, validate, and seek truth.

To navigate the intricate slippery landscape of 'information,' cultivating a mindset that prioritizes evidence-based reasoning and intellectual humility is crucial. Recognizing the prevalence of misinformation and understanding its origins empowers individuals to approach information with discernment. Only through education and open dialogue can we hope to counteract the tide of misinformation and foster a society rooted in truth and understanding. The journey toward knowledge is not merely about acquiring information; it is about engaging in a thoughtful, critical examination of the world around us.

Students must cultivate traits of being unbiased, courageous, upright, and forward-looking as they navigate the vast sea of information confronting them daily. In an age where misinformation is rampant, fostering an unbiased mindset allows students to approach information without preconceived notions, enabling them to evaluate facts critically. Courage is equally vital; it empowers them to challenge widely accepted beliefs and speak out against inaccuracies, even when doing so may not be popular.

Integrity ensures that students maintain a commitment to truthfulness in both consuming and disseminating information. This trait compels them to uphold ethical standards, recognizing the weight their words carry in shaping perspectives. Furthermore, a forward-looking approach encourages students to seek not only immediate solutions but also long-term implications of the information they encounter.

A teacher can embolden and empower students to effectively deal with information by fostering an environment of critical inquiry and open dialogue, where students feel safe to question, explore, and challenge prevailing narratives. By integrating lessons on media literacy and information evaluation into the curriculum, teachers can equip students with essential tools to discern credible sources from misinformation. Encouraging collaborative projects and discussions allows students to share diverse perspectives, enhancing their analytical skills and confidence in articulating their viewpoints. Moreover, teachers can model a growth mindset by demonstrating their own learning processes, embracing mistakes, and encouraging students to view challenges as opportunities for growth. By cultivating a culture of curiosity, resilience, and respect for diverse opinions, teachers can empower students to navigate the complexities of information with clarity and conviction, ultimately preparing them for informed citizenship in an increasingly complex world.

To support these traits, stringent filters should be implemented regarding the information that enters their knowledge base. This could involve rigorous evaluation of sources, critical questioning of the content, and discernment in sharing information with peers. By adopting these practices, students can contribute to a more informed and responsible society, ultimately becoming guardians of truth in a world teeming with noise and distraction.

In an era characterized by an overwhelming influx of information, the ability to discern truthful information from falsehoods is essential for students. Here are several methods students can adopt to filter and assess the reliability of the information they encounter:

1. Source Evaluation
 - Credibility of Sources: Students should consider the credibility of the source of information. Reliable sources are typically well-known publications, academic journals, or reputable organizations. Websites ending in .edu, .gov, or .org are often more trustworthy.
 - Author Expertise: Investigating the author's qualifications and background can provide insight into their expertise and potential biases. An author with relevant credentials or experience in the field is more likely to provide accurate information.

2. Cross-Verification
 - Fact-Checking: Utilizing fact-checking websites (e.g., Snopes, FactCheck.org, or PolitiFact) can help confirm the accuracy of specific claims or stories.
 - Multiple Sources: Students should seek confirmation from multiple sources before accepting information as true. If several reputable sources report the same information, it is more likely to be accurate.

3. Critical Thinking
 - Questioning Assumptions: Students should question the underlying assumptions of the information presented. What

evidence supports the claim? Are there logical fallacies or biases in the argument?

- Analyzing Intent: Understanding the purpose behind the information can provide context. Is the information designed to inform, persuade, entertain, or provoke an emotional response? Recognizing intent can help identify potential biases.

4. Look for Evidence

- Supporting Data: Reliable information is often accompanied by data, research, or references that support its claims. Students should look for well-cited studies or empirical evidence rather than anecdotal stories.

- Corroborating Evidence: Students should assess whether other evidence or sources corroborate the claims. If multiple independent studies or reports reach similar conclusions, the information is likely to be more credible.

5. Identifying Bias and Perspective

- Recognizing Bias: Understanding the political, social, or commercial biases of a source can help students critically assess the information. Biased reporting may distort facts or present them in a misleading way.

- Evaluating Perspectives: Students should consider various perspectives on an issue. Engaging with a range of viewpoints can provide a more comprehensive understanding of a topic and highlight differing interpretations of the same data.

6. Understanding Media Literacy

- Training in Media Literacy: Educating students about media literacy is crucial. This involves understanding how media works, recognizing the techniques used to convey messages, and analyzing the impact of media on public perception.

- Identifying Misinformation Tactics: Familiarizing students with common tactics used in misinformation—such as sensational headlines, emotional appeals, and manipulated images—can enhance their critical assessment skills.

7. Reflective Practices
 - Self-Reflection: Encouraging students to reflect on their biases and preconceived notions can promote more objective information processing. This involves questioning their beliefs and considering how they may influence their interpretation of information.
 - Discussion and Debate: Engaging in discussions or debates with peers can expose students to alternative viewpoints and challenge their understanding, fostering deeper critical thinking and analysis.

By implementing these methods, students can develop the skills necessary to navigate the complex landscape of information critically. This process not only enhances their ability to discern truth from falsehood but also prepares them to engage thoughtfully and responsibly with the world around them. Ultimately, fostering a culture of inquiry and skepticism will contribute to a more informed and engaged society.

Everything learned is knowledge, including insights gained from personal experience.

Testing uncertain times: what is true and what to do?

At times of uncertainty, the very foundation of knowledge becomes precarious. It is not just about what we know but about how we know it, how we discern truth from falsehood, and how we navigate the labyrinth of conflicting information. The answer lies in fostering a mindset that combines intellectual courage with critical thinking. Students and individuals alike must learn to stay calm in the face of uncertainty, to critically evaluate information, and to remain steadfast in their pursuit of the truth. One of the most important lessons from the COVID-19 pandemic is that knowledge is not always readily available or certain, and in times of crisis, it may take time to emerge. This does not mean that we should succumb to fear or misinformation. Instead, it calls for an even greater sense of responsibility toward seeking out reliable sources, engaging in rational discourse, and resisting the temptation to jump to conclusions.

The role of education is pivotal in preparing students for such uncertain times. It is essential to inculcate in them the ability to think critically and to develop mental resilience. Critical thinking involves the capacity to assess the reliability and validity of information. It requires the ability to ask questions like: Where is this information coming from? What evidence supports this claim? What are the potential biases at play? By honing this skill, students learn to separate fact from fiction, enabling them to make informed decisions even in the most uncertain situations.

Moreover, students must learn to deal with ambiguity and incomplete knowledge. The nature of science, especially in a rapidly evolving crisis like the COVID-19 pandemic, is that answers do not always come immediately. The process of scientific discovery is iterative, often involving trial and error, adjustments, and corrections over time. In such situations, the intellectual path may not be clear from the start. It requires patience and a willingness to adapt to new information as it becomes available. This adaptability is a crucial skill that students must cultivate— recognizing that knowledge is dynamic and ever-changing, and what may be considered true today could be revised tomorrow.

One powerful example of this is the initial treatment strategies for COVID-19. In the early days, treatments ranged widely, from antivirals to experimental drugs, with varying degrees of success. Some treatments that were initially thought to be effective were later proven to be ineffective or even harmful. This is where the ability to adapt to new knowledge becomes critical. The medical community did not stop at the first discovery but continued to test, research, and refine their understanding of the virus and how to combat it. This iterative process eventually led to more effective treatments and vaccines. Had the scientific community or the general public been rigid in their thinking, progress would have been stifled, and more lives would have been lost.

Students must also develop the mental strength to resist panic and maintain a sense of calm during uncertain times. Uncertainty can breed fear, and fear can cloud judgment. However, staying calm allows individuals to process information more clearly and make rational decisions. Mental strength, in this context, is about cultivating emotional resilience and maintaining focus on the long-term goal of seeking truth rather than being swayed by short-term anxieties. In times of crisis, it is easy to fall into the trap of believing that immediate answers are necessary. However, true knowledge often requires time, patience, and a steady commitment to inquiry.

The ability to navigate uncertainty with intellectual courage is a skill that should be at the core of education. Students should be encouraged to engage in dialogue, debate, and discussion, not just about what is known but about the process of knowing itself. They should be taught to value the journey of discovery as much as the destination, recognizing that knowledge is often provisional and subject to refinement and revision. This intellectual humility, combined with a strong sense of inquiry, will prepare students to face future uncertainties with confidence and clarity.

Chapter 4: Teaching knowledge and memorization

<u>Methods to teach different types of knowledge</u>

In a previous chapter, we studied different types of knowledge, and we noticed that they have significant differences, which implies that there are different cognitive or mental activities. Each knowledge type may require a different type of method. As a matter of fact, most of us teachers already employ them. However, the following section could help reflect on our methods and consolidate our skills in recognizing the type of knowledge.

To engage different types of knowledge in the classroom, teaching methods must be tailored to both the content and the cognitive processes involved. Below are examples of teaching methods corresponding to various types of knowledge, each illustrated with a STEM-related example.

1. Factual Knowledge: Direct Instruction

Factual knowledge refers to specific pieces of information that are universally accepted and easily articulated. Direct instruction is an ideal method for effectively imparting factual knowledge, where the teacher presents clear, concise information.

Example: In a biology class, the teacher explains the structure of a cell, providing factual knowledge such as the number of chromosomes in a human cell (46). The teacher might use visual aids like diagrams and charts to reinforce these facts, ensuring that students can recall specific data points.

2. Conceptual Knowledge: Concept Mapping

Conceptual knowledge involves understanding relationships between facts and grasping broader ideas. Concept mapping is a powerful tool for helping students visualize these relationships.

Example: In a chemistry class, students create a concept map linking various types of chemical bonds (ionic, covalent, hydrogen) to their respective characteristics (electronegativity, bond strength). This helps students understand how these different bonds are interconnected and how they govern the structure of molecules.

3. Procedural Knowledge: Demonstration and Practice

Procedural knowledge refers to knowing how to perform tasks or processes. Demonstrations followed by student practice are highly effective in this context.

Example: In a physics class, the teacher demonstrates how to set up a simple electrical circuit, explaining the role of each component (battery, resistor, wires, etc.). Students then replicate the process, wiring their own circuits to understand the procedure of circuit construction.

4. Principles: Socratic Questioning

Principles are fundamental truths or propositions that form the basis of reasoning. Socratic questioning encourages students to explore principles through guided inquiry.

Example: In a physics class discussing Newton's laws of motion, the teacher uses Socratic questioning to explore Newton's First Law: "What happens to an object in motion if no external force acts on it? Can you think of an everyday example?" This method helps students uncover and internalize the principle behind the law through critical thinking.

5. Logical Knowledge: Problem-Based Learning (PBL)

Logical knowledge involves reasoning and understanding the structure of valid arguments. Problem-based learning is an ideal method for cultivating this type of knowledge.

Example: In a computer science class, students are tasked with debugging a faulty algorithm. They must apply logical reasoning to trace the source of the error, correct logical fallacies and ensure that each line of code follows valid reasoning structures. Through this process, students develop a deep understanding of logical patterns and inferences.

6. Strategic Knowledge: Case Study Analysis

Strategic knowledge involves knowing how to apply knowledge in specific contexts. Case study analysis is an effective method to engage students in strategic thinking.

Example: In an engineering class, students analyze the case study of a failed bridge project. They must use their strategic knowledge to identify what went wrong and propose solutions, considering factors like material choice, structural integrity, and environmental impact. This method helps them apply theoretical knowledge to real-world scenarios.

7. Declarative Knowledge: Lecture with Active Recall

Declarative knowledge involves knowing facts and information explicitly. A traditional lecture supplemented with active recall exercises can reinforce declarative knowledge.

Example: In a geology class, a teacher lectures about different types of rocks (igneous, sedimentary, metamorphic). After the lecture, students engage in an active recall exercise where they are asked to write down all the key rock types and their characteristics from memory, reinforcing their declarative knowledge.

8. Tacit Knowledge: Apprenticeship or Mentorship

Tacit knowledge is difficult to articulate and often gained through experience. Mentorship or apprenticeship is a teaching method that allows students to learn by observing and imitating an expert.

Example: In a robotics lab, students work closely with a mentor who has years of experience building robots. Through hands-on work and observing the mentor's approach to problem-solving and design, students acquire tacit knowledge about the nuances of robot construction, troubleshooting, and innovation that cannot be easily explained through formal instruction alone.

By employing these varied teaching methods, educators can effectively target and nurture different types of knowledge, fostering a comprehensive learning experience for STEM students.

Teaching techniques for easy reception and long-term retention

All forms of knowledge, including facts, principles, and phenomena, should be learned, memorized, and recalled. Memory and recall are essential and foundational cognitive skills. Too often, we dismiss these abilities with terms like "rote learning" and "memorization," viewing them with a certain disdain. In many discussions—and even in my own books—memory tends to be underrated and sometimes even disparaged. Yet, memory is the bedrock of all other cognitive functions. Without it, we would need to relearn the same concept every day. For instance, individuals with Alzheimer's disease must often be reminded or told the same information repeatedly.

Every cognitive skill relies on the ability to remember and retrieve information, as memory is the foundation of all higher-level thinking. Memory, encompassing facts, principles, and their applications is foundational for intelligence. For example, mastering mathematical concepts requires recalling basic arithmetic operations. Without this recallable knowledge, students would struggle to progress to more complex problem-solving. Thus, students should be encouraged to develop techniques for enhancing memory and recall. Ultimately, strong memory skills serve as the bedrock upon which other cognitive abilities are developed, emphasizing the importance of effective memory strategies to enhance learning and cognitive development. A person's knowledge is as strong as their memory.

Teaching knowledge, fostering methods of memorization, and encouraging the use of associative maps can significantly enhance students' learning experiences and memory retention. Here are ten points on how to achieve this:

1. Active Learning Techniques
Active learning requires students to actively engage with the material through discussions, problem-solving, or hands-on activities. This method not only consolidates knowledge but also improves long-term retention by making learning interactive and dynamic.

Example of Implementation: In a chemistry class, instead of lecturing about chemical reactions, the teacher can have students perform small experiments, such as mixing vinegar and baking soda. The teacher can then guide discussions about the underlying principles of reactions, ensuring that students understand the concepts through direct experience.

2. Chunking Information
Chunking breaks complex information into smaller, manageable pieces. This aligns with cognitive psychology, as the brain is more

adept at processing information when it is presented in bite-sized chunks.

Example of Implementation: When teaching a chapter on cellular biology, break the content into smaller topics, such as cell organelles, functions, and processes. Each section can be taught in isolation, ensuring that students thoroughly understand one component before moving on to the next.

3. Repetition and Spaced Learning
Spaced repetition involves reviewing material at increasing intervals, which strengthens memory and reduces forgetting over time. This method allows knowledge to be transferred from short-term to long-term memory.

Example of Implementation: In a history class, after teaching a lesson on World War I, the teacher can schedule reviews of key events every few weeks, gradually extending the time between reviews. Students could engage in periodic quizzes or group discussions, ensuring that information remains fresh.

4. Use of Mnemonics
Mnemonics help students remember facts or concepts by associating them with easily recallable acronyms, rhymes, or stories.

Example of Implementation: To help students remember the order of taxonomic classification (Kingdom, Phylum, Class, Order, Family, Genus, Species), the teacher can introduce a mnemonic such as "King Philip Came Over For Good Soup." This mnemonic simplifies recall through association.

5. Visualization and Associative Maps
Visual aids like mind maps, diagrams, or charts help students organize information and make connections between concepts. Associative maps enhance understanding and recall by showing relationships between ideas.

Example of Implementation: In an economics class, the teacher could use a flowchart to visualize supply and demand cycles. Students could then create their own diagrams to explain other economic principles, helping them structure and retain the information.

6. Storytelling and Narrative Techniques
Embedding information within a story or narrative helps students relate to abstract concepts by providing context and making it easier to remember.

Example of Implementation: When teaching physics, a teacher could explain the story of Isaac Newton's discovery of gravity by describing how an apple allegedly fell on his head. The narrative helps contextualize the law of gravity, making it more memorable.

7. Encouraging Curiosity
Curiosity leads students to explore topics more deeply. By presenting thought-provoking questions or real-world applications, teachers can engage students and encourage deeper learning.

Example of Implementation: In a mathematics class, instead of just presenting the Pythagorean theorem, the teacher could ask, "Why is this formula so essential in architecture and design?" This question encourages students to think about the real-world importance of abstract mathematical principles.

8. Analogies and Real-World Examples
Analogies bridge the gap between new information and prior knowledge, making it easier for students to grasp complex concepts.

Example of Implementation: When explaining electricity, a teacher might use the analogy of water flowing through a pipe to explain electrical current, with resistance compared to narrow points in the pipe. This relatable comparison helps students grasp the abstract concept.

9. Interactive and Cooperative Learning
Cooperative learning allows students to engage with each other through group work or peer teaching. It deepens knowledge by encouraging different perspectives and reinforcing understanding.

Example of Implementation: In a literature class, the teacher could divide students into groups to analyze different aspects of a poem. Afterward, each group would present their interpretation to the class, fostering collaboration and reinforcing their understanding of poetic elements.

10. Reflection and Metacognition
Metacognitive practices encourage students to reflect on their learning processes, helping them become more aware of how they learn and what they need to improve.

Example of Implementation: At the end of each lesson, students can be asked to write a brief reflection on what they found challenging and what strategies helped them understand the material. This exercise not only encourages self-awareness but also enhances the learning process by helping students recognize their cognitive strengths and weaknesses.

The Power of Mind Maps in Memorization and Recall

Mind maps are increasingly recognized as potent tools for memorization and recall, serving as visual frameworks that organize information around a central idea. By utilizing keywords, images, and colors, mind maps engage both cognitive and visual processes, facilitating deeper connections between concepts. Each branch represents a related idea, allowing learners to clearly see relationships and hierarchies. This visual arrangement enhances memory retention by leveraging the brain's natural ability to recognize patterns, ultimately transforming complex information into manageable and easily retrievable knowledge.

Cognitive and Visual Engagement

The dual engagement of cognitive and visual faculties in mind mapping significantly amplifies learning. For instance, in the field of biology, a student studying the human circulatory system can create a mind map with the "Circulatory System" at the center. Branches may include "Heart," "Blood Vessels," and "Blood," with further sub-branches detailing functions, types, and interrelations. By visualizing these components and their connections, the student can better understand how the system operates as a whole, enhancing recall during examinations.

In psychology, mind maps can illustrate theories and models, such as Maslow's Hierarchy of Needs. A central node labeled "Maslow" can branch out to "Physiological Needs," "Safety Needs," "Love/Belonging," "Esteem," and "Self-Actualization." Each branch can incorporate keywords or images representing examples or implications of each need. This visual representation aids students in remembering the theory's structure and facilitates discussions on its application in real-world scenarios, such as workplace motivation or educational settings.

Diverse Applications Across Fields

Mind maps have applications across a wide range of fields, demonstrating their versatility. In education, teachers can use mind maps to outline course content, allowing students to visualize the scope of their studies. For example, a history class might use a mind map to explore the causes and consequences of World War II, with branches detailing political, economic, and social factors, making the information easier to digest and recall.

In the business sector, mind maps can enhance strategic planning. A project manager might create a mind map centered on a new product launch, with branches for market research, marketing strategies, budget, and timeline. This visual overview allows team members to see the project's complexity and interdependencies, fostering collaborative discussions and efficient problem-solving.

Moreover, in creative fields such as writing or design, mind maps serve as brainstorming tools. An author could use a mind map to outline a novel, starting with the title at the center and branching out into characters, plot points, and themes. This approach not only organizes thoughts but also sparks creativity by visually connecting disparate ideas.

Enhancing Active Learning

Mind maps also promote active learning, making the study process more interactive and engaging. Unlike traditional note-taking, which can often lead to passive absorption of information, mind mapping requires students to actively participate in structuring their knowledge. This active engagement fosters critical thinking and encourages learners to make connections between concepts, thereby deepening their understanding.

Mind Maps: An Overview

Mind maps are a visual tool that organizes information in a structured, non-linear format, radiating from a central concept. Designed to reflect how the brain processes and stores information, mind maps encourage the clustering of related ideas through associations. The central idea or concept forms the core, and branches (representing categories or sub-concepts) extend outward, creating a web-like structure. These branches can have further subdivisions, allowing for deeper exploration of complex topics. The use of colors, images, and keywords enhances the effectiveness of mind maps by engaging both the logical and creative sides of the brain, making learning more dynamic and memorable.

Benefits of Mind Maps in the Classroom

Mind maps are a powerful tool for learning because they promote active engagement with the subject matter and improve recall by encouraging students to visualize relationships between concepts. This visualization helps students see the bigger picture, making complex subjects easier to understand. Furthermore, creating mind maps develops critical thinking and organizational skills, fostering deeper comprehension.

Implementing Mind Maps in the Classroom

1. Introduce the Concept of Mind Mapping:
 Begin by explaining what a mind map is and how it works. Show students an example, perhaps using an online tool like MindMeister or drawing one on the board. For instance, if the

lesson is on ecosystems, write "Ecosystem" in the center and branch out to categories such as "Producers," "Consumers," "Decomposers," and "Food Chain."

2. Choose a Central Topic:
 The next step is to choose a central theme for the mind map. This theme could be the main topic of the lesson, such as "Photosynthesis" in a biology class or "Shakespeare" in a literature lesson. The central topic should be a broad concept that can easily branch out into related sub-topics.

3. Create Branches for Key Concepts:
 Have students identify the major ideas or categories related to the central concept. These will serve as the first level of branches extending from the main topic. For example, in a mind map on photosynthesis, the branches could be labeled "Light Reactions," "Calvin Cycle," "Chloroplasts," and "Stomata." Each branch should represent a distinct category of information that can be broken down further.

4. Encourage Subdivisions and Associations:
 Once the main branches are established, students should start adding more detailed sub-branches for related ideas. For example, under the "Light Reactions" branch in the photosynthesis map, students can add subdivisions like "Chlorophyll," "ATP," and "NADPH." Encouraging students to ask "how" and "why" questions about each topic fosters deeper connections and critical thinking. Additionally, using different colors for each branch can make the map visually distinct, helping with retention and clarity.

5. Incorporate Visuals and Keywords:
 Encourage students to use images, symbols, or drawings that represent the key ideas. Visual elements help to stimulate both hemispheres of the brain, enhancing memory and understanding.

Keywords should be succinct, avoiding full sentences to keep the map uncluttered. In the mind map about photosynthesis, students could draw a sun next to the "Light Reactions" branch or leaves near the "Chloroplast" branch to symbolize plant cells.

6. Group Activity:
 Crafting mental maps alongside students in real-time is a highly effective teaching method that fosters deep engagement and active learning. While AI tools offer a convenient way to generate mental maps, simply providing these pre-made resources to students diminishes the potential for meaningful cognitive engagement. When students are merely handed completed maps, they become passive recipients of information rather than active participants in the process of structuring knowledge.

By contrast, building mental maps with students during class transforms the learning environment into a dynamic and collaborative space. This interactive method encourages students to actively participate in organizing the information, fostering critical thinking as they contemplate the relationships between ideas and the hierarchy of concepts. The process of co-creating these maps leads to a more profound understanding of the material, as students internalize the connections while engaging with the content in real-time. This live construction of mental maps also enhances retention, as students are not simply reviewing but actively forming the knowledge themselves.

Though labor-intensive, this approach stimulates more meaningful cognitive activity, cultivating an active learning environment. The teacher's role in guiding this process empowers students to develop their own mental frameworks, which can become valuable tools for future learning and problem-solving.

This method can also be adapted into a group activity, fostering cooperative learning. For example, in a history lesson on World War II, dividing the class into groups to create separate mind maps—on the causes, key battles, or aftermath—promotes collaboration. Each group's presentation of their mind map reinforces knowledge while encouraging peer learning and engagement.

Mind maps provide a flexible and visually engaging way for students to organize, process, and recall information. Implementing mind maps in the classroom not only enhances students' understanding of complex topics but also develops essential skills like critical thinking and creativity. By encouraging active participation, mind maps transform learning into a more interactive and collaborative experience, helping students connect ideas and improve long-term retention.

Ways of Acquiring Knowledge

1. Observation: Gaining knowledge by closely watching and interpreting natural phenomena, behaviors, or events.
In a biology class, students can observe plant growth over time by setting up an experiment in which they monitor different environmental conditions, such as light and water. Over a few weeks, students record their observations of how the plants grow, change, and adapt. This method allows students to develop scientific thinking and interpret natural phenomena directly.
Implementation: Teachers can organize field trips or lab activities where students observe real-world phenomena. For instance, during a visit to a zoo, students can observe animal behavior, analyzing their feeding habits or social structures. Teachers should encourage note-taking and subsequent class discussions to interpret the observations.

2. Experience: Learning through personal interaction and involvement in various situations over time.

In a culinary arts class, students can acquire cooking skills by directly preparing meals. By consistently participating in practical cooking sessions, they develop a deeper understanding of techniques, ingredients, and flavors. **Implementation:** Practical exercises can be incorporated in a variety of subjects. In history, for example, students could role-play historical events or debates. In physics, students could build simple machines or conduct hands-on demonstrations to internalize the principles of mechanics. The key is to provide opportunities for experiential learning that relates to the subject matter.

3. Education/Instruction: Gaining knowledge through formal education, such as lectures, classes, and structured training.

A chemistry teacher might give structured lectures about chemical bonding, followed by laboratory instruction on how to test different reactions. This formal teaching approach combines theoretical knowledge with practical application. **Implementation:** Teachers should integrate both instruction and application. Lectures can be followed by interactive activities like group problem-solving or lab work. Instructors can further solidify understanding by holding class discussions, asking reflective questions, or using real-world applications to illustrate key points.

4. Reading and Research: Acquiring knowledge from books, academic journals, and articles.

As emphasized in the previous book, reading stands as the ultimate form of learning, enhancing cognition and deepening intellectual capacity. Only independent experimental research surpasses it in difficulty, as research demands extensive effort, resources, and time. Reading, however, requires little beyond the book itself—everything else comes from within the learner's time, dedication, and focus. A committed reader is compelled to engage actively, constructing mental imagery and grasping abstract concepts from every sentence. This imaginative process nurtures deeper thinking and reflection, fostering a profound connection with the material that ultimately cultivates a more insightful, critical mind. This is the training of the mind!

In a STEM classroom, reading plays a similarly crucial role in enhancing understanding and critical thinking. For instance, in a biology class, students can be assigned primary research papers on genetic engineering or stem cell research, along with textbook readings that cover foundational principles. To deepen their understanding, students can research recent developments or ethical discussions surrounding these topics.

Implementation: Teachers should assign a combination of textbooks, peer-reviewed articles, and case studies relevant to the subject. After completing the reading, students can engage in mini-research projects, where they explore current advancements or potential applications, write summaries or analysis reports, or deliver presentations. This approach reinforces their comprehension while fostering critical engagement with both theoretical and practical aspects of the subject.

5. Experimentation: Gaining knowledge by conducting experiments, testing hypotheses, and analyzing outcomes.
In a chemistry class, students might conduct lab experiments to test hypotheses, such as analyzing the chemical composition of different household products to determine pH levels.
Implementation: Teachers should regularly incorporate experiments or simulations. For example, in a psychology class, students could simulate memory or perception experiments and analyze the results to understand how cognitive processes work. Experimentation encourages critical thinking and the application of theory to practice.

6. Reflection and Analysis: Developing knowledge by thinking critically and reflecting on personal experiences and information. In a philosophy class, after studying various philosophical arguments, students could reflect on their own beliefs and evaluate the arguments' strengths and weaknesses. **Implementation:** Reflection should be incorporated into every lesson. Teachers can ask students to maintain journals, where they reflect on what they have learned, or hold discussions that encourage them to question and critique the material. Reflection deepens learning by connecting theory to personal experience. Reflection and analysis are pure thinking, one of the best ways of honing the mind.

7. Social Learning: Learning from others through conversation, mentorship, or collaboration.
 In a computer science class, students might work on a group project to develop a simple software program. By collaborating, they learn from one another, share knowledge, and solve problems together. **Implementation:** Teachers should design group activities and projects that foster teamwork. Peer teaching, where students explain concepts to one another, can also be effective. Social learning taps into collaborative knowledge-building, making learning dynamic and interactive.

8. Trial and Error: Gaining practical knowledge by repeatedly attempting something until a successful outcome is achieved. In a music class, students learn to play instruments by trying different techniques and adjusting based on mistakes. The process of repeated practice and feedback helps them improve their skills. **Implementation:** Teachers should allow students to engage in trial-and-error learning by giving them open-ended problems or projects with no definitive answers. For example, in coding or design classes, students can be encouraged to test different solutions and learn from failures.

9. Intuition: Gaining insights or knowledge through instinctive understanding, often developed through repeated exposure and practice.

In a physics class, students working on projectile motion problems might develop an intuitive sense of how objects will behave based on their prior experience with similar problems. Instead of consciously calculating every step, they may instinctively predict the trajectory or speed of an object, relying on their familiarity with the underlying principles.

Implementation: Teachers can encourage intuitive thinking by providing students with ample opportunities to solve real-world problems without rigid step-by-step instructions. For example, in an engineering design project, students can be tasked with building structures or solving fluid dynamics problems, allowing their instincts and experience to guide their solutions. Teachers should create a balance between supporting intuitive approaches and guiding students to refine their insights through analysis and reflection.

10. Media and Technology: Acquiring knowledge through digital platforms such as documentaries, podcasts, online courses, and webinars.

In language classes, students might use online apps like Duolingo to practice new vocabulary and grammar. The gamified experience keeps them engaged and facilitates self-paced learning.
Implementation: Teachers should leverage digital tools—documentaries, podcasts, or online learning platforms—to enrich the learning experience. In a flipped classroom model, students could watch instructional videos at home and engage in more interactive and problem-solving activities during class.

The media and technology formats present information in a structured, engaging way, making it easy to absorb. However, while these tools are excellent for introducing concepts, I believe over-reliance on them limits deeper intellectual engagement. Passive consumption of information without supplementary practices such as reading, critical reflection, and active questioning undermines the mental rigor required for true learning. These traditional methods demand more effort but cultivate a disciplined, analytical mindset, essential for the long-term development of deep thinking and cognitive resilience. In the end, we must determine whether our priority is fostering understanding or cultivating the ability to think critically.

Teaching students efficient ways of acquiring knowledge requires fostering active learning and critical thinking. Encouraging participation in discussions, hands-on activities, and problem-solving tasks helps students engage more deeply with the material. By creating a classroom environment that promotes curiosity, teachers can motivate students to ask questions and explore subjects in greater depth. For instance, using open-ended questions during discussions or assigning projects that relate to real-world scenarios enhances students' ability to apply knowledge practically and contextually.

Rhetoric in Teaching Knowledge: Enhancing Depth and Retention of Learning

Teaching, as described in *TEACH I: Cultivating Persona and Building Characters,* is the art of selling knowledge and skills to often unwilling learners. The challenge lies in ensuring this "sale" takes place, as the learners have paid for it, and both their parents and administrators expect us to make them "buy" the knowledge and skills.

At the most fundamental level, teaching knowledge revolves around the effective transmission of information. Facts, data, and well-established principles form the core of any academic discipline, and students must first grasp these foundational elements before they can engage in higher-level thinking and problem-solving. However, the method by which this knowledge is delivered significantly impacts its depth, retention, and application. This is where rhetoric, the art of persuasive and effective communication, proves invaluable.

The word "rhetoric" originates from ancient Greece, where it referred to the art of persuasive speaking or writing. In its modern definition, rhetoric encompasses techniques used to influence, persuade, or inform an audience, often through effective communication strategies, including the use of language, style, and argumentation. Rhetoric, when used purposefully in teaching, goes beyond mere information delivery. It serves to engage students at multiple levels—intellectually, emotionally, and logically—enhancing their ability to internalize and apply knowledge. By employing rhetorical techniques such as logos (appealing to logic and reasoning), ethos (establishing credibility), and pathos (eliciting emotional engagement), teachers can present knowledge in a more engaging, understandable, and memorable manner. This essay explores how rhetoric enriches the teaching of knowledge, using examples to illustrate its profound impact on learning outcomes.

Logos: Teaching Knowledge Through Logic and Reasoning

One of the most effective rhetorical strategies for teaching knowledge is the use of logos, or appealing to logic and reasoning. Knowledge in any discipline, whether it be mathematics, science, or humanities, is built upon logical sequences and structured argumentation. By breaking down complex concepts into smaller, manageable steps, teachers guide students through the material in a way that is not only comprehensible but also intellectually stimulating.

Consider a science teacher explaining the concept of genetic inheritance. This topic, while fundamental to biology, can be abstract and difficult for students to grasp. To make the concept more concrete, the teacher might employ an analogy—another rhetorical device under the umbrella of logos—by comparing genetic inheritance to the passing of a family heirloom from one generation to another. Just as a precious artifact is passed down through generations, genetic traits are transferred from parents to offspring through genes. This analogy not only simplifies the concept but also connects it to something familiar, helping students assimilate the new information into their existing cognitive frameworks.

Moreover, structured argumentation is central to logos. Teachers often guide students through a logical progression of ideas, starting from basic principles and leading to more complex conclusions. In a history lesson, for example, a teacher might begin by discussing the economic conditions of pre-revolutionary France, then introduce the political factors, and finally, the social unrest that culminated in the French Revolution. By presenting information in a logical sequence, the teacher ensures that students not only memorize the facts but also understand the causal relationships between events. This approach enables students to think critically about the material, fostering a deeper, more integrated understanding.

Rhetorical Questions: Engaging Students in Reflective Thinking

Another powerful rhetorical device in teaching knowledge is the use of rhetorical questions. Rhetorical questions are not meant to elicit immediate answers but rather to stimulate reflective thinking. When teachers pose thought-provoking questions, they encourage students to engage actively with the material, prompting them to reflect on their understanding and make connections between different pieces of knowledge.

For example, in a literature class discussing Shakespeare's Hamlet, the teacher might ask, "Why does Hamlet delay his revenge? What does this reveal about his character?" Such questions force students to go beyond the surface of the text and consider deeper psychological and thematic elements. The rhetorical question challenges them to synthesize their knowledge of the plot with their interpretation of Hamlet's motivations, fostering critical thinking and analysis. This active engagement with the material leads to a more profound and lasting understanding than passive memorization of facts alone.

Rhetorical questions can also be used to introduce new topics or concepts, sparking curiosity and motivating students to explore the answers themselves. For instance, a physics teacher might begin a lesson on Newton's laws of motion with the question, "Why do we feel a jolt when a car suddenly stops?" This question taps into students' everyday experiences, drawing them into the lesson and piquing their interest in the underlying physical principles. By connecting abstract concepts to real-world phenomena, rhetorical questions make knowledge more accessible and engaging.

Here are ten rhetorical sentences designed to appeal to logos, or logical reasoning, that can be effectively used in the context of teaching knowledge:

1. "If we consider the evidence presented in these studies, it is clear that a strong foundation in mathematics significantly enhances problem-solving skills across various disciplines."

2. "By analyzing the historical data, we can conclude that societies that invest in education experience higher economic growth rates compared to those that do not."

3. "Research shows that students who engage in active learning strategies outperform their peers in traditional lecture-based environments, underscoring the importance of participation in knowledge acquisition."

4. "If we apply the scientific method consistently, we can systematically verify our hypotheses, thus reinforcing the credibility of our findings."

5. "Given the alarming increase in climate-related disasters, it is imperative to adopt sustainable practices, as the cost of inaction far exceeds the investment in preventive measures."

6. "Statistical analysis indicates a direct correlation between regular physical activity and improved cognitive function, supporting the notion that a healthy body contributes to a healthy mind."

7. "If we examine the principles of economics, it becomes evident that supply and demand dictate market behavior, influencing our understanding of consumer choices."

8. "Logical reasoning dictates that if we prioritize critical thinking in education, we equip students with essential skills for navigating complex real-world problems."

9. "The principles of genetics clearly demonstrate that understanding heredity can lead to advancements in medicine, thereby enhancing our overall quality of life."

10. "When we evaluate the success rates of different teaching methods through empirical research, it becomes apparent that differentiated instruction leads to improved student outcomes."

Ethos: Establishing Credibility to Facilitate Knowledge Transfer

The use of ethos, or credibility, in rhetoric enhances the authority and trustworthiness of the information presented. In teaching, ethos is crucial because students are more likely to engage with and retain knowledge from sources they deem credible and reliable. Teachers, therefore, must establish themselves as knowledgeable, competent, and trustworthy figures in the eyes of their students.

Credibility can be established in several ways. First, teachers must demonstrate mastery of the subject matter. This may involve not only presenting facts but also engaging with current research, drawing on personal experience, or citing reputable sources. For example, a professor teaching economics might reference the works of prominent economists such as Adam Smith or John Maynard Keynes to support their explanations of economic theories. By aligning themselves with respected authorities in the field, the teacher reinforces their credibility, making the knowledge they impart more persuasive and trustworthy.

Moreover, ethos is not limited to intellectual authority; it also encompasses the teacher's character and rapport with students. Teachers who show empathy, fairness, and a genuine interest in their students' learning cultivate an environment of trust and respect. When students trust their teacher, they are more likely to engage actively with the material, ask questions, and seek clarification when needed. This trust is essential for effective knowledge transfer, as students are more inclined to internalize and apply information when they feel supported by a credible and reliable teacher.

Here are ten rhetorical sentences designed to appeal to ethos, or credibility and ethical appeal, that can be effectively used in the context of teaching knowledge:

1. "As educators, we bear a profound responsibility to ensure that our students not only acquire knowledge but also develop the integrity and ethical judgment necessary for their future roles in society."

2. "Drawing from my years of experience in the field, I can assure you that understanding diverse perspectives enriches our learning environment and fosters respect among peers."

3. "When we engage in discussions that challenge our beliefs, we demonstrate the courage to grow and learn, embodying the very principles we hope to instill in our students."

4. "By upholding the highest standards of academic integrity, we set an example for our students, emphasizing the value of honesty and the pursuit of truth in all endeavors."

5. "As a community of learners, we must recognize that our commitment to lifelong learning reflects not only our personal growth but also our duty to contribute positively to society."

6. "Consider the contributions of influential thinkers and innovators; their ethical choices and dedication to their fields serve as powerful reminders of the impact we can have when we prioritize knowledge for the greater good."

7. "In today's interconnected world, it is our ethical obligation to teach students the importance of cultural competence and empathy, preparing them to navigate and contribute to a diverse society."

8. "When we foster an environment of mutual respect and collaboration, we affirm our commitment to not only academic excellence but also to the ethical development of our students."

9. "Reflecting on the values we uphold in education, it becomes evident that nurturing curiosity and critical thinking in our students empowers them to become responsible and ethical citizens."

10. "As we explore complex issues, let us remember that our role as educators is not only to impart knowledge but also to inspire ethical reasoning and informed decision-making in our students."

Pathos: Creating Emotional Connections to Enhance Engagement

While logos and ethos are essential for teaching knowledge, the emotional appeal of pathos should not be underestimated. Human cognition is deeply influenced by emotion, and students are more likely to engage with and remember material when they feel emotionally connected to it. By appealing to students' emotions, teachers can make knowledge more relatable, meaningful, and memorable.

One of the most effective ways to invoke pathos in teaching is through storytelling. Stories have a unique ability to humanize abstract concepts and bring them to life. For instance, a history teacher discussing the horrors of the Holocaust might share personal accounts of survivors, bringing historical facts into a deeply personal and emotional context. These stories not only make the material more engaging but also help students connect with the subject matter on a human level, fostering empathy and a deeper understanding of the historical event.

Humor is another rhetorical device that taps into pathos. When used appropriately, humor can lighten the mood, reduce anxiety, and make challenging material more approachable. A mathematics teacher, for example, might use a humorous analogy to explain a difficult concept like quadratic equations, comparing it to the challenges of navigating a maze. This lighthearted approach makes the material less intimidating and more accessible, encouraging students to engage with the lesson.

Personal anecdotes also serve as powerful tools for invoking pathos. When teachers share their own experiences—whether they are stories of struggle, success, or curiosity—they create an emotional connection with their students. For example, a teacher explaining the scientific method might recount a personal story of a failed experiment and the lessons learned from it. This anecdote not only makes the abstract concept of the scientific method more tangible but also humanizes the teacher, fostering a sense of shared experience and emotional engagement with the material.

Here are ten rhetorical sentences designed to appeal to pathos, or emotional appeal, that can be effectively used in the context of teaching knowledge:

1. "Imagine the joy of discovery when a student finally grasps a challenging concept; that moment is what drives us as educators to inspire a love for learning."

2. "Think about a time when you faced a difficult problem; the determination you felt is what we want to cultivate in our students as they navigate their own challenges."

3. "When we share personal stories of struggle and triumph, we create connections that foster empathy, showing students that perseverance is as important as knowledge."

4. "As we discuss the impact of climate change, let us remember that the future of our planet rests in the hands of our students, who are capable of making a difference."

5. "Every time we ignite a spark of curiosity in our students, we open the door to endless possibilities, allowing them to dream beyond their current reality."

6. "Reflect on the stories of individuals who overcame adversity through education; these narratives serve as powerful reminders of the transformative power of knowledge."

7. "When we highlight the voices of marginalized communities in our lessons, we not only educate but also honor their experiences, making learning more inclusive and impactful."

8. "As we delve into historical events, let us not forget the human experiences behind the facts; these stories connect us and deepen our understanding of the world."

9. "Consider the excitement in a student's eyes when they achieve a goal; that feeling of accomplishment is the emotional reward that validates our efforts as educators."

10. "In moments of uncertainty, it is our duty to reassure students that their voices matter, empowering them to share their thoughts and feelings in a supportive environment."

The effective use of rhetoric in teaching enhances students' cognitive engagement, emotional investment, and critical thinking, ultimately leading to deeper learning and improved retention. By blending logical reasoning, credibility, and emotional appeal, rhetoric transforms the classroom into a dynamic environment where knowledge is not only acquired but also internalized and applied.

Chapter 5: What is intelligence

Definitions of intelligence

Intelligence is a complex and multifaceted concept that has been defined in various ways across academic disciplines and traditional frameworks. Below is a compilation of several definitions from both perspectives:

Traditional Definitions of Intelligence

1. Classical Definition:
 - Aristotle: "Intelligence is the ability to understand and reason, often associated with wisdom and practical knowledge."

2. Philosophical Definition:
 - Plato: "Intelligence is the capacity to apprehend the eternal truths and the essence of things, emphasizing the philosophical pursuit of knowledge."

3. Pragmatic Definition:
 - John Dewey: "Intelligence is the ability to adapt to the environment and engage in effective problem-solving in real-life situations, emphasizing practical application over abstract reasoning."

4. Traditional Educational Perspective:
 - "Intelligence is the capacity to acquire and apply knowledge and skills, often measured through standardized testing and assessments in educational contexts."

5. Common Sense Definition:
 - "Intelligence is the ability to think, understand complex ideas, learn quickly, and adapt to new situations in everyday life."

6. Street-smart Definition:
"Intelligence is the ability to solve problems in real-time using the least amount of resources and whatever limited tools or information are available."

7. Indian Traditional Definition:
"Intelligence, or *buddhi*, is the faculty of discernment, reasoning, and moral judgment, extending beyond cognitive abilities to include spiritual wisdom and ethical clarity."

Academic Definitions of Intelligence

1. Psychometric Definition:
 - Spearman (1904): "Intelligence is the general mental ability that underlies performance on various cognitive tasks, often measured through IQ tests."

2. Cognitive Psychology Definition:
 - Anderson (2009): "Intelligence is the ability to learn from experience, solve problems, and use knowledge to adapt to new situations."

3. Gardner's Multiple Intelligences Theory:
 - Gardner (1983): "Intelligence is the ability to solve problems or create products that are valued within one or more cultural settings, encompassing various modalities such as linguistic, logical-mathematical, spatial, musical, and interpersonal intelligences."

4. Sternberg's Triarchic Theory of Intelligence:
 - Sternberg (1985): "Intelligence consists of three aspects: analytical intelligence (problem-solving), creative intelligence (the ability to deal with novel situations), and practical intelligence (the ability to adapt to everyday life)."

5. Emotional Intelligence:
- Goleman (1995): "Intelligence is the capacity to recognize and manage one's own emotions, as well as the emotions of others, which plays a crucial role in social interactions and personal decision-making."

6. Cultural Definition:
- Nisbett et al. (2001): "Intelligence varies across cultures and contexts, reflecting different values and practices that influence how cognitive abilities are perceived and developed."

The definitions of intelligence illustrate its multifaceted nature, reflecting a range of cognitive, emotional, and practical dimensions. Academic perspectives often emphasize measurable abilities and theoretical frameworks, while traditional definitions highlight wisdom, adaptability, and moral considerations. Together, these definitions provide a comprehensive understanding of intelligence, demonstrating its relevance across diverse contexts and disciplines.

Intelligence and change

If the universe remained static—if every object, thought, or being stayed exactly as it was from the moment of its creation—knowledge alone would suffice. In such a world, once one has acquired knowledge of something, the need for further cognitive engagement would be minimal; the act of knowing would be finite. We would not need to think beyond what we have already learned because nothing would alter our understanding.

However, the world does not operate in this manner. Everything, from the most microscopic particles to the broad expanse of human emotion and thought, is in a perpetual state of transformation. A tree grows and sheds its leaves; societies rise and fall; technology advances; and even our emotions shift with every experience. Change demands intelligence because knowledge alone cannot anticipate or adapt to new forms, situations, and realities. Intelligence allows us to interpret these shifts, understand their roots, and forecast their outcomes.

Consider the evolution of a person's personality. A child's personality may be shaped by early experiences, but as that child grows, they encounter new challenges, people, and environments, all of which influence who they become. The intelligent mind sees not only the immediate shifts in behavior or outlook but understands the underlying causes—perhaps a new friendship or a traumatic event—and can predict how these changes may continue to evolve over time. This awareness extends beyond mere knowledge of personality traits; it involves an active, ongoing engagement with the changing nature of the person.

In life, psychology, or even simple day-to-day experiences, intelligence helps us navigate the complexities of change. Consider the technological advancements we witness daily. If one simply knows how to operate a machine today, that knowledge might be obsolete tomorrow when the machine's design evolves. Intelligence, however, enables us to adapt, learn anew, and stay ahead of the curve because we are constantly sensing, processing, and adjusting to change.

Understanding the nature of change—its degree, direction, causes, and consequences—is central to intelligence. Change is the driving force behind all progress and adaptation, and everything around us is in a constant state of flux. This is fundamentally how evolution works: change (variation), the adoption of beneficial changes, the elimination of detrimental changes (selection), and the transfer of information from one person to another, even across generations (inheritance). Whether we examine life itself, the ever-evolving realms of psychology, or even personalities and individuals, the one constant is change.

Intelligence, therefore, is the ability to not only recognize that things are changing but to deeply comprehend the nuances of these changes and their implications. It is this intricate understanding that sets intelligence apart from mere knowledge. Intelligence is fluid, adaptable, and responsive. Intelligence allows us to perceive not only surface-level changes but also the deeper, more profound shifts occurring beneath. It helps us adjust our methods, strategies, and thinking to meet the new realities that emerge. Intelligence is about having the cognitive flexibility to respond to the world as it becomes. This is why intelligence is essential—because change is inevitable, and to navigate it successfully, we must think, adapt, and grow.

My definition of intelligence, therefore, is "***Intelligence is the dynamic mental engagement that enables individuals to detect, predict, process, direct, and regulate changes in the environment, themselves, and others.***" It involves the active application of cognition to foresee and understand the nature and direction of change, strategically influence outcomes, and adapt to evolving circumstances. It is the intellectual force that integrates awareness, foresight, and adaptability to master change. When we address someone as intelligent, we should refer to a person who can predict, process, direct, and regulate changes to solve a problem that has arisen instantly or is anticipated. For example, imagine a pilot who faces sudden engine failure mid-flight. The ability to assess the situation, predict outcomes, process possible solutions, and take immediate corrective action to safely land the plane is intelligence. This process involves real-time mental engagement and decision-making under pressure, which goes beyond just recalling pre-learned knowledge. Similarly, consider a scientist encountering a novel research question in a lab. The ability to hypothesize, design experiments, and interpret results to uncover previously unknown information is an intellectual process. When individuals solve a problem for the first time, they are actively engaged in the process of intelligence. However, upon encountering the same issue again, they can draw upon their prior experience or knowledge, requiring less deep cognitive effort. In this second instance, what may simply be knowledge for them could still represent intelligence for others who have not faced that problem before. Intelligence is thus the capacity to generate solutions to changing circumstances, while repeated application of solutions becomes knowledge. Objective-oriented thinking, which solves problems within the domain of change, defines intelligence. The best form of intelligence is revealed in scenarios of absolute uncertainty.

It takes a lifetime to become the best possible intelligent person one can be. Intelligence is not a fixed attribute but an evolving process shaped and sharpened by the challenges one faces. Importantly, the act of confronting as many problems as possible, pondering deeply upon them, and solving them based on contextual needs or constraints serves as the essential nourishment for intelligence. Each problem presents a unique set of circumstances that demands real-time mental engagement, creativity, and adaptability. By continually engaging with new and diverse challenges, intelligence is not only practiced but expanded. The more varied and complex the problems, the more nuanced and sophisticated the intelligence becomes.

In this way, intelligence thrives on variety, complexity, and context. The more we immerse ourselves in solving problems, adapting to change, and applying novel approaches, the closer we come to realizing our full intellectual potential. This lifelong pursuit ensures that intelligence remains dynamic, continually evolving in response to the ever-changing world around us.

Teachers should challenge students to think critically, solve complex problems, and engage deeply with material beyond memorization. They should encourage inquiry by asking open-ended questions that demand analysis, reflection, and application. Students should be pushed to make connections between concepts, explore multiple perspectives, and learn how to adapt knowledge to new situations. Teachers should foster an environment of experimentation, allowing students to learn through trial and error. By promoting independent thinking, collaborative learning, and real-world problem-solving, teachers can cultivate the skills needed for students to not only gain knowledge but also develop true intelligence.

Stages of intelligence

As a mental construct, intelligence can be understood as a dynamic and multifaceted process that transcends the functioning of our sensory organs. It involves three core components: sensing, processing, and output. All of these require a degree of mental engagement. Sensing, for instance, can occur with or without active cognitive involvement; we can perceive the world passively, but when mental engagement is introduced, the experience deepens. Similarly, actions can be performed automatically, but when mental focus is applied, the outcome is more thoughtful, deliberate, and reflective.

The essence of intelligence lies in the quality of mental engagement across these stages. The more intricate, real-time mental involvement in the intake of information, its analysis, and the eventual expression of an outcome, the more intellectual the process becomes. For example, when students learn to solve a mathematical problem, the intelligence shown lies not just in the solution but in their ability to understand the problem, think critically through each step, and derive an answer. This continuous mental engagement transforms raw sensory input into knowledge, insight, or action. Intelligence, therefore, is not just about what we sense or do but how deeply we engage mentally with those experiences to produce meaningful outcomes.

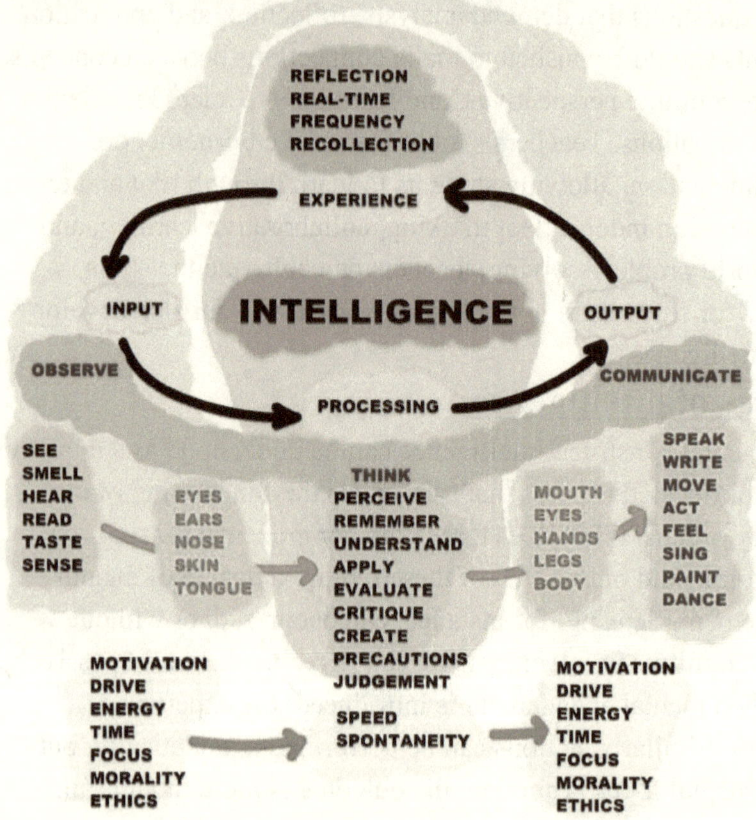

Sensing

The initial stage of intelligence is sensing, which refers not only to the reception of stimuli through the traditional five senses—sight, hearing, touch, taste, and smell—but also to a more profound cognitive form of perception. This cognitive sensing involves the ability to interpret and understand nuances in the environment, including subtle cues that may not be readily observable. For instance, a teacher may sense a student's confusion not just through their body language but also by interpreting the emotional undertones in their responses.

Intelligence demands a heightened awareness and the ability to perceive the world through a lens that integrates both sensory input and cognitive insights. This involves being attuned to the broader context, discerning patterns and relationships within the information received, and understanding the implications of what is sensed. It is this comprehensive awareness that allows individuals to gather rich, contextual information, enhancing their capacity for intelligent decision-making.

Processing
The second aspect of intelligence is processing, which encompasses the mental operations that occur after information is sensed. This purely cerebral work involves analyzing, synthesizing, and evaluating the information gathered. It requires higher-order thinking skills such as critical thinking, problem-solving, and creativity.

During the processing phase, individuals draw on their existing knowledge and experiences to make sense of new information. For example, when confronted with a complex mathematical problem, a student engages in cognitive processing by recalling relevant concepts, formulating strategies, and evaluating potential solutions. This process is not merely mechanical; it involves an active engagement of the intellect, where individuals challenge assumptions, explore alternatives, and generate new ideas.

Moreover, processing information entails overcoming cognitive biases that may hinder clear thinking. This involves questioning one's initial reactions or beliefs, re-evaluating sources of information, and integrating diverse perspectives. The depth of processing correlates strongly with the quality of outcomes, influencing how effectively individuals can understand and apply knowledge.

Output
The final stage of intelligence is output, which refers to the expression of processed information. This output can take various forms, including verbal communication, written expression, artistic creation, or even physical actions. In some cases, even inaction is an output! The way information is expressed reflects the depth of understanding and the quality of processing that has occurred.

For instance, a researcher who has thoroughly analyzed data may present their findings through a compelling presentation that combines clear language, visual aids, and emotional appeal, effectively engaging their audience. Alternatively, an artist may express complex emotions and ideas through their work, providing a different yet equally valid form of output.

Intelligence accumulates knowledge—both factual and procedural. The more knowledge one attains, the more likely one is to solve complex problems quickly. Intelligence depends on knowledge, and knowledge provides opportunities to enhance intelligence. Intelligence is an iterative process that increases exponentially with the variety, frequency, and complexity of the problems one faces.

The Interdependence of Intelligence and Knowledge

Knowledge is what we learn, and intelligence is what we practice.

Intelligence, often characterized as the capacity to learn, reason, and solve problems, fundamentally relies on a robust foundation of knowledge. This knowledge encompasses a spectrum of facts, principles, logic, and rationale, which together form the cognitive toolkit necessary for intelligent functioning. Without a solid grasp of these elements, the ability to think critically and adaptively is significantly impaired.

Acquiring knowledge is the first step in developing intelligence. Facts provide the raw data that individuals draw upon to make informed decisions. Principles offer the underlying frameworks that guide reasoning, while logic serves as the structured approach to problem-solving. Rationale, encompassing the reasoning behind actions and decisions, is crucial for understanding the implications of those choices. For instance, a scientist must not only know various biological facts but also understand the principles of experimental design and logical reasoning to derive meaningful conclusions from research data.

Moreover, intelligence is not only about possessing knowledge; it is equally about the ability to process and apply that knowledge efficiently. This involves filtering information to arrive at solutions that are viable within specific constraints, such as time and energy. For example, a project manager must assess a multitude of variables, prioritize tasks, and make decisions that maximize productivity while minimizing resource expenditure. This economic processing of information reflects a nuanced understanding of both the context and the constraints at hand.

The relationship between intelligence and knowledge is reciprocal. Knowledge provides the foundational elements necessary for intelligent thought, while the processing of this knowledge within constraints determines the effectiveness of intelligent actions. Cultivating both aspects is essential for fostering true intelligence in any domain.

In contemporary discourse, what we often label as "stupid" is, in fact, a reflection of our natural state, whereas intelligence is a learned attribute. We learn our intelligence through the accumulation of knowledge, which is dependent on experiences, communication, and imagination. The true measure of intelligence lies in the ability to solve problems, which often requires applying knowledge gained from others. In essence, much of what we consider 'intelligence' today is, in fact, knowledge that we have heard from others.

Any new information that arises within a mind is a direct product of that mind's intelligence, reflecting its unique capacity for understanding and processing. In contrast, all other information obtained from external sources constitutes knowledge. This distinction emphasizes the significance of knowledge acquisition, as it serves as the very foundation upon which the tools of intelligence are built. The interplay between intelligence and knowledge is crucial, for it is through the assimilation of knowledge that individuals can refine their intelligence, enabling them to navigate complexities and engage with the world more effectively.

Imagine intelligence as the only mouth and alimentary canal of knowledge to find, eat, digest information and assimilate that 'knowledge' to keep growing. Intelligence serves as the medium through which knowledge is acquired, functioning as a suction conduit that draws in diverse streams of information. This influx of knowledge manifests as solutions, facts, processes, or even tools that enhance one's cognitive capabilities. Even to absorb knowledge from external sources, the mind should have intelligence tools and a knowledge base to make sense of the 'information' and assimilate that knowledge. The broader and more versatile 'mouth' (the individual's intelligence tools), the more effectively they can assimilate knowledge, leading to a richer understanding of complex concepts. Each new piece of knowledge not only enriches the individual's cognitive toolkit but also enhances their ability to address future challenges.

Knowledge in one scenario may simply be information, but in another, it becomes the cornerstone of intelligence. The ability to apply the most relevant knowledge to a given situation defines modern intelligence. In my opinion, the true form of intelligence—or absolute ingenuity—manifests when an individual approaches and solves a problem without having prior knowledge of it.

Intelligence is a process grounded in factual knowledge, utilizing procedural knowledge to acquire deeper or more knowledge. While intelligence represents the process, knowledge is the product. Intelligence works by processing existing information to uncover new insights or enhance current understanding. It is an active, dynamic cognitive function that transforms knowledge into deeper comprehension or more advanced applications, ultimately driving intellectual growth.

Intelligence is a fusion of cognition and personality.

Why would anyone want to solve so many problems? Is there an immediate or delayed benefit to the individual? In an educational context, why would a student willingly choose to tackle a diverse array of problems? For the average person, what compels them to confront a problem when evasion is an option? What if the problem is not that significant? What if a person is content with the status quo? Why should they do more, especially when it involves the draining cognitive work that problem-solving often demands?

The questions posed suggest a fundamental relationship between cognitive capacity and motivation. They imply that while individuals may possess the cognitive ability to solve problems, the drive to engage in such efforts is often influenced by perceived relevance and personal contentment. Thus, understanding this interplay is crucial in fostering a desire for learning and problem-solving among students. The motivation to solve problems increases the likelihood of iteration, through which intelligence grows. Therefore, I prefer to view intelligence as a dual construct comprising two interrelated components: cognitive traits and personality traits. Each of these dimensions plays a crucial role in shaping an individual's overall intelligence and ability to navigate the complexities of life.

Cognitive Traits

The cognitive aspect of intelligence refers to a set of skills and processes that facilitate the acquisition, processing, and application of knowledge. These skills are instrumental in how individuals perceive and interact with their environment. Key cognitive traits include:

1. Knowledge: Serving as the foundation of intelligence, knowledge encompasses the information, facts, concepts, and principles that individuals acquire through education and experience. A robust knowledge base is vital for informed decision-making and effective problem-solving.

2. Analytical Thinking: This skill involves breaking down complex information into manageable components, allowing individuals to understand relationships and draw logical conclusions.

3. Critical Thinking: Critical thinking enables individuals to evaluate arguments and evidence critically, assessing the validity of information and forming reasoned judgments based on rational thought.

4. Problem-Solving: The ability to identify issues, generate viable solutions, and implement effective strategies is a key cognitive trait that reflects intelligence in action.

5. Logical Reasoning: This trait involves systematic thinking and the capacity to follow a sequence of steps, leading to valid conclusions derived from given premises or data.

6. Systems Thinking is an analytical approach that emphasizes understanding the interconnections and interdependencies within a complex system, enabling effective problem-solving by recognizing how changes in one part can impact the whole.

7. Memory: Memory, encompassing both short-term and long-term retention of information, is essential for learning and the application of knowledge over time.

8. Attention: The ability to focus on specific information while filtering out distractions is critical for effective learning and processing of new information.

9. Information Synthesis: This cognitive skill allows individuals to integrate various pieces of information into a coherent understanding, fostering informed decision-making.

10. Pattern Recognition: Recognizing trends, relationships, and regularities in data helps individuals predict outcomes and make sound judgments.

11. Creativity: Creativity represents the capacity for divergent thinking, enabling individuals to generate novel ideas, solutions, or approaches to problems, which is crucial for innovation.

12. Metacognition: Metacognition involves awareness and regulation of one's cognitive processes, including the ability to reflect on and adjust one's learning strategies.

Together, these cognitive traits form a comprehensive framework that underpins the processing of information and problem-solving capabilities, allowing individuals to adapt to new situations effectively.

Personality Traits

While cognitive traits are essential for understanding and applying information, personality traits significantly influence how individuals approach learning and interaction with their environment. These traits often determine a person's motivation, resilience, and overall attitude toward challenges. Key personality traits associated with intelligence include:

1. Courage: The willingness to take risks and face challenges is crucial for intellectual growth and exploration.

2. Grit: Persistence and determination in the face of obstacles are vital for overcoming difficulties and achieving long-term goals.

3. Patience: The ability to remain calm and composed while navigating complex problems fosters a more thorough understanding of difficult concepts.

4. Motivation: Intrinsic motivation drives individuals to pursue knowledge and engage actively in the learning process, contributing to overall intelligence.

5. Adaptability: The capacity to adjust one's thinking and behavior in response to changing circumstances is essential for effective problem-solving and learning.

6. Empathy: Understanding and relating to the emotions of others can enhance collaborative efforts and foster a supportive learning environment.

7. Confidence: A belief in one's abilities can empower individuals to tackle challenging tasks and engage more fully in the learning process.

8. Curiosity: An innate desire to explore and learn is a powerful driver of intellectual engagement and discovery.

9. Resilience: The ability to bounce back from setbacks and maintain a positive outlook is essential for sustaining motivation and continued learning.

10. Self-discipline: The capacity to regulate one's actions and maintain focus on long-term goals is critical for achieving success in academic and personal pursuits.

Cognitive traits provide the necessary skills for processing information, solving problems, and adapting to new situations, while personality traits shape individuals' attitudes, motivations, and responses to challenges. Together, these dimensions of intelligence enable individuals to navigate their environments effectively, fostering both personal and academic growth. Personality traits belong to the humanities side of intelligence, which is a vast subject that includes psychology. That is why a whole book, *TEACH II: Motivating Minds and Enhancing Productivity*, was dedicated to teaching some of these personality traits to students.

Principles of Intellectual Development in Education

Let us recall the definition of intelligence in the light of change.

"Intelligence can be defined as the dynamic mental engagement that enables individuals to detect, predict, process, direct, and regulate changes in the environment, themselves, and others."

Based on this definition, intelligence is all about how one is prepared, cognitively and personality-wise, to predict, deal with, or regulate change. In the following sections, we shall discuss some cognitive training that can be used to improve intelligence.

In the realm of education, fostering an environment conducive to intellectual growth necessitates an understanding of various principles that guide students toward becoming critical thinkers and problem solvers. Below, I elaborate on a few fundamental principles: Root Cause Analysis, Causes and Consequences, Most Probable of All the Possibilities, Systems Thinking, Critical Inquiry, Hypothesis Testing, Iterative Learning, Design Thinking, Learning, Unlearning, and Relearning. Using this vocabulary of intelligence is a good practice to reinforce the learning of intelligence.

1. Root Cause Analysis

Root cause analysis serves as a foundational principle in education, enabling students to delve beneath the surface of problems. This method involves identifying the underlying factors contributing to an issue, thus equipping students with the skills to address problems effectively rather than merely treating their symptoms. For instance, consider a student struggling with academic performance. Instead of attributing this to a lack of intelligence, educators can guide the student to explore various potential root causes—be it ineffective study habits, emotional distress, or external distractions. By focusing on these deeper issues, students can develop targeted strategies for improvement, fostering a mindset that values investigation and resolution over superficial fixes.

2. Causes and Consequences

The principle of causes and consequences emphasizes the intricate relationship between actions and their outcomes. In an educational context, this principle encourages students to analyze not just the effects of their choices but also the rationale behind them. For example, in a science class, students might examine how pollution (cause) leads to climate change (consequence). Understanding this relationship fosters a deeper appreciation for the interconnectedness of actions within complex systems. As students recognize the repercussions of their decisions, they cultivate a sense of responsibility and foresight, essential traits for effective problem-solving and ethical decision-making.

3. Change, interactions and emergence

The principle of "Change, Interactions, and Emergence" embodies the essence of intelligence by teaching us how systems evolve, respond, and give rise to new properties. Intelligence thrives in recognizing that change is inherent in every process, both within and around us. To understand change, one must observe the factors influencing it, be it environmental, biological, or social. Here, interaction becomes essential: elements within any system— molecules in a chemical reaction, individuals within a community, or neurons within a brain—interact in ways that shape and are shaped by one another.

This interplay creates emergent phenomena or outcomes that cannot be easily deduced by examining individual parts alone.

Emergence in complex systems often yields innovative solutions, novel patterns, and insights that exceed the sum of their parts. In learning, this principle encourages flexibility and the development of critical thinking, recognizing that intelligence is not only about accumulating information but also about understanding relationships and anticipating transformations.

4. Certainties, Probabilities and Possibilities

In a world characterized by uncertainty and variability, understanding the interplay between certainties, probabilities, and possibilities is essential. Certainties represent established knowledge and facts that provide a solid foundation for decision-making, serving as benchmarks against which we can evaluate the unknowns. Probabilities emerge when we assess various scenarios and evaluate their likelihood, enabling individuals to weigh potential outcomes based on available evidence and leading to informed predictions. For instance, in a project examining renewable energy, students might analyze different energy sources, predicting the environmental and economic impacts of each, and by prioritizing the most likely scenarios, they can develop realistic solutions and enhance their decision-making skills. Possibilities encompass the range of outcomes that may arise from uncertain situations; while not every outcome can be predicted with certainty, recognizing the breadth of possibilities allows students to think creatively and adaptively. By integrating certainties with probabilistic thinking and acknowledging various possibilities, individuals are better equipped to navigate complexities with confidence and clarity, fostering a nuanced understanding of the multifaceted nature of real-world challenges.

5. Systems Thinking

Systems thinking is a holistic approach that encourages students to recognize the interconnectedness of various components within a system. This principle fosters an understanding that issues do not exist in isolation; rather, they are often part of larger systems. For example, when studying ecosystems, students learn how changes in one species can impact the entire food web. By applying systems thinking, they develop critical skills for analyzing multifaceted problems, enabling them to craft more comprehensive solutions. This principle also cultivates empathy, as students appreciate how their actions can ripple through interconnected systems, fostering a sense of collective responsibility.

6. Critical Inquiry

Critical inquiry is essential for nurturing independent thinkers. This principle involves engaging students in questioning and investigating the validity and reliability of information. In an age of misinformation, teaching students to scrutinize sources and assess arguments is paramount. For instance, in a history class, students might explore differing narratives of a significant event, encouraging them to critically evaluate the perspectives and motivations behind each account. This process not only strengthens their analytical skills but also fosters open-mindedness, enabling them to appreciate diverse viewpoints. By nurturing a culture of inquiry, educators empower students to develop sound arguments and judgments, vital for active participation in democratic societies.

7. Hypothesis Testing

The principle of hypothesis testing promotes an empirical approach to learning, allowing students to formulate and test hypotheses to explore relationships and causation. In a biology lab, for instance, students might hypothesize that increasing light exposure will enhance plant growth. By conducting experiments to test their hypothesis, they learn the importance of the scientific method, experiencing firsthand the iterative nature of inquiry. This principle cultivates critical thinking as students analyze data and draw conclusions based on evidence rather than assumptions.

8. Iterative Learning

Iterative learning embodies a continuous process of learning through trial and error. This principle encourages students to refine their understanding and strategies based on feedback and outcomes. For example, during a design project, students may create prototypes, receive critiques, and subsequently improve their designs. By embracing iteration, they learn that failure is not a final endpoint but a valuable part of the learning process. This principle nurtures a growth mindset, instilling resilience and adaptability in students. As they encounter challenges, they become more inclined to persist, ultimately fostering a sense of confidence in their abilities.

9. Design Thinking

Design thinking is a user-centered approach to problem-solving that emphasizes empathy, creativity, and iterative testing. This principle encourages students to define problems, ideate solutions, prototype, and test their ideas, fostering innovation and practical application of knowledge. For example, in a community service project, students might identify a local issue, brainstorm solutions, develop a prototype, and gather feedback from community members. This hands-on approach not only cultivates creativity but also reinforces the importance of collaboration and feedback in the learning process. Design thinking empowers students to become proactive problem solvers, prepared to tackle real-world challenges with confidence.

10. Learning, Unlearning, and Relearning

The principle of learning, unlearning, and relearning acknowledges the necessity of adapting to new insights and perspectives. In an ever-evolving world, the ability to discard outdated or incorrect information and embrace fresh knowledge is essential for intellectual growth. For instance, consider the rapid advancements in technology and how they necessitate a shift in skill sets. Students must be encouraged to recognize that the pursuit of knowledge is not a linear process; rather, it involves continuous evolution. By fostering an environment that values adaptability, educators empower students to thrive in a landscape characterized by constant change. This principle underscores the importance of lifelong learning, equipping students with the mindset necessary to navigate an uncertain future.

Chapter 6: Intelligence and human nature

Encountering and Evading Problems

Human behavior is profoundly influenced by a complex interplay of drives, motivations, and inherent natures. These elements shape not only how individuals perceive the world but also how they respond to the challenges they encounter. In the current context, this differentiation becomes particularly evident: some individuals might instinctively evade problems, while others might confront and solve them. This divergence in behavior likely forms the foundation of what one would become by nature, as the repeated choice between evasion and confrontation gradually molds a person's character and life trajectory.

Interestingly, the tendency to evade problems can also be viewed as a form of intelligence. This instinct to avoid challenges is innate, as problems often carry the risk of injury, loss, or the depletion of our limited resources. Thus, avoiding problems can be seen as a calculated decision prioritizing immediate safety or mental peace. However, in a world inherently filled with challenges, this avoidance may result in a life characterized by limited experiences and inactivity. While such an approach might preserve a sense of security, it ultimately restricts personal growth and the wisdom that emerges from confronting and overcoming obstacles.

A life dominated by the evasion of problems, though not devoid of intelligence, may ultimately become minuscule in its scope and significance. It is a life that lacks the richness of experience and the depth of understanding that comes from active engagement with the world's complexities. That is not enough of a life. To truly live is to encounter and navigate difficulties to embrace the uncertainties and trials that are an inescapable part of existence. Thus, while evasion might offer a temporary refuge, it is not enough to constitute a life fully lived.

Survival through problem-solving, particularly with the goal of ensuring a prolonged and comfortable existence for oneself and others, is the essence of what education strives to achieve. Education equips individuals with the knowledge, skills, and critical thinking necessary to navigate life's challenges effectively. By fostering the ability to solve problems, education not only supports individual survival but also contributes to the well-being and advancement of society as a whole.

The process of learning and problem-solving is not merely about overcoming immediate obstacles but about creating sustainable solutions that enhance the quality of life for future generations. In this sense, education serves as the foundation for both personal and collective progress, enabling us to build a world where survival is not just about meeting basic needs but about thriving in a way that benefits everyone.

Real-Time or Instantaneous Intelligence

Intelligence can be understood in two temporal contexts: real-time or instantaneous intelligence and future-oriented intelligence. In this sense, with the available data, the output should be delivered immediately or at a later time, which could be one hour, one day, a year, a decade, or a century.

Intelligence operates on different timescales, reflecting the ability to process information and make decisions both in the present and with foresight toward the future. Immediate solutions require a swift response to current challenges, while future-oriented solutions involve strategic planning for potential scenarios. Immediate solutions are characterized by practical intelligence, facilitating rapid problem-solving in real-time contexts. Conversely, future-oriented solutions are grounded in strategic intelligence, promoting long-term planning and innovation to effectively address anticipated challenges.

Real-time intelligence refers to the immediate processing and application of information as situations unfold. This type of intelligence is characterized by quick decision-making and problem-solving capabilities, enabling individuals to respond effectively to dynamic environments. For instance, during a crisis, a leader must assess the situation, evaluate available information, and make decisions rapidly. This involves utilizing cognitive traits such as analytical thinking, pattern recognition, and emotional regulation.

Examples of real-time intelligence can be found in various domains:

- Emergency Response: First responders must evaluate complex, rapidly changing situations, requiring them to apply their knowledge and problem-solving skills instantly.
- Sports: Athletes demonstrate real-time intelligence by making split-second decisions based on their opponents' actions, adjusting their strategies accordingly.
- Negotiations: Skilled negotiators need to assess verbal and non-verbal cues from counterparts to adapt their strategies and responses in real-time.

In contrast, future-oriented intelligence focuses on the anticipation of challenges and opportunities that lie ahead. This type of intelligence involves strategic thinking, foresight, and planning, requiring individuals to synthesize information, assess potential scenarios, and devise long-term solutions. Future-oriented intelligence is heavily influenced by cognitive traits such as creativity, critical thinking, and metacognition, alongside personality traits like curiosity and resilience.

Examples of future-oriented intelligence include:

- Strategic Planning: Business leaders engage in future-oriented intelligence by analyzing market trends and forecasting potential shifts, allowing them to develop sustainable strategies for growth.
- Education: Educators who adopt future-oriented intelligence prepare students not just for immediate assessments but also equip them with skills that will be valuable in their future careers.
- Research and Development: Scientists and innovators utilize future-oriented intelligence to anticipate technological advancements and societal needs, guiding their research towards impactful discoveries.

Understanding intelligence in terms of both real-time and future-oriented contexts allows for a more nuanced appreciation of how individuals navigate their environments. While real-time intelligence emphasizes immediate responsiveness and adaptability, future-oriented intelligence focuses on planning and strategic foresight. Both forms are essential for effective decision-making and problem-solving, highlighting the dynamic nature of intelligence as it applies to various aspects of life.

Intelligence, Dynamics of Dominance, and Cooperation in Human Behavior

As members of a social species, humans, like other animals, exhibit innate propensities for dominance, which have evolved as crucial mechanisms for establishing hierarchies and securing resources. In the animal kingdom, dominance behaviors are primarily expressed through physical prowess and aggressive interactions, serving as essential components for survival and social order. In animals, **might is right**! However, in humans, intellectual capabilities have become the new currency of dominance.

Brain is the superpower and bright is the new might.

This shift reflects an evolutionary adaptation where cognitive skills, knowledge acquisition, and problem-solving abilities play pivotal roles in gaining status and influence within social groups. As a result, intellectual superiority can manifest in social dynamics, shaping interpersonal relationships and societal structures in ways that physical dominance once did.

Here, we shall explore how knowledge and intelligence, while beneficial, can sometimes lead to the manifestation of 'dominance.' It also examines strategies for balancing dominance with cooperative behaviors to foster a more inclusive and productive social environment.

Dominance Instincts and Social Structures
Dominance instincts are deeply rooted in our evolutionary history and play a critical role in the social structures of many species. In human societies, these instincts are moderated by cultural norms and social expectations that prioritize cooperation and collective well-being over raw competition. Cultural practices, parenting, and educational systems are designed to nurture cooperative behaviors, promoting skills such as empathy, collaboration, and conflict resolution.

These social structures help balance our inherent dominance instincts with the need for harmonious social interactions. By emphasizing the value of working together and supporting one another, societies aim to channel dominance instincts into positive outcomes and productive relationships.

Intelligence and intolerance to ignorance

In the early days of my teaching career, I grappled with a growing sense of frustration, often disheartened when some students struggled to grasp concepts despite repeated explanations. As teachers, we naturally stand on a higher pedestal of knowledge, but this advantage can sometimes obscure our ability to empathize with students who take longer to understand. I eventually realized that my frustration wasn't solely rooted in my desire for their success; it also stemmed from a subconscious expectation that they should quickly reach my level of understanding. Over time, I came to see that my impatience reflected my own limitations in addressing diverse learning needs rather than any deficiency on their part.

Intelligent individuals, or those who are simply knowledgeable, often display a low tolerance for ignorance, stemming from their deep appreciation for knowledge and critical thinking. This intolerance is driven by several psychological factors. First, those with high cognitive abilities may have a heightened need for cognitive closure, seeking clear, evidence-based answers and feeling frustration when confronted with ambiguity or unfounded perspectives. Moreover, they may engage in social comparison, evaluating their self-worth by measuring their intellectual capabilities against others. This can foster a sense of superiority and intensify their disdain for ignorance. The principle of cognitive dissonance also plays a role; when intelligent individuals encounter beliefs that conflict with their own, it creates discomfort, prompting them to reject those viewpoints outright. As a result, their intolerance for ignorance is both a reflection of their values and a product of the cognitive mechanisms shaping their interactions.

One typical trait of intelligent individuals is their drive to improve existing systems, enhance processes, and devise novel solutions. Their inclination to challenge the status quo often leads to friction with others, as change can disrupt established norms, creating tension between innovative thinkers and those resistant to transformation. An intelligent person often holds alternative views that challenge prevailing norms. When these views are expressed, they may provoke resistance and be perceived as arrogance. This tension creates mutual intolerance between the intelligent individual and others, making open dialogue more strained. This intellectual intolerance often appears as arrogance, as highly intelligent individuals may come across as condescending or dismissive toward differing views. Their confidence in their abilities may cause them to undervalue alternative perspectives, fostering a sense of superiority that alienates others. Additionally, the desire for validation can prompt them to assert dominance in discussions, further reinforcing the perception of arrogance. When they prioritize their own understanding over collaborative dialogue, it gives the impression that they are unwilling to engage with or respect others' insights. This behavior hampers meaningful discourse and limits the potential for mutual learning and growth, perpetuating a cycle of intellectual elitism that can be damaging to both individuals and broader social dynamics.

As a teacher, I should have exercised greater compassion, recognizing that each student's learning process is unique and shaped by different factors. Instead of allowing frustration to build, I needed to approach their struggles with patience and cultivate tolerance. Compassion means stepping into their shoes and understanding that learning difficulties are not obstacles but opportunities for growth. Teaching demands adaptability, especially when some students find certain concepts harder to grasp. By fostering tolerance and emotional resilience in myself, I could have created a more supportive environment, empowering students to feel motivated and encouraged. Compassion and tolerance not only enhance the classroom dynamic but also lay the foundation for more meaningful and effective learning.

While knowledge and intelligence are crucial for personal and societal progress, they can paradoxically lead to arrogance—an inflated sense of superiority that undervalues others' contributions. This arrogance often arises from cognitive overconfidence, where highly intelligent individuals overestimate their abilities and dismiss differing perspectives. Social comparison, where knowledge is treated as a status symbol, further entrenches this sense of superiority. The pursuit of recognition can exacerbate the problem, driving individuals to assert intellectual dominance through condescending behavior. Both teachers and students must recognize the connection between intelligence and intolerance toward ignorance as a fundamental aspect of educational behavior. Teachers should remain mindful of their ability to engage empathetically with students, while students must stay aware of their capacity to collaborate respectfully with peers. Such awareness is essential for nurturing constructive interpersonal relationships and group cohesion, underscoring the importance of humility and openness in intellectual discourse.

Balancing Dominance and Cooperation

To balance dominance with cooperation and mitigate the risk of arrogance, several strategies can be employed:
- Cultivating Self-Awareness: Developing self-awareness through reflective practices, feedback, and mindfulness helps individuals recognize and address their own tendencies toward arrogance.
- Promoting Humility: Emphasizing humility encourages individuals to appreciate and value the contributions of others, fostering a more inclusive and respectful environment.

- Fostering Emotional Intelligence: Enhancing emotional intelligence helps individuals navigate social interactions with empathy and respect, reducing the likelihood of arrogance.
- Encouraging Collaborative Learning: Collaborative learning environments that value diverse perspectives and collective problem-solving can mitigate the effects of dominance and promote mutual respect.

In the educational setting, the dynamics between intelligence, ignorance, intolerance, arrogance, and dominance have profound implications for both teaching and learning. Intelligent students or educators, due to their cognitive abilities, often exhibit a low tolerance for ignorance. This intolerance stems from their frustration with a perceived lack of critical thinking or disregard for evidence-based reasoning. While intelligence is a valuable asset, this intolerance can sometimes be misinterpreted as arrogance, where intellectually gifted individuals may project an inflated sense of superiority over those less informed or less capable. This not only alienates others but can also create an environment where meaningful discourse is stifled and opportunities for collaborative learning are diminished.

Psychologically, this can be explained by cognitive overconfidence, where individuals overestimate their intellectual capacities and undervalue the contributions of others. This behavior, especially if left unchecked, risks creating power imbalances in classroom dynamics, where dominant individuals may overshadow less confident students, reducing inclusivity and discouraging participation. Additionally, the constant social comparison prevalent in educational environments can exacerbate these issues, with knowledge becoming a tool for social hierarchy, furthering feelings of inadequacy among peers.

To mitigate these risks, educators must foster an atmosphere of mutual respect, emphasizing the value of diverse perspectives. Encouraging humility in intellectual exchanges is essential, reminding students that knowledge is not static and that learning is a continuous, collective process. Teachers should cultivate empathy and emotional intelligence, guiding students to understand that intelligence does not justify dismissiveness. Importantly, educators themselves must model this behavior, avoiding intellectual dominance and promoting open dialogue. By reinforcing a culture of curiosity over competition, the classroom becomes a space where intelligence is celebrated without becoming a tool for arrogance or social dominance, ensuring a more inclusive, supportive learning environment for all.

Here are a few psychologically driven sentences that a teacher can say to the class to reduce the perceptions of intellectual intolerance between teachers and students.

1. "Each of us learns at a different pace, and that's perfectly okay—what matters is that we keep moving forward together."

2. "If something is unclear, please ask questions; your curiosity helps me understand how I can support you better."

3. "Learning is not about being right all the time but about exploring, making mistakes, and growing from them."

4. "I value every question, no matter how simple or complex it may seem—each question brings us closer to understanding."

5. "Do not feel discouraged if you don't grasp something immediately; often, the most profound insights come with patience and persistence."

6. "Remember, I am here to guide you, not to judge you; your progress is what truly matters to me."

7. "We are all here to learn from each other—your perspective is as important as anyone else's."

8. "If a concept seems challenging right now, it only means you are on the brink of mastering something new."

9. "Your efforts, no matter how small they may seem, are steps towards greater understanding, and I appreciate every single one."

10. "Let's embrace the learning process as a journey—sometimes slow, sometimes fast, but always moving us toward greater knowledge and confidence."

Sentences that a teacher can say to reduce intellectual intolerance between students

1. "Everyone here has a unique way of thinking, and that diversity of thought enriches our learning experience."

2. "We all come from different backgrounds, so let's respect how each person approaches a problem—there is no one right way to learn."

3. "Remember, collaboration is key; the best solutions often come when we combine our different strengths and perspectives."

4. "No question is too simple or too advanced—every contribution helps the entire class grow and understand better."

5. "Just because something comes naturally to one person doesn't mean it should for everyone else—let's support each other in our individual learning journeys."

6. "Learning is not a competition; we're here to help one another succeed, not to compare or criticize."

7. "Be patient with one another—what may be easy for you might be a challenge for someone else, and vice versa."

8. "The goal is to improve together, not to outshine anyone; when one person learns, we all benefit."

9. "It is important to listen to others' ideas with an open mind, even if you think you already know the answer—you might see things from a new perspective."

10. "We grow the most when we challenge our assumptions and engage respectfully with viewpoints different from our own."

Sentences to promote intellectual humility

1. "Balancing your natural drive to lead with humility allows you to appreciate and elevate the contributions of others."

2. "Intelligence is powerful, but true wisdom lies in recognizing the value of collaboration and shared knowledge."

3. "By cultivating self-awareness, you can transform dominance into a positive force that fosters cooperation and mutual respect."

4. "Harnessing your instincts for leadership without overshadowing others is key to creating a more inclusive and productive environment."

5. "Emotional intelligence helps you navigate the fine line between confidence and arrogance, ensuring that you uplift rather than undermine your peers."

6. "Collaboration isn't a sign of weakness; it is a testament to your strength in recognizing the power of collective effort."

7. "Humility in the face of knowledge doesn't diminish your abilities—it amplifies your capacity to grow alongside others."

8. "Embracing the contributions of others while maintaining your own drive for excellence leads to richer, more dynamic learning experiences."

9. "By tempering your dominance instincts with cooperative values, you create a balance that enhances both individual and group success."

10. "True leadership is not just about guiding others but also about fostering an environment where everyone's voice is valued and heard."

Diligence Beats Intelligence: The Unyielding Power of Persistent Effort

Only doing gets things done.

Thinking, no matter how deep or insightful, is merely the first step. It is the spark, the catalyst for action, but it is the action itself that propels us forward. Too often, we fall into the trap of overthinking—dwelling on plans, imagining outcomes, anticipating challenges—without ever taking that crucial step into execution. The mind may dream up possibilities, but those dreams remain dormant until they are brought into the realm of doing. We must remember that the actions resultant of the thinking are a part of intelligence. It is through doing that we learn, grow, and make things happen. Thinking gives us direction, but doing leads us to the destination.

In the modern discourse on success and personal achievement, the debate between the value of intelligence and diligence has been long-standing. Intelligence is often heralded as the key to innovation, creativity, and leadership. However, as society advances and the demands for consistent performance increase, it becomes evident that diligence is the primary determinant of success. While intelligence may offer a head start, it is diligence—the unwavering commitment to hard work and perseverance—that ensures sustained progress and eventual success. Diligence trumps intelligence, with 99% of the diligent achieving success, compared to only 1% of the intelligent. The argument rests on the premise that intelligence, without the accompanying discipline of diligence, lacks value and impact. In essence, thinking is not enough—doing is a must.

The Overwhelming Success of the Diligent Majority

In contrast to intelligence, diligence is a universally accessible trait. It requires no inherent talent, only the willingness to work hard, persevere, and remain committed to one's goals. The diligent individual is characterized by a relentless pursuit of improvement, an unwavering focus on tasks, and resilience in the face of challenges. This trait is the cornerstone of success in any field—be it academics, business, sports, or the arts. Empirical evidence supports the assertion that the vast majority of successful individuals owe their achievements to diligence rather than innate intelligence. In practice, 99% of diligent people reach their goals because they consistently apply themselves, learn from their mistakes, and push through obstacles. They cultivate the habits and work ethic that, over time, yield tangible results.

The Inextricable Link Between Doing and Thinking

Intelligence can guide one's thoughts and provide a framework for decision-making, but without action, these thoughts remain in the realm of theory. Thinking alone does not produce results; it is the execution of ideas that leads to success. In the context of personal and professional growth, actions—rooted in diligent effort—speak louder than intellectual prowess. The diligent individual understands that the application of intelligence requires sustained effort. Thinking must be accompanied by doing, as it is through action that ideas are tested, refined, and realized. The value of intelligence is maximized only when it is channeled into productive activities. That is why doing is a part of intelligence!

The phenomenon where intelligent individuals may exhibit tendencies towards laziness is a topic of considerable interest in psychology. While it is important to acknowledge that not all intelligent people are lazy, and laziness itself can be subjective, there are several psychological explanations for why intelligence might correlate with a lack of motivation or a propensity to engage in less effortful behavior.

1. Cognitive Efficiency and Energy Conservation
Intelligent individuals often excel at problem-solving and analytical thinking, which allows them to find solutions quickly and efficiently. This cognitive efficiency can lead to the perception that less effort is required to achieve the same results as others. As a result, intelligent people may develop a habit of exerting minimal effort to achieve satisfactory outcomes, leading to what might be

perceived as laziness. From an evolutionary perspective, energy conservation has been a crucial survival strategy. If an intelligent person can achieve goals with less effort, they might subconsciously opt to conserve energy for other tasks, leading to behaviors that could be labeled as lazy.

2. Boredom and Lack of Stimulation

Intelligent individuals often require more stimulation to remain engaged in a task. Routine tasks that do not challenge their cognitive abilities can lead to boredom, which in turn can manifest as laziness or disengagement. This lack of motivation can be particularly pronounced in environments that do not cater to their intellectual needs, such as monotonous work settings or traditional educational systems that do not offer sufficient opportunities for advanced learning or creativity. When intelligent people are not sufficiently challenged, they may struggle to find the motivation to apply themselves fully, leading to a decrease in productivity and the appearance of laziness.

3. Perfectionism and Fear of Failure

Intelligence can sometimes be accompanied by high expectations and a desire for perfection. The fear of not meeting these expectations can lead to procrastination or avoidance of tasks altogether, which can be perceived as laziness. This phenomenon is often referred to as "perfectionistic procrastination." Intelligent individuals may become paralyzed by the fear that their work will not live up to their own or others' standards, leading them to delay starting or completing tasks. In some cases, they may avoid tasks entirely if they do not believe they can perform them perfectly.

4. Overconfidence and Underestimating Effort

Intelligent individuals might develop overconfidence in their abilities, leading them to underestimate the amount of effort required to complete tasks successfully. This overconfidence can result in procrastination, as they might believe they can accomplish tasks quickly at the last minute without the need for sustained effort. This behavior can be seen as laziness, especially when it leads to rushed or incomplete work. The tendency to rely on their intellectual abilities rather than consistent effort can create a pattern of behavior where tasks are only tackled when absolutely necessary, often with minimal investment of time or energy.

5. Intrinsic vs. Extrinsic Motivation

Intelligent people are often more intrinsically motivated, meaning they are driven by internal rewards such as personal satisfaction, curiosity, or the joy of learning. However, if they find themselves in environments where extrinsic motivation (e.g., rewards, grades, or recognition) is emphasized over intrinsic factors, they may become disengaged. This misalignment between their internal motivations and external demands can lead to a lack of effort in tasks that do not align with their personal interests, which might be perceived as laziness.

6. Social and Environmental Factors

Social and environmental factors can also contribute to the perception of laziness in intelligent individuals. For instance, if an intelligent person grows up in an environment where their natural abilities are constantly praised without the need for effort, they may develop a fixed mindset. This mindset, as opposed to a growth mindset, can lead to a belief that effort is unnecessary or even undesirable. Consequently, they may avoid challenges or hard work, relying solely on their innate intelligence, which can result in behaviors that appear lazy.

7. Sensory Processing Sensitivity

Some intelligent individuals may possess a trait known as sensory processing sensitivity, where they are more attuned to their environment and may process information more deeply. This heightened sensitivity can lead to quicker mental exhaustion, particularly in overstimulating or stressful environments. As a result, these individuals might conserve their energy by avoiding tasks that they perceive as overwhelming or unnecessary, which can be misconstrued as laziness.

Productivity Vs. Creativity

The notion that productivity is against creativity arises from the distinct demands and goals associated with these two concepts. Productivity typically emphasizes efficiency, output, and the completion of tasks within a defined framework. It is concerned with maximizing results in a given time and optimizing processes to achieve measurable success. This approach, while necessary for many aspects of life, can often limit the freedom needed for creative expression. Creativity, by contrast, thrives in open-ended, explorative environments where innovation, experimentation, and the challenging of existing norms are encouraged. It requires time for reflection, the freedom to make mistakes, and a willingness to deviate from predefined paths.

When productivity becomes the primary focus, creativity may be stifled due to the pressure to deliver results quickly. The emphasis on deadlines and measurable outcomes can inhibit the mental space necessary for the incubation of new ideas. Creative processes often involve detours, trial and error, and nonlinear thinking— qualities that are not easily quantified or aligned with a productivity-driven mindset. Consequently, workers or students may feel compelled to prioritize productivity over creativity, completing tasks efficiently rather than exploring new ideas or approaches that might lead to more innovative outcomes.

Moreover, creativity often requires periods of rest and downtime, which are perceived as unproductive from a conventional standpoint. Yet, these intervals are crucial for the brain to make new connections, leading to breakthrough ideas. When the emphasis is on continuous productivity, individuals are less likely to take the time necessary for such cognitive processes to occur.

However, it is important to recognize that productivity and creativity need not be entirely at odds. When balanced thoughtfully, productivity can support creativity by providing the structure and discipline needed to bring creative ideas to fruition, while creativity can inspire new, more effective ways of working. The key lies in creating environments that nurture both, allowing individuals the freedom to innovate within productive frameworks.

Flexibility of the Mind: Challenging One's Own Ideas as Intelligence

Fixity of mind can be seen as a virtue that aligns with basic instincts and the necessities of group living, providing individuals with a sense of stability and security within their communities. This steadfastness fosters a shared understanding and trust among group members, reinforcing social cohesion and collective identity. By valuing consistency in beliefs and practices, individuals contribute to a harmonious environment, enabling groups to function effectively while adhering to common norms and values essential for survival. The flexibility of the mind is an acquired trait that develops through challenging training and diverse experiences, enabling individuals to adapt to new situations and perspectives. This cognitive adaptability is often cultivated through deliberate practice, exploration of contrasting viewpoints, and the willingness to confront discomfort. As individuals navigate complex challenges and engage with unfamiliar concepts, they expand their cognitive frameworks, ultimately enhancing their ability to think critically and respond creatively in various contexts.

The process of challenging one's own ideas and solutions is a crucial aspect of intellectual development and intelligence. It involves a reflective practice where individuals critically examine their own thoughts and approaches, seeking to identify flaws, biases, or areas for improvement.

The Interplay of Work, Knowledge, Intelligence, and Confidence in Education

In the educational landscape, the notion that "the more a student works, the more knowledge, intelligence, and confidence they gain" stands as a fundamental principle. This perspective posits that productivity is the ultimate goal of education, achievable through the cultivation of work skills and intrinsic motivation. A student's ability to engage in productive work fosters not only academic success but also personal growth, preparing them for the challenges of adulthood and professional life. However, the perception of workload often varies with age, leading to discussions about the balance between effort and expected outcomes.

Understanding the Role of Work in Education

At its core, education is designed to empower students with the knowledge and skills necessary for navigating the complexities of life. This empowerment hinges significantly on the amount of work students are willing to undertake. Engaging with academic material, participating in discussions, and completing assignments fosters a deep understanding of concepts and cultivates critical thinking abilities. The process of working through problems and grappling with challenging ideas enhances cognitive skills, enabling students to approach issues from multiple perspectives.

As students immerse themselves in their studies, they cultivate intellectual curiosity and a desire for lifelong learning—qualities essential for navigating an increasingly complex world.

The Impact of Work on Intelligence

Intelligence, often perceived as an innate trait, is significantly influenced by environmental factors, including the amount and quality of work a student engages in. According to psychologist Carol Dweck's research on the growth mindset, individuals who believe in the malleability of intelligence are more likely to embrace challenges and persist in the face of setbacks. This mindset fosters a willingness to work hard, leading to greater intellectual growth.

When students actively engage in problem-solving, critical thinking, and creative endeavors, they expand their cognitive abilities. For example, participating in hands-on laboratory activities allows students to apply theoretical knowledge, reinforcing their understanding of scientific concepts. Similarly, writing assignments compel students to articulate their thoughts clearly, honing their analytical skills. The cumulative effect of such activities leads to increased intelligence as students learn to approach problems methodically and creatively.

Building Confidence Through Productive Engagement

Confidence is a crucial component of successful learning and personal development. The more a student works, the more opportunities they have to experience success, which in turn fosters confidence. Completing challenging tasks, whether in academics or extracurricular activities, instills a sense of accomplishment. For instance, a student who dedicates time to mastering a complex mathematical concept will not only improve their grades but also develop confidence in their ability to tackle difficult subjects.

Moreover, when students engage in productive work, they receive feedback that helps them recognize their strengths and areas for improvement. This feedback loop encourages a growth mindset, where students view challenges as opportunities for growth rather than as insurmountable obstacles. As they witness their progress over time, students become more self-assured in their abilities, laying the foundation for future success in both academic and personal pursuits.

Productivity as the Ultimate Goal of Education

In the context of education, productivity transcends mere output; it encompasses the ability to work effectively, manage time efficiently, and produce meaningful results. This holistic view of productivity is particularly relevant in a world that increasingly values skills such as problem-solving, collaboration, and adaptability.

However, achieving this level of productivity requires a shift in how students perceive their workload. It is not uncommon for students to voice complaints about having too much work, especially in the context of school versus college. A school-aged child, for instance, may have a heavier workload than a college student, particularly in developing countries where educational systems often emphasize rote memorization over critical thinking.

In colleges, students should ideally be self-motivated to work independently, engaging in learning without the constant oversight of teachers. This autonomy is a hallmark of adulthood, preparing students to take responsibility for their education and professional development. It is essential to create an environment where students are encouraged to pursue knowledge and productivity for their own sake rather than merely for grades or approval.

Personal Reflection: Lessons from Experience

Reflecting on my own educational journey, I recognize the impact of my choices on my current professional life. As a college student, I did not engage deeply with my studies beyond what was necessary for exams. This lack of productive engagement stunted my growth and instilled a mindset of passive learning. I often found myself overwhelmed by tasks in my professional life, primarily due to a lack of motivation for productivity. I realized that thinking critically is essential, but the act of *doing* yields results.

My experience highlights the importance of instilling a strong work ethic in students from an early age. As an educator, I have made it my goal to promote productivity among my students. I encourage them to work diligently for every mark they receive, particularly in internal assessments. I emphasize the value of effort and process over mere outcomes. This approach not only fosters a sense of ownership over their learning but also reinforces the idea that hard work and dedication lead to tangible results.

The Challenge of Balancing Workload

While promoting productivity is essential, it is equally important to recognize the need for balance. The volume of work assigned should be age-appropriate and commensurate with the students' developmental stage. Younger students, especially those in primary education, may require a more moderate workload, with an emphasis on play and exploration, to foster a love for learning. In contrast, college students should be expected to manage their time effectively and take initiative in their studies.

Unfortunately, many students, especially in developing countries, face an overwhelming workload that can lead to burnout and disengagement. Striking a balance between encouraging productivity and avoiding excessive pressure is crucial. Educators must be mindful of the challenges students face and provide appropriate support, including time management strategies and resources for effective study habits.

The Connection Between Productivity, Happiness, and Confidence

Productivity is not just a pathway to academic success; it significantly contributes to students' happiness and confidence. Engaging in productive work instills a sense of purpose and accomplishment, enhancing overall well-being. When students invest time in meaningful tasks, they experience fulfillment, positively affecting their happiness. Working towards goals, such as mastering challenging concepts or completing projects, fosters a sense of agency, empowering students to tackle challenges with resilience and confidence. As they see the results of their efforts, their belief in their abilities strengthens, reinforcing their motivation.

Additionally, productivity cultivates essential life skills, including time management, organization, and goal-setting, which are vital for academic success and personal growth. Students who develop these skills are better prepared for the complexities of adult life, enhancing their independence and self-assurance. Productive individuals often enjoy greater success and satisfaction, leading to increased happiness. Engaging in meaningful work creates a sense of accomplishment, as they regularly set and achieve goals. This progress boosts self-esteem and reinforces a positive self-image. Furthermore, productivity fosters resilience and adaptability, enabling individuals to navigate challenges effectively. A proactive mindset allows for efficient time and resource management, reducing stress and creating space for personal interests and relationships.

As both a teacher and a learner, I have come to recognize that productivity is not just a means to an end but a transformative process that enriches students' academic journeys. My mission is to instill in my students the belief that their efforts will yield meaningful results, shaping their futures and preparing them to become proactive, confident individuals capable of facing the challenges of adulthood. When students embrace productivity, they not only achieve academic success but also cultivate the happiness and confidence essential for navigating life's complexities.

Redefining Intelligence

Let me refine my definition of intelligence once again!!

Intelligence is a complex interplay of cognitive and personality traits that enables individuals to detect, predict, process, regulate, and direct change effectively within contextual constraints.

In its simplest form, intelligence is the ability to manipulate information for improvement, where information encompasses any form of knowledge. All matter, energy, expression, emotion, complexity, emergent properties, and entities (including abstract ones) are part of knowledge.

Every existence and change is information, and all of it is knowledge.

Intelligence is the ability to manipulate information effectively, where information encompasses any form of knowledge. This information may manifest as sound, words, actions, perceptions, being, light, emotion, and more. Fields of intelligence can be categorized based on the type of information manipulated and the resultant products. For instance, **linguistic intelligence** involves the manipulation of words to convey ideas, while **musical intelligence** pertains to the processing of sound patterns and rhythms. **Kinesthetic intelligence** is linked to physical actions and bodily movement, whereas **interpersonal intelligence** focuses on the perception and understanding of emotions and social dynamics. **Intrapersonal intelligence** is rooted in self-awareness and personal understanding. Additionally, **logical-mathematical intelligence** encompasses reasoning, problem-solving, and the manipulation of numbers, while **naturalistic intelligence** pertains to the recognition and classification of flora and fauna. **Visual-spatial intelligence** engages with light and visual representation, while **existential intelligence** relates to deep philosophical questions about existence. Each category reflects unique cognitive processes and outcomes, highlighting the diverse dimensions of human intelligence.

The difference between knowledgeable people and intelligent people is that intelligent people possess flexibility of mind, self-awareness, and mental audacity.

Chapter 7: Teaching Intelligence

In my life, the most significant part of my intellectual growth took place during my schooling. This growth was neither intentional on my part nor structured by the curriculum; it happened by sheer coincidence. I attended a non-profit residential school, Sri Satya Sai Gurukulam, in Rajamahendravaram, Andhra Pradesh. I studied there for ten years, from first through tenth grade, living with my peers in one close-knit community, day in and day out. We fought and played, fought again, and then played some more—every day, all day. Returning home during vacations felt almost unsettling as if I were out of place. My schooling and friends shaped my perception of belonging; that community was my world, as formative as it was familiar. The intellectual growth I experienced emerged from interactions with my classmates during non-academic hours.

When we were about eight years old (in third grade), we once peeled a raw coconut for Ganesh Pooja, smuggling it from nearby fields into our hostel room. Armed with only small iron rods, we dug into the coconut, peeling it together, discussing, and improvising on each other's ideas until we achieved our goal. We only knew that we needed a coconut for the pooja; everything else was unknown. We were physically weak, the coconut was raw, we had no sharp tools, and we had to do all this without our wardens' knowledge. That was intellectual training in itself.

We improvised a version of cricket, secretly playing while sitting during study hours. The bat and ball were crafted from aluminum foils from tablet sheets. We constructed a projector from cardboard. We decorated rooms in ingenious ways on different occasions. We engineered ways of packing all the class stuff into one room. We explored almost everything, largely unguided, unmonitored, and unhindered—inhabitants of our own small world. Every day offered something new, often outside classroom hours. These experiences, which shaped the little intelligence I have, are aspects I owe entirely to my school. I am sure each teacher would agree that their schooling has been more intellectual while college was more knowledgeable.

Exploring the unknown with peers is the best intellectual exercise.

Engaging with peers to explore the unknown fosters genuine intellectual growth, as it encourages curiosity, creativity, and independent problem-solving. Excessive teacher involvement, however, can shift this dynamic, transforming exploration into knowledge transfer rather than intellectual discovery. Intellectual learning thrives in environments where students lead, discuss, and challenge ideas independently.

Reflecting on these experiences, and now as a teacher, I have identified a few principles for fostering intelligence:

(i) The teacher's role is primarily to set the target and establish the constraints and then, importantly, vanish;

(ii) Students should have the freedom to explore independently, with minimal intervention from the teacher;

(iii) These exercises should be integrated daily, turning intelligence into a lifestyle rather than a task;

(iv) The best learning occurs outside the classroom, solely among students, free from external guidance or interference.

These approaches emphasize autonomy and daily practice, cultivating intelligence through self-guided discovery. However, in today's educational setting, the strategies mentioned may not be fully feasible. Homes often serve as spaces for nurturing, comfort, and leisure rather than for fostering intelligence. Furthermore, with abundant accessible knowledge readily available to answer any question, students may rely on external sources instead of exploring and improvising. Consequently, the responsibility to instill intelligence increasingly rests on educators. In the following sections, we will explore methods for adapting classes and teaching strategies to foster intelligence. Presently, most people develop "academic intelligence," which is useful in academic and professional realms, yet intelligence is rarely embraced as a lifestyle.

Intelligence and teaching

Intelligence is a complex interplay of cognitive and personality traits that enables individuals to detect, predict, process, regulate, and direct change effectively within contextual constraints.

Here, the changes include all forms of energy, matter, emergence, emotions, and anything that can be malleable. Intelligence is the inclination to challenge and improve the status quo. In this chapter, we shall discuss the principles of what intelligence could be instilled in students and how it could be instilled in them.

Intelligence is an attitude, a style, a habit, and an instinct that improves with practice. As the application of knowledge, intelligence is best demonstrated when solving a problem or directing a course of action. Yet, our natural tendency is to seek an alternative, an 'expert' to ease our mental burden, ensure the job is done properly, or avoid causing further issues. For similar reasons, we often resist changing our methods. Students frequently say, "I find this comfortable, which is why I do not want to try something new!" These are real-life and real-time problems that we evade solving, which could have been the best part of our personalities with the flexibility of the mind and willingness to solve problems. These are two of the ways we miss the chance to practice intelligence. Intelligence demands curiosity, boldness, playfulness, and a willingness to explore. In an academic setting, students are supposed to practice intelligence and hope that it spills into their profession and every other sphere of life.

A teacher's role is about igniting curiosity, fostering analytical thinking, and, importantly, empowering the student with the courage to deal with the problem. We should certainly aim to spark their interest and enhance their learning outcomes. The richness of a subject lies not just in its facts but in the analytical dimensions it offers. As educators, we are tasked with guiding students through this intricate landscape of knowledge, intelligence and personality.

A wealth of resources exists to help illuminate the analytical aspects. It is our responsibility to tap into this reservoir and utilize examples that can resonate with our students. Engaging them in philosophical inquiries is one effective method. Asking questions such as, "If you were in this situation, what actions would you take to improve it?" encourages students to think critically and personally about the material. Such questions compel them to move beyond rote memorization and towards a more profound understanding. The classroom should never be a space where superficial engagement is acceptable; every session should challenge students to reach analytical levels of thought.

Data analysis and research should become integral components of our teaching strategies. We must encourage students to think deeply and not simply accept information at face value. For instance, when discussing a scientific principle, we could analyze real-world data to illustrate its implications or test its validity. This practice helps students develop critical thinking skills and fosters an environment of inquiry and exploration. In every lesson, we must create an atmosphere where students are not just passive recipients of knowledge but active participants in the learning process.

Moreover, the teaching process should not be confined to a rigid curriculum. If the syllabus dictates that we teach ten points on a topic, why not extend this to thirteen? Teaching is inherently service-based, and there is no detriment in offering a little more. This approach not only enriches the learning experience but also enhances our fulfillment as educators. We should view this as an opportunity to elevate our reputation and achieve our professional goals. When we teach with the intention of serving our students' intellectual growth, we create a positive ripple effect that extends beyond the classroom. By fostering an environment where students feel empowered to explore, question, and analyze, we can cultivate thinkers, innovators, and problem-solvers equipped to navigate the complexities of the world.

Educators must commit to teaching with depth and purpose, encouraging critical and analytical thinking that encompasses the 'what,' 'why,' and 'how' of subjects. An inquiry-driven classroom allows students to leave not only with knowledge but also with the ability to apply it meaningfully in their lives. The fulfillment of teaching is magnified when we witness our students thriving, armed with essential skills to confront future challenges.

Teaching intelligence involves nurturing critical thinking and intellectual curiosity, elevating the teacher's role beyond mere knowledge conveyance. Every discipline—whether science, literature, or mathematics—offers opportunities for analysis and interpretation. By guiding students through these processes, teachers can create an environment rich in inquiry. For example, a science teacher can facilitate data analysis, while a literature teacher can prompt thematic interpretations, enhancing understanding and empowering students to derive their own solutions. The more a teacher encourages students to think critically and actively engage with the material, the greater the impact they have on their intellectual development. Ultimately, a teacher's success is measured by the extent to which they inspire their students to think deeply, question assumptions, and apply their knowledge creatively.

Educational submission is the enemy of intelligence.

Educational submission refers to a model of learning where students are expected to adhere strictly to prescribed norms, rules, and behaviors established by educators or the educational system. In this paradigm, students may be conditioned to prioritize obedience and compliance over independent thought, creativity, and critical analysis. This submission can manifest through various mechanisms, such as rigid curricula, punitive discipline policies, and an emphasis on rote memorization. Educational submission is used excessively in primary and secondary schools to manage the crowd and increase productivity. However, this approach stifles the courage and willingness to explore alternatives, and that is where intelligence dies for the rest of life.

Submission, when used as an educational tool through excessive conditioning and stringent rules for obedience, can stifle creativity and, consequently, intelligence. Creativity thrives on freedom and liberty, enabling individuals to transcend existing boundaries and explore new ideas. A sense of mental freedom is essential for fostering innovative thinking; without it, students may find themselves trapped within rigid frameworks that discourage divergent thought.

The fear of failure, humiliation, punishment, disengagement, loss, or disgrace serves as a formidable barrier to intellectual growth. Therefore, the first critical step for educators is to cultivate an environment in which students feel affection and respect rather than fear of the teacher. Teachers should build a reputation and persona of intelligence, liberty, knowledge and motivation to better the ambience for teaching intelligence. When students are at ease, they are more likely to engage in creative exploration without the constraints of anxiety.

Once this foundation is established, teachers should grant students the freedom to explore their imaginations to the fullest. It is equally important for educators to provide structured approaches for thinking critically and solving problems, guiding students toward effective methodologies. As students become more adept at navigating challenges, teachers should gradually step back, allowing students to take ownership of practicing intelligence. The teacher's role should evolve to focus on eliminating fear and encouraging students rather than dictating solutions.

Submission may be good for acquiring knowledge and productivity, but it obstructs intelligence. This shift fosters an ideal atmosphere for teaching intelligence, empowering students to develop their own ideas and solutions while nurturing their innate creativity and critical thinking skills. By embracing this approach, we can cultivate a generation of thinkers who are confident and capable of transforming their insights into actionable knowledge.

Formal education in imparting knowledge and intelligence

The role of formal education in this process cannot be overstated. Schools primarily focus on imparting the accumulated knowledge of humanity, which has been gathered over thousands of years.

This education system has transformed society for the better. While criticisms of the education system abound, it is important to consider the alternative: without schools, how would humans solve problems? How much progress would have been possible? Would complex and prolonged thinking, such as that required in mathematics, even exist? Would we all be operating cohesively on the same level and direction?

Just imagine if there were no school system at all—how would humans be? Even now, if we were to abolish the entire education system, it is likely that future generations would regress to a state of ignorance, beating back our Gen Z to what we might call stupidity. Reading is important, learning is important, and subjects like language, science, and mathematics are crucial. Schools are irreplaceable in fostering abstract thinking, imagination, and creativity and ensuring a uniform foundation of essential knowledge among members of society.

In the educational landscape, the mission of cultivating socially responsible and productive citizens transcends the mere provision of refined knowledge. It involves imparting information and developing the essential tools that enhance intelligence. While knowledge is important, it can often become static; it is the tools of intelligence—such as critical thinking, problem-solving, and adaptability—that empower individuals to effectively navigate the complexities of modern society. Consider two groups of students: those who possess knowledge and those who have the means and motivation to acquire knowledge independently. Clearly, the latter represents the true goal of education.

By equipping students with these tools, educators foster an environment where learners can engage meaningfully with real-world challenges. This approach nurtures their ability to synthesize information, innovate, and contribute positively to their communities. Furthermore, this focus on intelligence aligns with the demands of an ever-evolving global landscape, where adaptability and practical application of knowledge are crucial.

Systems Thinking and Design Thinking as Intellectual Methodologies

One of the most effective approaches to teaching analytical concepts is through the lens of systems thinking. This method encourages students to consider the entirety of a problem by examining all the factors involved, recognizing the interconnectedness of these factors, and understanding the degree of influence each one has on the overall system. By doing so, students can grasp the complexity of real-world issues and develop a holistic approach to problem-solving.

Systems thinking is an approach that emphasizes understanding the complex interrelationships and dynamics within a system rather than viewing components in isolation. Its core principles include:

1. Holistic Perspective: Systems thinking advocates for viewing the system as a whole, recognizing that the behavior of individual parts affects the entire system. This perspective helps identify patterns and interactions that may not be apparent when examining components separately.

2. Interconnections: It highlights the importance of relationships and interactions between different elements within the system. Understanding these interconnections can reveal how changes in one area impact others, fostering a comprehensive understanding of system dynamics.

3. Feedback Loops: Systems thinking emphasizes the role of feedback loops, which can be reinforcing or balancing. These

loops illustrate how actions within the system can lead to positive or negative consequences over time, influencing future behavior.

4. Emergent Properties: It recognizes that systems often exhibit properties that cannot be understood by analyzing parts in isolation. Emergent properties arise from the interactions among components and can lead to unexpected outcomes.

5. Dynamic Complexity: Systems thinking acknowledges that systems are dynamic and constantly evolving. This principle encourages ongoing analysis and adaptability, allowing for better responses to changing conditions and challenges.

Starting Simple: Begin by introducing the students to a problem that involves just two factors. Encourage them to analyze the interaction between these factors and understand how they influence each other. This initial step allows them to build a solid foundation in identifying relationships and dependencies within a system.

Gradual Complexity: With each iteration, introduce an additional factor into the problem. As the system grows more complex, guide the students in accounting for these new variables, helping them see how each additional factor adds layers of complexity and interconnectedness. This iterative approach gradually enhances their ability to manage and analyze intricate systems.

Acknowledging Depth and Breadth of Thought: Throughout the process, it is crucial for the teacher to acknowledge the depth of thought the students are employing. Regularly highlight how many factors they have considered, the connections they've identified, and the thoughtful analysis they've applied to reach their conclusions. Phrases like, "Look at how many variables you've accounted for" or "Notice how deeply you've analyzed the system to understand the full scope of the problem" can reinforce their efforts and build confidence.

Emphasizing the Magnitude of the Problem: Finally, make sure to emphasize the complexity and magnitude of the problem they are tackling. By doing so, you help them appreciate the significance of their analytical journey and the value of their critical thinking skills. Remind them that real-world problems are often vast and multifaceted, and their ability to dissect and understand these problems using systems thinking is a powerful tool in both academic and practical settings.

Psychologically driven sentences to infuse systems thinking.

1. "You've done an incredible job connecting all the pieces of this puzzle—your systems thinking is truly impressive."

2. "Each layer of complexity you uncover brings you closer to mastering this concept—keep pushing forward!"

3. "By considering every factor, you're not just solving problems; you're building a deeper understanding of how the world works."

4. "Your ability to see the bigger picture and analyze the interconnections is a skill that will set you apart."

5. "I'm amazed at how you've managed to break down this complex issue into manageable parts—this is what great analytical thinking looks like."

6. "Remember, the more factors you consider, the stronger your analysis becomes. You're doing fantastic work."

7. "Every new element you account for adds depth to your understanding—keep exploring, you're on the right path."

8. "The way you've tackled these challenges shows a high level of critical thinking—your effort is paying off."

9. "You're turning what seemed like an overwhelming problem into a series of solvable steps—this is exactly how systems thinking should be applied."

10. "Your persistence in analyzing all these interconnected factors is leading you to insightful conclusions—excellent work!"

While systems thinking involves dissecting and deeply understanding a problem, design thinking focuses on developing solutions. Design thinking is a human-centered approach to innovation that emphasizes understanding users' needs and iteratively creating solutions. Its core principles include:

1. Empathy: Understanding the users' experiences, needs, and emotions is foundational. This involves engaging with users through interviews, observations, and interactions to gain insights that inform the design process.

2. Define: After gathering insights, the next step is to clearly articulate the problem you are trying to solve. This stage synthesizes information to identify key challenges, ensuring the design efforts are focused on addressing real user needs.

3. Ideation: This phase encourages brainstorming and generating a wide range of ideas without judgment. Diverse perspectives are welcomed to explore innovative solutions, fostering creativity and collaboration.

4. Prototyping: Creating tangible representations of ideas—
whether through sketches, models, or digital mockups—allows
teams to explore concepts in a concrete way. Prototypes facilitate
quick experimentation and feedback.

5. Testing: Testing prototypes with users provides critical
feedback. This iterative process allows designers to refine and
improve solutions based on real-world use, ensuring that the final
product effectively meets users' needs.

Integrating systems thinking and design thinking provides a robust
framework for addressing complex problems and creating
innovative solutions. These methodologies enhance problem-
solving and innovation. For example, a team faced with a
challenge can first apply systems thinking to analyze the broader
context and relationships within the system, identifying underlying
issues. Subsequently, design thinking can be employed to ideate
and prototype solutions that address those specific problems,
ensuring that the final design resonates with users.

Approaches to instill intellectual traits in students:

1. Audacity: Teach students to be bold and courageous in their
pursuits. Encourage them to take risks, challenge the status quo,
and pursue innovative ideas with confidence.

2. Motivation: Instill a strong sense of purpose and drive. Help
students identify their personal goals and passions and cultivate an
intrinsic motivation to achieve them.

3. Curiosity: Foster a deep and enduring curiosity about the world.
Encourage students to ask questions, seek out new knowledge, and
explore various subjects with enthusiasm.

4. Critical Thinking: Develop the ability to analyze information, evaluate different perspectives, and make reasoned decisions. Teach students to approach problems with a thoughtful and analytical mindset.

5. Resilience: Build the capacity to recover from setbacks and challenges. Encourage students to persevere through difficulties and view failures as opportunities for growth.

6. Grit: Cultivate determination and sustained effort towards long-term goals. Teach students the importance of working hard and maintaining focus despite obstacles.
These steps collectively enhance students' ability to tackle challenges effectively and achieve their full potential, preparing them for both academic and real-world success.

Practice is important for improving any skill. Let us define what a skill is. A skill is typically a repetitive activity measured against scales at the personal level and/or community level to decide the expertise level. All activities that are done by the body and mind are involved in input, processing and output: skills of speaking, thinking, writing, reading, intelligence, gaining knowledge, playing, typing, singing, driving, etc.

Often, we hear that graduates are not market- or industry-ready. This sentiment typically arises from two key deficits. The first is a lack of personality traits, particularly in terms of communication skills and confidence. The second is the inability to solve real-world problems. In academia, the focus is on imparting knowledge and understanding the broader context of concepts and theories. In industry, however, the focus shifts to applying that knowledge in practical settings, where workers must operate machines or processes while mitigating any issues that arise. These are two related yet distinct levels of learning. Expecting a fresh graduate to seamlessly solve industry-level problems is, therefore, an unrealistic expectation. However, in the academic setting, it is crucial to train students to solve problems.

One way to build this competency is by challenging students daily with at least one contextual problem—one that is new to them. This form of intelligence training is invaluable as it helps students develop the mental agility needed to understand a problem, analyze the factors involved, and arrive at the best possible solution based on the constraints at hand. Such exercises equip students not just with theoretical knowledge but also with the cognitive tools to tackle problems creatively and effectively, a skill that will serve them well in any industry.

The challenge of teaching intelligence through problem-solving lies in the discomfort it often causes students. A new problem demands immediate focus, and finding a solution, especially in a theoretical context without the aid of real-world objects like equipment or machines, adds to the difficulty. The absence of tangible tools hampers their ability to concentrate fully, as students are required to rely solely on their imagination. They must not only visualize the problem but sustain and build upon this mental image until the solution is found—a task that can be overwhelming.

However, despite this difficulty, I believe this form of intellectual exercise is the most valuable training a teacher can provide. It forces students to stretch their cognitive abilities, fostering creativity, critical thinking, and mental endurance. These are the very skills that will distinguish them in both academic and professional environments. By navigating through such discomfort, students not only strengthen their problem-solving capabilities but also prepare themselves for the complexities of real-world challenges, where clear-cut solutions and perfect tools are rarely at hand. This rigorous mental training equips them with resilience and adaptability, traits essential for success in any field.

Teaching intelligence involves cultivating various cognitive skills, fostering a mindset of curiosity, and providing students with tools and strategies to enhance their cognitive abilities. Rather than focusing solely on the rote acquisition of facts, effective teaching of intelligence encompasses developing critical thinking, problem-solving skills, and adaptive learning strategies. Here are several key approaches to teaching intelligence:

1. Promote Critical Thinking
Encourage students to engage in activities that require analysis, evaluation, and synthesis of information. Use open-ended questions, debates, and case studies to stimulate higher-order thinking. Critical thinking exercises help students to question assumptions, consider multiple perspectives, and make reasoned decisions.

2. Foster Problem-Solving Skills
Incorporate problem-based learning where students tackle complex, real-world problems. This approach helps them develop problem-solving skills by applying knowledge in practical situations. Encourage experimentation, iterative testing, and creative solutions.

3. Encourage Metacognition
Teach students to be aware of their own thinking processes. Metacognition involves self-reflection on how one learns, understands, and solves problems. Techniques such as self-assessment, reflective journaling, and goal-setting help students become more effective and independent learners.

4. Promote Curiosity and Inquiry
Stimulate curiosity by encouraging students to ask questions and explore topics of interest. Create an environment where inquiry is valued and supported. Allow students to pursue individual research projects and explore subjects beyond the standard curriculum.

5. Utilize Diverse Learning Strategies
Incorporate a variety of learning strategies to cater to different cognitive styles. Techniques such as visualization, analogies, mind mapping, and mnemonic devices can enhance understanding and retention. Provide opportunities for hands-on learning and experiential activities.

6. Develop Adaptive Learning Skills
Teach students how to adapt their learning strategies based on the task and context. This includes recognizing when different approaches are needed and being flexible in their use of cognitive strategies. Encourage students to experiment with different methods and reflect on their effectiveness.

7. Encourage Collaborative Learning
Promote teamwork and collaborative projects that require students to share ideas, negotiate solutions, and learn from each other. Collaborative learning fosters interpersonal skills, creativity, and collective problem-solving.

8. Teach Emotional Intelligence
Emotional intelligence (EQ) is crucial for effective problem-solving and decision-making. Teach students to manage their emotions, empathize with others, and handle interpersonal relationships judiciously. Activities and discussions on emotional awareness and regulation can enhance EQ.

9. Provide Constructive Feedback

Offer timely and specific feedback to help students understand their strengths and areas for improvement. Constructive feedback encourages growth and learning, helping students to refine their cognitive strategies and approaches.

10. Model Lifelong Learning

Demonstrate a commitment to lifelong learning by continually pursuing new knowledge and skills. Share your learning experiences with students and emphasize the importance of ongoing intellectual growth. Modeling curiosity and a passion for learning can inspire students to adopt similar attitudes.

Teaching intelligence is a multifaceted endeavor that involves more than simply imparting knowledge. It requires fostering critical thinking, problem-solving abilities, and adaptive learning strategies. By promoting metacognition, curiosity, and emotional intelligence and by employing diverse learning strategies and collaborative methods, educators can help students develop a well-rounded intellectual capacity. Ultimately, teaching intelligence equips students with the cognitive tools necessary for navigating complex problems, making informed decisions, and continuing their intellectual development throughout their lives.

Looking for "All Possibilities and the Most Probable of Them": A Caveat in Intelligence

In the realm of intelligence and decision-making, the pursuit of "all possibilities and the most probable of them" represents a nuanced approach to evaluating options and making informed choices. This concept underscores the importance of comprehensive exploration and critical assessment in the process of intelligent decision-making. While seeking all possibilities and focusing on the most probable outcomes can significantly enhance decision-making and problem-solving, it also comes with inherent caveats that must be navigated carefully. Understanding these caveats is crucial for applying this approach effectively.

1. The Comprehensive Exploration of Possibilities

The first aspect of this approach involves identifying and exploring all potential options available in a given situation. Comprehensive exploration is essential for ensuring that no viable solutions or opportunities are overlooked. This process involves gathering a wide range of information, considering diverse perspectives, and evaluating different scenarios. By casting a broad net, individuals can uncover novel solutions and avoid the pitfalls of narrow thinking.

However, this exhaustive approach can lead to information overload, where the sheer volume of possibilities becomes overwhelming. In such cases, the challenge is to balance thoroughness with manageability. It is crucial to develop systematic methods for organizing and evaluating the possibilities to prevent analysis paralysis—a state where the decision-making process is stalled due to excessive analysis.

2. The Importance of Evaluating Probabilities

Once all possibilities are identified, the next step is to assess the likelihood of each option's success or feasibility. This involves analyzing each possibility's potential outcomes, risks, and benefits to determine which is the most probable and viable. Evaluating probabilities requires a combination of quantitative analysis, such as statistical modeling, and qualitative judgment, including experience and intuition.

While focusing on the most probable outcomes is essential for making realistic and practical decisions, it also introduces the risk of overemphasizing probability at the expense of innovation and creativity. Prioritizing the most probable options can lead to a conservative approach that favors familiar and safe choices over potentially disruptive but high-reward alternatives. As a result, individuals and organizations may miss out on groundbreaking opportunities that, while less probable, could offer significant long-term benefits.

3. Cognitive Biases and Decision-Making

Cognitive biases can significantly impact the process of evaluating possibilities and probabilities. Biases such as confirmation bias, where individuals favor information that supports their existing beliefs, or availability bias, where recent or easily recalled information is given undue weight, can skew the evaluation process. These biases may lead individuals to overlook important possibilities or misjudge the probabilities of outcomes.

To mitigate the effects of cognitive biases, it is important to adopt strategies such as seeking diverse opinions, using objective criteria for evaluation, and employing structured decision-making frameworks. These practices help ensure that the evaluation of possibilities and probabilities is as unbiased and comprehensive as possible.

4. The Dynamic Nature of Possibilities

Another caveat is the dynamic nature of possibilities and probabilities. Situations and contexts are often fluid, and what is considered probable today may change due to evolving conditions. Therefore, decision-makers must be adaptable and willing to reassess possibilities and probabilities as new information becomes available. This requires ongoing monitoring and flexibility in the decision-making process.

Incorporating a feedback loop into the decision-making process can help address the dynamic nature of possibilities. By regularly reviewing outcomes and adjusting strategies based on new insights, individuals and organizations can stay responsive to changing circumstances and improve their decision-making accuracy.

The approach of seeking "all possibilities and the most probable of them" is a valuable strategy in intelligent decision-making, emphasizing thorough exploration and realistic assessment. However, it is accompanied by several caveats, including the risk of information overload, the potential for cognitive biases, and the need for adaptability in a dynamic environment. By acknowledging and addressing these caveats, individuals can leverage this approach more effectively, enhancing their decision-making processes and achieving more informed and innovative outcomes. The key is to balance comprehensive exploration with practical evaluation, ensuring that all viable options are considered while maintaining a focus on the most probable and beneficial choices.

Teaching Systems Thinking in College: An Integrative Approach

Systems thinking is an approach that emphasizes understanding complex entities as integrated wholes rather than isolated parts. This perspective is increasingly recognized as essential in various fields, from engineering to social sciences, as it enables students to analyze interactions, dependencies, and feedback loops within systems. Teaching systems thinking in college involves fostering a holistic mindset that integrates various components into a cohesive understanding of how systems operate and evolve. This essay explores effective strategies for teaching systems thinking at the collegiate level and highlights its importance in preparing students for complex problem-solving and interdisciplinary work.

1. Introducing Systems Thinking Concepts

The initial step in teaching systems thinking is to introduce students to its fundamental concepts. These include the notions of systems, boundaries, feedback loops, and dynamic behavior. Systems can be defined as sets of interrelated components working together towards a common purpose. Feedback loops illustrate how outputs of a system can loop back as inputs, influencing the system's behavior. Educators should use real-world examples, such as ecosystems, organizational structures, or urban systems, to illustrate these concepts. By providing concrete examples, students can better grasp how systems thinking applies to diverse contexts.

2. Employing Interactive Learning Methods

Interactive learning methods are crucial for engaging students with systems thinking. Case studies, simulations, and modeling exercises provide practical experiences that illustrate system dynamics. For instance, using software tools to model complex systems, such as climate models or economic systems, allows students to visualize and manipulate variables, observing how changes affect the overall system. Role-playing exercises can also help students understand different perspectives within a system, fostering a deeper appreciation of how various components interact and influence one another.

3. Integrating Systems Thinking into Curriculum

To ensure systems thinking is effectively integrated into the college curriculum, it should be incorporated across various disciplines. This interdisciplinary approach helps students apply systems thinking to different fields, reinforcing its relevance and utility. For example, in engineering courses, systems thinking can be applied to design and optimization processes. In business courses, it can enhance understanding of organizational behavior and supply chain management. By embedding systems thinking into core courses and projects, students learn to approach problems from a systems perspective and recognize the interconnectedness of various factors.

4. Encouraging Collaborative Learning

Collaborative learning enhances the application of systems thinking by encouraging students to work together on complex problems. Group projects and team-based activities require students to communicate, negotiate, and integrate diverse viewpoints. These collaborative efforts mimic real-world scenarios where complex problems often involve multiple stakeholders with differing perspectives. Through collaboration, students learn to appreciate the value of diverse inputs and the necessity of considering multiple factors when analyzing systems.

5. Fostering Critical Thinking and Reflection

Critical thinking and reflection are integral to systems thinking. Students should be encouraged to analyze and question the assumptions underlying system models and to reflect on their own learning processes. Activities such as reflective journaling and group discussions can help students develop a critical mindset, enabling them to question and refine their understanding of system dynamics. This reflective approach fosters a deeper comprehension of how systems function and the implications of various interventions.

6. Highlighting Real-World Applications

To demonstrate the practical relevance of systems thinking, educators should emphasize real-world applications and case studies. Highlighting how systems thinking is used in fields such as environmental management, healthcare, and urban planning can inspire students and illustrate the impact of their learning. Guest lectures from professionals who apply systems thinking in their careers can also provide valuable insights and real-world context.

Conclusion

Teaching systems thinking in college is essential for preparing students to tackle complex, interdisciplinary problems. By introducing fundamental concepts, employing interactive learning methods, integrating systems thinking across curricula, encouraging collaboration, fostering critical thinking, and highlighting real-world applications, educators can effectively impart this valuable approach. Systems thinking equips students with the skills to analyze and address multifaceted issues, preparing them for successful careers and informed decision-making in an increasingly interconnected world.

Methods of imparting intelligence

A moment's intelligence is the next moment's knowledge; your knowledge is my intelligence, and vice versa.

Intelligence encompasses the capacity to learn, reason, solve problems, and adapt to novel situations. It integrates various cognitive functions, such as logical reasoning and the understanding of complex ideas, and manifests in analytical, creative, practical, and emotional forms. Essentially, intelligence is the information derived from within oneself. What I discover as my own information can become your intelligence. Intelligence is not something to learn but to practice. In this sense, the role of the teacher is only to challenge and create an ambience for thinking and acting to solve a problem.

A teacher, as has been the tradition for centuries, must impart the knowledge of facts and principles to students. However, to truly fulfill the role of an educator, one must go beyond mere knowledge transfer. Teaching becomes a half-hearted engagement if we stop there. It is essential to cultivate an environment where students practice the process of intelligence daily. Intelligence is not just a static trait; it is a habit and an attitude. By encouraging students to think critically, solve problems, and apply their knowledge actively, we empower them to develop their intellectual capabilities and foster a lifelong love for learning.

A teacher who is bent on teaching will work more before class than during class.

The teacher has to plan a directed activity to attain student thinking, solving and communicating. During the class, the teacher only poses questions and challenges and conducts the process of intelligence. The less the teacher does during the class, the more outcomes there will be!

To instill intelligence in students, teachers can implement the following methods that foster critical thinking, problem-solving, and adaptability:
1. Socratic Questioning
 - Method: Use open-ended, probing questions that require students to analyze, evaluate, and synthesize information. This encourages deeper thinking and exploration of underlying principles.
 - Example: In a history class, instead of asking, "What happened during the French Revolution?" ask, "How might the French

Revolution have unfolded differently under modern economic conditions?"

2. Problem-Based Learning (PBL)
- Method: Present real-world problems that require students to apply knowledge and develop solutions through research, discussion, and collaboration.
- Example: In a science class, students could be asked to design a solution for reducing plastic waste in oceans, integrating concepts of chemistry, environmental science, and engineering.

3. Case Studies and Scenario Analysis
- Method: Use case studies relevant to the subject to promote the application of theory to practical situations. Encourage students to analyze cases, discuss possible outcomes, and propose solutions.
- Example: In a business class, students analyze the rise and fall of a major corporation, identifying the key factors that influenced its success and downfall, then suggest strategies for future stability.

4. Collaborative Learning
- Method: Facilitate group work where students collaborate to solve complex problems or complete projects. Peer-to-peer learning fosters collective intelligence and helps students view problems from multiple angles.
- Example: Assign groups to research different historical empires and compare their political, social, and economic structures. Each group presents their findings and engages in a class-wide discussion.

5. Reflective Journals
- Method: Encourage students to maintain reflective journals where they document their thought processes, challenges, and insights during learning. Reflection helps develop metacognitive awareness, a key component of intelligence.

- Example: In a literature class, students write weekly reflections on how their interpretations of a novel's themes evolved after classroom discussions or further readings.

6. Simulation and Role-Playing
- Method: Create simulations or role-playing activities where students must assume roles and solve problems in dynamic, changing environments. This method promotes adaptability and forward-thinking.
- Example: In a political science class, students role-play as members of a United Nations council, negotiating solutions to a global crisis such as climate change or a humanitarian disaster.
7. Interdisciplinary Projects
- Method: Encourage students to undertake projects that span multiple subjects, pushing them to integrate knowledge from different fields to address a common problem.
- Example: In a project on urban planning, students combine knowledge from geography, economics, environmental science, and architecture to design a sustainable city model.

8. Design Thinking
- Method: Use the principles of design thinking, which involve empathy, ideation, prototyping, and testing, to help students innovate solutions to complex problems.
- Example: In a technology class, students design and prototype apps to solve local community issues, refining their ideas based on user feedback.

9. Mind Mapping and Concept Mapping
- Method: Use visual tools like mind maps and concept maps to help students organize information, see relationships between concepts, and deepen their understanding.

- Example: In a biology class, students create a mind map of the human circulatory system, linking each part to its function and relating it to other systems in the body.

10. Gamification
- Method: Turn learning into a game-like experience where students face challenges, earn rewards, and track progress. This method increases engagement and motivates students to think strategically.
- Example: In a math class, use a point-based system where students earn badges for solving increasingly complex problems, encouraging them to continuously push their limits.

A teacher who challenges more than instructs is the one truly teaching intelligence.

Rhetoric in teaching intelligence

Rhetoric in teaching intelligence plays a transformative role in shaping how students think, solve problems, and apply knowledge in dynamic contexts. Unlike the teaching of knowledge, which centers on the transfer of facts and established principles, teaching intelligence focuses on cultivating students' abilities to analyze, synthesize, and generate new ideas from existing knowledge. It involves guiding them to think critically and approach problems from diverse perspectives.

By engaging students through logical argumentation (logos), fostering creative thinking through analogies and metaphors, inspiring emotional engagement (pathos), and building credibility and trust (ethos), teachers can cultivate the intellectual abilities that define true intelligence. Whether through encouraging structured debate, using rhetorical questions to prompt critical thinking, or making emotional appeals to stir curiosity, rhetoric enhances both the cognitive and emotional dimensions of learning. Rhetoric in teaching intelligence not only sharpens students' analytical and problem-solving skills but also fosters the intellectual curiosity and flexibility necessary for lifelong learning and real-world problem-solving.

Here are ten rhetorical sentences that can be used to teach intelligence and encourage critical thinking, creativity, and problem-solving skills in students:

1. "What if the solution you are searching for is hidden within a perspective you have not yet considered?"
2. "Is it not true that the greatest innovations come from questioning the very assumptions we take for granted?"
3. "Imagine if every problem you encountered had multiple solutions—what would you do differently?"
4. "If we cannot explain this concept simply, do we truly understand it at all?"
5. "Why settle for one way of thinking when the world presents us with countless alternatives?"
6. "Could it be that failure is not the opposite of success, but rather the key to unlocking deeper understanding?"
7. "What happens when we stop asking 'what is' and start asking 'what could be'?"
8. "Is it possible that the real challenge is not in finding the right answer, but in asking the right question?"
9. "If knowledge is power, then is not intelligence the wisdom to apply that power in meaningful ways?"
10. "How can we use what we know today to solve the problems of tomorrow?"

Intrigue as an educational tool

Intrigue is the art of sparking curiosity by introducing elements of novelty, mystery, or the unexpected. It captivates attention and stimulates the desire to explore further, making individuals more engaged and invested in the subject or experience. In both personal and professional settings, intrigue fosters curiosity, encourages deeper thinking, and motivates people to seek answers or solutions. The psychological effect of intrigue lies in its ability to disrupt routine patterns, making people more alert, receptive, and open to learning. In educational and creative environments, it can enhance focus, promote innovation, and lead to greater retention of information. The anticipation generated by intrigue stimulates curiosity, prompting individuals to engage deeply with the subject matter. This cognitive engagement fosters critical thinking as learners seek connections and explore the unknown. Furthermore, the intellectual excitement that accompanies anticipation encourages innovative problem-solving as students actively seek answers and solutions.

Intrigue is the art of creating curiosity and excitement about the subject matter, encouraging deeper engagement and exploration. Teachers can effectively use intrigue by presenting content in novel ways, raising unanswered questions, or offering surprising perspectives. By fostering an environment where students are eager to know more, teachers can transform passive learners into active participants. Intrigue drives intellectual curiosity, making learning more dynamic, enjoyable, and impactful.

Ten Methods to Use Intrigue to Generate Interest and Attention:

1. Pose Thought-Provoking Questions
Start the lesson with a challenging or puzzling question that relates to the topic but doesn't have an immediately obvious answer. For

example, "What would happen if gravity suddenly stopped working?" This stimulates curiosity and sets the stage for a deeper exploration of the subject.

2. Introduce Mystery into the Subject Matter
Present a mystery or unsolved problem related to the topic. Let students work through the clues or data to solve it over the course of the lesson. For example, in history, you could ask, "What led to the disappearance of this ancient civilization?" Intrigue keeps them engaged as they seek answers.

3. Use Real-Life Connections and Stories
Share intriguing stories or case studies that connect the lesson to real-world situations or famous discoveries. Students are naturally drawn to narrative structures, especially when they involve unusual or surprising elements. For instance, linking a biology lesson to the strange life forms in deep-sea ecosystems can captivate interest.

4. Change the Learning Environment
Occasionally, altering the learning space or tools can spark curiosity. For example, moving the class outdoors, introducing a new technology tool, or re-arranging the seating arrangement can generate novelty and intrigue, leading to increased focus.

5. Offer a Teaser
Begin the class by hinting at something fascinating that will be revealed by the end, but only after certain steps of learning are completed. For example, "By the end of this lesson, you'll be able to explain how light can bend around objects."

6. Incorporate Unusual Props or Visual Aids
Bring in an unexpected object, image, or video clip that is tied to the lesson in a unique way. If you're teaching chemistry, for example, bringing an old alchemist's book or using an unusual

experiment setup can generate intrigue. The novelty will pique students' curiosity.

7. Present Contradictory or Paradoxical Statements
Start the lesson with a statement that seems counterintuitive or contradicts common knowledge. For example, "Did you know that there are places on Earth where water can boil and freeze at the same time?" This triggers curiosity as students work to resolve the seeming contradiction through learning.

8. Use Puzzles and Challenges
Incorporate puzzles or brain teasers related to the subject matter that students must solve. These challenges engage students actively and can be designed in a way that they uncover the core concepts of the lesson. For example, math or logic puzzles can stimulate problem-solving while keeping students intrigued.

9. Gradual Revelation of Information
Instead of presenting all the information at once, reveal content piece by piece. For instance, you could present a scientific problem or phenomenon and let students make observations and hypothesize before explaining the underlying theory. This keeps them guessing and engaged throughout the process.

10. Encourage Curiosity-Driven Research
Assign small, intriguing research tasks where students must explore a concept or find out why something works the way it does. Give them just enough information to start, but leave out key details they must discover themselves. This independent exploration stimulates a deeper interest in the subject.

Here are ten sentences a teacher can use to create intrigue and capture students' excitement and attention:

1. "What if I told you that everything we know about this topic might be completely wrong?"

2. "By the end of this class, you will have learned a skill that most people don't even know exists."

3. "There's a hidden connection between this lesson and something you use every day – can you guess what it is?"

4. "Today, we are going to explore something so bizarre that it might change the way you think about this entire subject."

5. "Imagine being able to predict the future—by the end of this lesson, you might be able to."

6. "The answer to this question is simple, yet only a few people in the world truly understand why it works."

7. "Let me share with you one of the biggest mysteries scientists are still trying to solve."

8. "What you are about to learn will help you see the world in a way you've never thought possible."

9. "There is something so strange about this topic that it has left experts puzzled for centuries—let's figure it out."

10. "I'm about to show you something that could completely change how you approach your future studies."

Teaching the flexibility of the mind

The flexibility of the mind is perhaps the most intellectual lesson a teacher can impart, as it empowers learners to adapt, question, and evolve in the face of changing circumstances and knowledge. However, this flexibility faces significant hindrances. Psychologically, humans are inherently born with cognitive fixity, a preference for consistency and familiar patterns. The brain is wired to conserve energy by reinforcing established beliefs and routines, making it difficult to challenge deeply held convictions. This is known as cognitive dissonance, where the mind experiences discomfort when encountering ideas that conflict with preexisting beliefs.

Socially, the flexibility of mind can cause tension, as individuals are often shaped by the norms, expectations, and rules of their communities. To deviate from these is not only intellectually challenging but also socially costly. Breaking away from societal conventions may lead to alienation, disapproval, or even ostracism. Furthermore, cultural and religious beliefs, which are often deeply ingrained, provide a sense of identity and stability. Questioning these frameworks is not only difficult on a personal level but can also invoke societal backlash.

Thus, teaching flexibility of mind requires more than fostering intellectual agility; it demands sensitivity to these psychological, social, religious, and cultural implications, ensuring learners can navigate the discomfort of change without losing their sense of belonging.

When teaching flexibility of mind, it is essential for the teacher to also inculcate in students an awareness of the risks, nuances, and strategies required for its responsible use. Flexibility, though intellectually liberating, can come with significant social risks, such as isolation, alienation, or even expulsion from certain communities. The teacher must emphasize that while questioning beliefs and systems is an important part of intellectual growth, doing so without careful consideration of timing and placement can lead to unintended social consequences.

Psychologically, students must be prepared to navigate the discomfort of going against the grain. This involves recognizing that cognitive flexibility is not always welcomed in environments where conformity is expected. Teachers should encourage students to develop a nuanced understanding of when and how to express dissenting views, balancing courage with social awareness. Timing plays a crucial role—knowing when to challenge ideas and when to remain tactful is key to ensuring that intellectual flexibility does not alienate individuals from their social or cultural environments.

Furthermore, teachers must guide students in understanding the importance of respecting social and cultural contexts, helping them weigh the potential consequences of their actions. Flexibility of mind, when applied with careful navigation and consideration, can lead to progress without risking unnecessary social disruption.

Here are five carefully designed activities to help inculcate flexibility of mind in students. Each activity emphasizes critical thinking, open-mindedness, and adaptability:

1. Cultural Exchange Debates
 - Objective: To expose students to diverse viewpoints and practice adapting their thinking.
 - Activity: Divide students into pairs or groups and assign them different cultural, historical, or ideological positions on a topic (e.g., education, government, or ethics). Students must first argue from their assigned perspective, then switch sides and argue from the opposing viewpoint. Afterward, have a reflective discussion about how they felt challenging their initial stance and what they learned from seeing both sides.
 - Outcome: Students develop an appreciation for multiple perspectives and learn the importance of flexibility in understanding complex issues.

2. Ambiguous Problem Solving

- Objective: To enhance cognitive flexibility by working through open-ended problems.
 - Activity: Present students with a real-world problem that does not have a clear solution (e.g., how to reduce pollution in their community or how to address an ethical dilemma). Working in teams, students must brainstorm several possible solutions, weigh their merits, and present them. Teams then rotate and critique each other's solutions, making adjustments based on feedback.
 - Outcome: Students practice creative problem-solving, adaptability in thinking, and collaborative evaluation of ideas.

3. Mindset Shifting Journals
 - Objective: To encourage self-awareness and reflection on fixed versus flexible thinking.
 - Activity: Assign students regular journaling tasks where they reflect on situations in which they felt strongly about an issue or resisted new information. Encourage them to write about why they felt this way and whether they could have approached the situation with more openness. Periodically, students will share their reflections in small groups and discuss how their mindsets have shifted.
 - Outcome: This activity builds metacognitive awareness, helping students recognize areas where their thinking is rigid and develop strategies for being more open to change.

4. "What If?" Scenarios
 - Objective: To help students explore alternate possibilities and outcomes, fostering adaptability.
 - Activity: Present students with a historical event, scientific discovery, or literary plot. Ask them to alter one key variable or decision and explore how that would change the outcome. For example, "What if the Internet had never been invented?" or "What if a character in a novel made a different decision?"

Students will present and discuss these alternate realities, considering the wider implications.
 - Outcome: This activity encourages students to think flexibly about cause and effect, consider multiple possibilities, and understand the interconnectedness of choices and consequences.

5. Role-Reversal Teaching
 - Objective: To build empathy, adaptability, and the ability to rethink concepts from different roles.
 - Activity: Assign students the role of teacher for a specific lesson or topic. Each student must prepare and teach the topic from a different perspective or to a different audience (e.g., explaining a scientific concept to young children or discussing a philosophical idea from the viewpoint of an opposing philosophy). After their teaching session, peers will critique how well they adapted the content to the new audience or perspective.
 - Outcome: Students practice adapting their communication and thinking based on audience needs, enhancing flexibility in how they convey and process information.

These activities help students develop a mindset capable of adapting to new ideas, challenges, and perspectives—skills essential for intellectual growth and resilience in an evolving world.

I have an activity where I organize a debate on a controversial topic, such as vegetarianism versus non-vegetarianism. I divide the students into two groups: vegetarians and non-vegetarians. Then comes the twist. I assign the vegetarians to argue in favor of non-vegetarianism and against vegetarianism, while the non-vegetarians must argue in favor of vegetarianism and against non-vegetarianism. This twist usually surprises the students. The debate typically goes on for three or four rounds. My aim is not to determine which diet is better but to have students take a stance that opposes their daily practice and beliefs. The goal is for them to experience and gracefully navigate the discomfort of defending a position contrary to their own.

Activity: Perspective Shift Debate on Abortion

Objective: To enhance cognitive flexibility and empathy by encouraging students to engage with opposing viewpoints on a highly controversial topic.

Overview: This activity involves a structured debate on the topic of abortion, designed to challenge students' existing beliefs and foster an understanding of diverse perspectives.

Procedure:

1. Introduction: Announce the debate topic—abortion. Explain the significance of understanding differing viewpoints and the skills students will develop through this activity, including critical thinking and respectful discourse.

2. Group Segregation: Divide the class into two groups: one consisting of students who identify as pro-abortion (supporting the right to choose) and the other as anti-abortion (against abortion).

3. Role Assignment: Introduce the twist: assign the pro-abortion group to argue against abortion and the anti-abortion group to advocate for abortion rights. This unexpected role reversal encourages students to step outside their comfort zones.

4. Debate Format: Conduct the debate in three to four rounds, allowing each group time to present their arguments and counterarguments. Emphasize the importance of respectful engagement and active listening during discussions.

5. Reflection: After the debate, hold a debriefing session where students can reflect on their experiences. Discuss how it felt to advocate for a position contrary to their own beliefs and what insights they gained from the exercise.

Outcome: This activity aims to cultivate cognitive flexibility by allowing students to experience the challenges of defending an opposing stance. It encourages them to navigate discomfort gracefully while enhancing their critical thinking skills and empathetic understanding of complex social issues.

Activity: Perspective Shift Debate on Belief and Doubt in Scientific Inquiry

Objective: To encourage cognitive flexibility and critical thinking by exploring the roles of belief and doubt in the process of scientific inquiry.

Overview: This activity involves a structured debate on the interplay between belief and doubt, aiming to challenge students' perspectives on how these concepts influence learning and knowledge acquisition in science.

Procedure:

1. Introduction: Introduce the debate topic—belief versus doubt in scientific inquiry. Discuss the significance of both concepts in fostering critical thinking, skepticism, and a deeper understanding of scientific processes.

2. Group Segregation: Divide the class into two groups: one advocating for the importance of belief in scientific progress (emphasizing trust in established theories and collaboration) and

the other advocating for the importance of doubt (focusing on skepticism, questioning established norms, and the need for continual inquiry).

3. Role Assignment: Introduce the twist: assign the group advocating for belief to argue in favor of skepticism and the group advocating for doubt to argue for the importance of belief in advancing scientific understanding. This role reversal encourages students to confront their own biases and engage with differing perspectives.

4. Debate Format: Conduct the debate in three to four rounds, allowing each group time to present their arguments, counterarguments, and rebuttals. Stress the importance of respectful engagement and active listening during discussions.

5. Reflection: After the debate, hold a debriefing session where students can reflect on their experiences. Discuss how it felt to argue against their own beliefs and what insights they gained regarding the dynamic between belief and doubt in the learning process.

Outcome: This activity aims to foster cognitive flexibility by encouraging students to experience the challenges of defending an opposing stance. It promotes critical thinking and a deeper understanding of how both belief and doubt can coexist in the pursuit of knowledge, ultimately enhancing their ability to engage thoughtfully with complex issues in scientific inquiry.

Teaching intellectual endurance

Engaging in games like Sudoku, Minesweeper, Chess and solving a Rubik's Cube serves as a powerful tool for sharpening cognitive skills, fostering sustained focus, and enhancing the efficiency of thinking. These games challenge the mind to process information rapidly and accurately, requiring the player to anticipate outcomes, recognize patterns, and strategize under pressure. Sudoku, for example, demands logical reasoning and attention to detail, while Minesweeper trains the mind to make calculated decisions based on incomplete information. Chess, often referred to as the game of kings, requires players to think several moves ahead, constantly evaluating the consequences of each action. Similarly, solving a Rubik's Cube involves a combination of memory, spatial reasoning, and algorithmic thinking, all of which are essential for developing quick and complex problem-solving abilities.

These games not only improve cognitive function but also build mental endurance, enabling individuals to sustain focus over extended periods—a crucial skill for academic and professional success. The mental agility required in these activities translates directly to real-life scenarios where quick, efficient, and complex thinking is needed. Regular engagement with such games can train the brain to think faster, navigate complexities with ease, and maintain sharp focus, which is particularly beneficial in the context of education. The goal of education is to cultivate a mind capable of sustained and efficient thinking, and these games provide a practical and enjoyable way to achieve that end, preparing individuals to tackle the intellectual challenges they will encounter throughout their lives.

The teacher teaches intelligence by getting out of the way.

Chapter 8: Inculcating Self-learning and Lifelong Learning Skills

Why lifelong learning?

The world is changing rapidly, with knowledge evolving daily and the problems we encounter also shifting. There is no way for a human being to remain unchanged in terms of cognitive skills; they must be upgraded continually. Unlike in ancient times, when knowledge was finite, contemporary society experienced an exponential acceleration of knowledge. This reality necessitates that every individual engages in lifelong learning throughout their lifespan.

Lifelong learning requires foundational knowledge, the skills to learn effectively, and intrinsic motivation for continued education. These essential skills are often cultivated during college. From that point onward, the direction and intensity of learning will depend on individual needs. However, it is crucial to keep learning even in the absence of immediate necessity; otherwise, the skills acquired can stagnate and become obsolete within a few years. For instance, consider someone who has never used a laptop. If such a person suddenly finds themselves in a situation where they must use one, the resulting struggles, anxieties, and feelings of humiliation can be overwhelming.

The consistent relevance of a human is dependent on lifelong learning.

Lifelong learning has become an essential requirement in the modern world, primarily due to the rapid acceleration of technology and the widening generation gap. As technology evolves at an unprecedented pace, new tools, platforms, and methods of communication emerge regularly. This constant change necessitates that individuals remain adaptable and continuously update their skills to stay relevant in their personal and professional lives. Those who engage in lifelong learning are better equipped to navigate the complexities of new technologies, improving their employability and ensuring they can contribute effectively in a dynamic workplace.

Moreover, the generational divide often leads to differing perspectives on technology and communication methods. Younger generations, having grown up with advanced technology, may approach problems and solutions differently than older generations, who may not be as familiar with recent innovations. Lifelong learning facilitates intergenerational collaboration by enabling individuals of all ages to bridge this gap, fostering mutual understanding and respect.

Additionally, as the world faces rapid globalization, individuals must understand diverse cultures, perspectives, and practices. Lifelong learning promotes cultural competence, which is essential for effective communication and collaboration in diverse environments.

The pursuit of lifelong learning encourages personal growth, critical thinking, and creativity. In an era where information is abundant and easily accessible, individuals equipped with a mindset for continuous learning are better positioned to think critically about information, innovate, and contribute to society positively. Thus, embracing lifelong learning is not only a personal imperative but also a societal necessity to thrive in an increasingly complex and interconnected world.

Types of Lifelong Learning

Lifelong learning refers to the continuous, voluntary, and self-motivated pursuit of knowledge for personal or professional development throughout an individual's life. It encompasses various forms of learning, including formal education, informal learning through experiences, and self-directed learning, where individuals take the initiative to identify their learning needs, set goals, and pursue knowledge independently.

Types of lifelong learning include:

1. **Formal Learning**: Structured learning through educational institutions, such as degrees, diplomas, or professional certifications.
2. **Informal Learning**: Unstructured, spontaneous learning from daily experiences, interactions, or social activities.
3. **Non-Formal Learning**: Organized learning outside formal education systems, such as workshops, seminars, and community courses.

Lifelong self-learning is a crucial aspect of lifelong learning, where individuals actively seek knowledge and skills without formal instruction. This process involves setting personal learning objectives, utilizing resources such as books, online courses, and mentorship, and reflecting on one's learning journey.

Risks of not learning lifelong

A person who remains unchanged after attaining adulthood leads a stagnant lifestyle, both in terms of personal growth and knowledge and can be described as embodying a "fixed stereotype." This indicates an adherence to outdated routines, perspectives, and skills, avoiding the dynamic, lifelong learning that fosters adaptability. Such a person may become a stereotype of inflexibility, resisting new ideas and experiences and embodying the notion of stagnation in a world that continuously evolves. This reluctance to grow can limit both personal fulfillment and the ability to engage meaningfully with a changing world.

Many people struggle with lifelong learning due to a combination of psychological, social, and environmental factors. First, a fixed mindset can hinder individuals from believing in their ability to learn and grow. This mindset often leads to fear of failure or embarrassment, which discourages the exploration of new ideas or skills. Additionally, a lack of motivation can stem from complacency; when individuals feel satisfied with their current knowledge or skills, they may not see the need to pursue further learning.

Moreover, time constraints play a significant role. Many individuals lead busy lives filled with personal and professional responsibilities, leaving little room for self-directed learning. This can result in prioritizing immediate tasks over long-term development.

Social and cultural influences also impact lifelong learning. In some environments, there may be a lack of encouragement or resources for continued education, leading individuals to feel unsupported in their learning endeavors. Finally, limited access to technology and learning opportunities can create barriers, particularly in underserved communities, preventing individuals from engaging with new information and ideas.

The absence of self-learning can lead to several significant risks and drawbacks in both personal and professional contexts:

1. Stagnation of Skills and Knowledge: Without self-directed learning, individuals may find their skills becoming outdated. In rapidly evolving fields, such as technology and science, failing to

keep pace with new developments can hinder career growth and competitiveness.

2. Decreased Adaptability: Self-learning fosters adaptability by encouraging individuals to engage with new concepts and approaches. Without this, people may struggle to adjust to changes in their environment or industry, making them less resilient in the face of challenges.

3. Limited Critical Thinking and Problem-Solving Skills: Self-learning promotes independent thinking and the ability to analyze situations critically. Without these skills, individuals may rely too heavily on established protocols or instructions, resulting in a lack of innovation and creativity.

4. Reduced Confidence and Initiative: Individuals who do not engage in self-learning may develop a dependency on structured learning environments. This can lead to diminished confidence in their ability to tackle new tasks or challenges independently.

5. Missed Opportunities for Personal Growth: Self-learning encourages exploration and curiosity, leading to personal development beyond formal education. Without it, individuals may miss out on enriching experiences that can enhance their knowledge, perspective, and overall quality of life.

6. Inability to Stay Current: In a world where information is constantly evolving, failing to engage in self-learning can result in a disconnect from current trends and knowledge. This can hinder effective communication and collaboration with peers and colleagues.

7. Career Limitations: Employers increasingly value self-learners who demonstrate a commitment to ongoing education and skill enhancement. Without self-learning, individuals may find

themselves less attractive candidates for promotion or new job opportunities.

Lifelong learning is fundamentally dependent on three critical components: skills for learning, time management, and intrinsic motivation. First, essential learning skills include proficient reading, the ability to learn by observation, and maintaining focus during the learning process. These skills are further enhanced by having prerequisite knowledge, which provides a solid foundation for acquiring new information. Additionally, the quality of learning is often influenced by grit—the perseverance and resilience to overcome obstacles and persist in the face of challenges.

Second, the allocation of time for learning hinges on individual priorities and constraints. In a world filled with competing demands, effectively managing time is crucial to making room for continuous education. Individuals must navigate their responsibilities, interests, and personal goals to carve out opportunities for learning.

The drive for lifelong learning is intrinsically linked to the perception of pleasure or necessity in the learning process. A genuine curiosity or a pressing need to acquire knowledge can serve as powerful motivators. This may stem from a passion for a particular subject or a desire to adapt to rapidly changing circumstances. The combination of skills, time management, and intrinsic motivation lays the groundwork for a fulfilling lifelong learning journey.

The beginning of a stereotype marks the point where change has halted because learning has ceased.

Inculcating lifelong learning in college

Lifelong learning can be effectively instilled in college students through various strategies that promote curiosity, independence, and adaptability.

1. Curriculum Design: Incorporating project-based learning and interdisciplinary courses encourages students to apply knowledge creatively, fostering a mindset of inquiry and exploration beyond the classroom.

2. Encouraging Critical Thinking: Implementing assignments that require analysis, evaluation, and synthesis of information helps students develop critical thinking skills essential for lifelong learning.

3. Promoting Self-Directed Learning: Providing opportunities for students to pursue independent research projects or self-study encourages them to take charge of their learning journey. Faculty can guide this process by offering resources and mentorship.

4. Utilizing Technology: Integrating online platforms for learning, such as MOOCs (Massive Open Online Courses) and webinars, exposes students to a wide range of topics and expertise, reinforcing the idea that learning can occur anywhere and anytime.

5. Fostering a Growth Mindset: Encouraging resilience and a positive attitude toward challenges can help students view failures as learning opportunities, motivating them to continue their educational pursuits beyond graduation.

The sole purpose of educational institutions is to provide learning skills. One of the skills listed above is the growth mindset, which is difficult to teach and train. It is not a skill or attribute that one can have for a while but, like intelligence, should be nurtured every day.

Fostering Growth Mindset in College

Fostering a growth mindset in students is a crucial endeavor that encourages them to embrace challenges, persist in the face of obstacles, and recognize that their abilities can be developed through dedication and hard work. This mindset not only enhances their academic and intellectual pursuits but also contributes to their physical skills and overall personal development. Here are several effective strategies to instill and nurture a growth mindset in students, enabling them to continuously upgrade their knowledge and skills.

1. Emphasize Effort Over Innate Ability:

One of the foundational principles of a growth mindset is the belief that effort leads to improvement. Educators should consistently reinforce the idea that intelligence and skills are not fixed traits but can be cultivated through perseverance and hard work. By praising effort rather than inherent talent, students are more likely to embrace challenges as opportunities for growth.

2. Create a Safe Learning Environment:

A supportive classroom atmosphere is essential for fostering a growth mindset. Students should feel safe to take risks, make mistakes, and learn from failures. Educators can encourage open discussions about setbacks and emphasize that failure is a natural part of the learning process. By normalizing mistakes, students are more likely to view them as stepping stones rather than barriers.

3. Encourage Goal Setting:

Setting realistic, achievable goals allows students to focus on their growth journey. Educators can guide students in setting both short-term and long-term goals, emphasizing the importance of incremental progress. When students can see the steps they need to take to achieve their goals, they are more likely to remain motivated and engaged in the learning process.

4. Promote Self-Reflection:

Encouraging students to reflect on their learning experiences is vital for developing a growth mindset. Self-reflection allows students to evaluate their strengths and weaknesses, identify areas for improvement, and recognize their progress over time. Journals or portfolios can serve as effective tools for students to document their growth journey and celebrate their achievements.

5. Draw Inspiration from Others:

Students can draw motivation from the successes of their peers or role models. Educators can share stories of individuals who have overcome challenges and achieved greatness through perseverance and hard work. By highlighting examples of resilience, students can see that success is attainable and that they, too, can progress despite constraints.

6. Foster a Love for Learning:

Cultivating a passion for learning is essential for maintaining a growth mindset. Educators should create engaging and stimulating lessons that spark curiosity and excitement about new concepts. Incorporating diverse teaching methods, such as hands-on activities, discussions, and multimedia resources, can make learning more enjoyable and relevant to students' lives.

7. Provide Constructive Feedback:

Timely and constructive feedback helps students understand their progress and areas for improvement. Educators should focus on specific behaviors and strategies rather than general assessments. This approach encourages students to view feedback as a valuable tool for growth rather than as a critique of their abilities.

8. Encourage Collaboration:

Group activities and collaborative projects can enhance students' sense of community and collective growth. Working with peers fosters a supportive environment where students can share ideas, learn from one another, and celebrate each other's successes. Collaboration also encourages students to step out of their comfort zones and embrace different perspectives.

9. Integrate Physical Skills and Well-Being:

Physical education and extracurricular activities play a significant role in fostering a growth mindset. Engaging in sports or physical challenges allows students to experience the benefits of perseverance and teamwork firsthand. Encouraging them to pursue physical fitness not only promotes overall well-being but also instills resilience and a commitment to continuous improvement.

10. Promote Lifelong Learning as a Value:

Lastly, educators should instill the belief that learning is a lifelong journey. Emphasizing that growth extends beyond formal education encourages students to see themselves as lifelong learners. By framing learning as a dynamic process that continues throughout life, students are more likely to cultivate a growth mindset that serves them in all areas of their lives.

Fostering a growth mindset in students requires a multifaceted approach that emphasizes effort, resilience, and a love for learning. By creating an environment where challenges are embraced, mistakes are viewed as opportunities, and progress is celebrated, educators can empower students to see growth as an eternal virtue. In this way, learning becomes synonymous with living, and a growth mindset serves as a powerful catalyst for lifelong development and fulfillment.

Encouraging lifelong learning of alumni

Nurturing a growth mindset in students is not only a responsibility that teachers undertake during their formal education but also a lifelong commitment that can extend beyond graduation. A teacher's role in fostering a growth mindset can profoundly impact their students' perspectives on learning, resilience, and personal development long after they have left the classroom. Here are several strategies that educators can employ to personally nurture and appreciate the growth mindset in their former students, facilitating their continuous growth even post-graduation.

1. Establish Lifelong Relationships:

Maintaining connections with students after graduation is crucial for nurturing a growth mindset. Teachers can use various platforms, such as social media, alumni networks, or school events, to stay in touch. By engaging with students through regular check-ins, sharing updates, and celebrating their achievements, teachers demonstrate that they care about their students' growth beyond the classroom. These relationships can provide a supportive framework for students as they navigate new challenges in their personal and professional lives.

2. Encourage Reflection on Growth:

Teachers can promote reflection on growth by encouraging former students to share their learning journeys. This can be facilitated through alumni newsletters, social media groups, or even virtual gatherings. By asking students to reflect on their challenges and successes, teachers can help them recognize their progress and reinforce the idea that learning is a lifelong process. Sharing stories of resilience can inspire other alumni and foster a community that values personal growth.

3. Provide Resources for Continued Learning:

Teachers can curate and share resources that promote lifelong learning, such as books, articles, online courses, or workshops related to personal and professional development. By creating a repository of resources that align with the interests and aspirations of their former students, teachers can encourage them to pursue knowledge and skills continuously. This proactive approach not only nurtures a growth mindset but also emphasizes the importance of self-directed learning.

4. Celebrate Alumni Achievements:

Recognizing and celebrating the achievements of former students is a powerful way to nurture a growth mindset. Teachers can showcase alumni accomplishments through newsletters, social media posts, or school events. Celebrating successes reinforces the notion that hard work and perseverance lead to positive outcomes, encouraging others to adopt a similar mindset. By highlighting diverse paths and achievements, teachers also demonstrate that growth can manifest in various forms.

5. Facilitate Networking Opportunities:

Teachers can play a crucial role in connecting former students with one another and with professionals in their fields of interest. Organizing alumni events, workshops, or mentorship programs allows graduates to share experiences, network, and learn from one another. These opportunities foster a collaborative environment that encourages continuous growth and learning. By facilitating such connections, teachers empower their former students to seek guidance and inspiration from their peers.

6. Model Lifelong Learning:

Teachers should embody the principles of a growth mindset by continuing their own learning journeys. Sharing personal experiences of growth, challenges, and successes can inspire students to view learning as a lifelong endeavor. By demonstrating curiosity, resilience, and a willingness to learn, teachers become role models for their former students. This modeling reinforces the idea that growth is a continuous process that does not end with graduation.

7. Encourage Goal Setting Beyond Graduation:

Teachers can encourage former students to set personal and professional goals after graduation. This can be done through informal conversations, alumni gatherings, or online discussions. By emphasizing the importance of setting achievable, incremental goals, teachers can help students stay focused on their growth journey. Encouraging students to share their goals with others can create accountability and a sense of community, further reinforcing the idea that growth is an ongoing process.

8. Foster a Supportive Community:

Creating a supportive community among former students can enhance the nurturing of a growth mindset. Teachers can facilitate online forums or social media groups where alumni can share experiences, seek advice, and offer support. These platforms provide a space for students to connect and learn from one another, reinforcing the idea that growth is often a collective journey.

Nurturing a growth mindset in students does not conclude at graduation. By establishing lifelong relationships, encouraging reflection, providing resources, celebrating achievements, facilitating networking, modeling lifelong learning, encouraging goal setting, and fostering a supportive community, teachers can continue to positively influence their former students' growth journeys. Ultimately, the cultivation of a growth mindset is a continuous process that extends far beyond the classroom, empowering students to embrace challenges and strive for lifelong learning and personal development.

Staying connected with alumni through social media serves as a meaningful way to foster a sense of community and ongoing support. Each time I come across a post showcasing their achievements or efforts toward upskilling, I make it a point to engage by liking and congratulating them. This simple act of recognition can significantly impact their sense of accomplishment, reinforcing the notion that their commitment to lifelong learning is valued and acknowledged.

By publicly celebrating their successes, I aim to create an environment where alumni feel appreciated and motivated to continue their personal and professional growth. Such interactions not only affirm their efforts but also cultivate a shared sense of pride within our educational community. For me, as a teacher, witnessing my former students thrive evokes a profound sense of fulfillment. It serves as a testament to the effectiveness of my teaching and the values we emphasized during their formative years. The acknowledgment of their growth inspires me to maintain this connection, as it highlights the transformative power of education and lifelong learning. Ultimately, these engagements reinforce the belief that learning extends beyond the classroom, fostering a culture of continuous improvement and support among all members of our educational family.

Chapter 9: Planning the Lesson Plans

A lesson plan is a comprehensive framework that delineates the objectives, content, teaching methods, and assessment strategies for a specific lesson or series of lessons. It acts as a roadmap for educators, guiding them in delivering structured and effective instruction while ensuring that students achieve the desired learning outcomes. The significance of lesson plans lies in their ability to provide clarity and focus, aiding in the organization of instructional materials and activities. Additionally, they facilitate the assessment of student progress and promote reflection on teaching practices, ultimately enhancing the overall learning experience. However, I must acknowledge that I do not create formal lesson plans for every class; rather, I typically outline my approach mentally, focusing primarily on planning for the most critical classes. I am acutely aware that developing lesson plans can be particularly challenging in higher education, where the content is often dense and requires a deep level of intelligence. In such contexts, creating comprehensive plans can become nearly impractical. As a result, I tend to focus on planning activities for only a select number of classes, prioritizing engagement and adaptability over rigid structure. **Teachers need to breathe, too!** The provided lesson plans can be tried at least occasionally. The huge number of classes to handle and the class size are the major impediments to implementing systematic class plans.

In my view, each chapter should encompass various types of lesson plans, including an introductory and vocabulary lesson plan, a knowledge lesson plan, an intelligence lesson plan, and a reflection lesson plan. Essentially, a lesson plan outlines the teaching objectives for that particular hour—whether it is to introduce new concepts, develop essential technical vocabulary, impart knowledge, or foster intelligence as a means of enhancing cognitive skills. Each lesson plan should incorporate student activities designed not only to promote cognitive development but also to build personality and increase productivity. This multifaceted approach ensures a holistic learning experience, enriching students' academic and personal growth. We shall see different types of lesson plans for the topic "The Interrelationship Between Philosophy, Psychology, and Pedagogy."

Ice Breaker Lesson Plan

Objective:
To foster a comfortable, open, and engaging environment where students and the teacher can build rapport, trust, and mutual respect.
Duration: 50 minutes

1. Introduction (5 minutes)
- Objective: Set a welcoming tone and briefly introduce the purpose of the session.
- Teacher's Role: Introduce yourself and explain that the goal of the activity is to break the ice and get to know each other better in a fun, relaxed manner.
- Student's Role: Listen and get comfortable with the idea of a participative activity.

2. Icebreaker 1: "Two Truths and a Lie" (15 minutes)
- Objective: Encourage students to share personal facts and engage in a fun guessing game.

Activity:
- Each student writes down two truths and one lie about themselves on an index card.

- One by one, students will read their statements aloud, and the class (including the teacher) will guess which statement is the lie.

Teacher's Role: Participate alongside students, making your own statements to contribute to the activity. Encourage all students to share and gently nudge any reluctant participants.
Student's Role: Participate by writing down their truths and a lie and actively engaging in guessing others' responses.

3. Icebreaker 2: "Common Ground" (15 minutes)
- Objective: Build connections between students and teachers by identifying shared interests or experiences.

Activity:
- Divide the class into small groups (3-4 students per group).
- Each group will discuss amongst themselves for 5 minutes to find at least three things they all have in common (e.g., hobbies, favorite food, books, etc.).
- After 5 minutes, each group will share their findings with the rest of the class.

Teacher's Role: Join different groups for a few moments to learn about their commonalities, demonstrating an active interest in their conversations.

Student's Role: Actively engage in the discussion to find common ground with their peers.

4. Icebreaker 3: "Teacher Trivia" (10 minutes)
- Objective: Allow students to learn about the teacher in a fun and interactive manner.

Activity:

- Prepare 5-7 interesting facts about yourself (as the teacher) in advance, both personal and professional.
- Present these facts to the class, but mix in a few fictitious ones as well.
- Students will guess which facts are true and which are false.

Teacher's Role: Share personal and professional facts to humanize yourself and encourage students to feel more comfortable asking questions and participating.

Student's Role: Actively guess which statements about the teacher are true or false.

5. Reflection and Wrap-Up (5 minutes)
- Objective: Summarize the importance of getting to know each other and fostering a collaborative environment.

Activity:
- Briefly discuss how building rapport will help throughout the course and encourage students to communicate freely whenever they need help or guidance.
- Allow students to share their impressions of the icebreaker activity.

Teacher's Role: Provide positive feedback on the activities and encourage students to approach future classes with openness.

Student's Role: Reflect on the activity and share their experience if they feel comfortable.

Follow-Up:
- Encourage students to continue engaging in class and to foster peer connections. Consider using similar icebreaker activities for future lessons to maintain rapport.

Introductory lesson plan

The introductory lesson plan should primarily focus on fostering motivation for studying the chapter by emphasizing its relevance in everyday contexts. It should also include the definitions of key terms and technical vocabulary, along with student activities that explore the sounds, speech, and meanings of these words. Following these activities, a quiz should be administered to assess understanding. Finally, the lesson should provide a seamless transition into the knowledge lesson plan for the chapter, which will be covered in the subsequent class.

Lesson Plan: Introductory-Vocabulary for "The Interrelationship Between Philosophy, Psychology, and Pedagogy"

Grade Level: Undergraduate
Subject: Education/Philosophy
Duration: 50 minutes

Objectives:

1. To motivate students for the study of the chapter by highlighting its relevance in daily contexts.
2. To introduce and define key terms and technical vocabulary related to the chapter.
3. To engage students in activities that enhance their understanding of vocabulary through sounds, speech, and meanings.
4. To prepare students for the subsequent knowledge lesson plan on the chapter.

Lesson Outline

1. Introduction (10 minutes)

- Engagement: Begin the class by asking students about their understanding of philosophy, psychology, and pedagogy. Facilitate a brief discussion on how these fields interrelate in education.
- Motivation: Explain the relevance of the chapter to their daily lives and future careers in education, emphasizing the importance of understanding these concepts.

2. Vocabulary Introduction (15 minutes)
- Key Vocabulary: Introduce key terms such as:
- Philosophy
- Psychology
- Pedagogy
- Epistemology
- Constructivism
- Behaviorism
- Definitions: Provide clear definitions and contextual examples for each term, encouraging students to think critically about how these concepts relate to their studies.

3. Student Activities (15 minutes)
- Activity 1: Sound and Speech Exploration
- Play audio recordings of the key terms and ask students to repeat them, focusing on pronunciation and intonation.

- Activity 2: Word Associations
- Have students work in pairs to create word associations or mind maps for each term. This will help them connect the vocabulary to broader concepts within the chapter.

4. Quiz (5 minutes)
- Assessment: Distribute a short quiz consisting of matching terms with their definitions or filling in the blanks to assess understanding of the key vocabulary introduced.

5. Transition to Next Lesson (5 minutes)
- Wrap-Up: Conclude the lesson by summarizing the importance of the vocabulary in understanding the chapter.
- Preview: Provide a brief introduction to the knowledge lesson plan for the next class, outlining what students can expect to learn.

Assessment:
- Evaluate student understanding through the quiz and participation in activities. Provide feedback to guide their learning in the subsequent lessons.

Knowledge Lesson Plan

A knowledge-based lesson plan must delve into the intricate details of facts, processes, and methods, encapsulating everything that is already known within the interconnected realms of philosophy, psychology, and pedagogy. This lesson plan serves as a foundational structure where educators can systematically present established theories and concepts, allowing students to grasp the complexities of these fields. By dissecting the interconnectedness of philosophy's principles, psychological theories, and pedagogical approaches, we lay the groundwork for deeper intellectual exploration. Such a knowledge lesson plan can extend across multiple lectures, fostering an environment where students can engage critically with the material. It is here that they will begin to draw connections, pose questions, and cultivate a rich understanding that transcends rote memorization. Ultimately, this approach not only enriches students' comprehension but also empowers them to apply their newfound knowledge in innovative ways, thereby enhancing their overall educational journey.

Lesson Plan: Knowledge Lesson on the Interconnected Realms of Philosophy, Psychology, and Pedagogy

Grade Level: Undergraduate
Duration: 50 minutes
Subject: Education/Pedagogy
Topic: The Interconnected Realms of Philosophy, Psychology, and Pedagogy

Objectives
- To understand the fundamental principles of philosophy, psychology, and pedagogy.
- To explore the interrelationships between these disciplines and their impact on educational practices.
- To analyze key theories and concepts from each field and their practical implications for teaching and learning.

Lesson Outline

1. Introduction (5 minutes)
 - Briefly introduce the topic and objectives of the lesson.
 - Pose a thought-provoking question: "How do philosophy, psychology, and pedagogy influence each other in the context of education?"

2. Presentation of Key Concepts (15 minutes)
 - Philosophy in Education: Discuss major philosophical theories (e.g., idealism, realism, pragmatism) and their implications for teaching.
 - Psychology in Education: Cover key psychological theories (e.g., behaviorism, constructivism, cognitive development) and their impact on learning processes.
 - Pedagogy: Explain various pedagogical approaches (e.g., traditional vs. progressive education) and their philosophical and psychological underpinnings.

3. Interconnectedness Discussion (15 minutes)

- Explore how philosophy informs psychological theories and pedagogical practices.
- Example: How does the constructivist approach in psychology align with pragmatic philosophy?
- Facilitate a group discussion, encouraging students to share their insights and make connections among the disciplines.

4. Group Activity (10 minutes)

- Divide students into small groups and assign each group a specific theory from one of the three disciplines.
- Task each group to discuss how their assigned theory can influence teaching practices and learning experiences.
- Ask groups to present their findings briefly.

5. Conclusion and Reflection (5 minutes)

- Summarize key points discussed in the lesson.
- Introduce the next lesson on Intelligence, highlighting that the upcoming session will focus on how the interrelationship between philosophy, psychology, and pedagogy can be utilized to foster intelligence in students. Explain that students will explore various types of intelligence, including practical applications in the classroom.
- Encourage students to reflect on the importance of understanding the interplay between these fields in shaping their teaching strategies.
- Assign readings or provide handouts for further exploration of the topic.

Assessment

- Participation in discussions and group activities.
- Submission of a reflective journal entry on how the interconnectedness of these fields can influence their own educational philosophies.

Additional Notes
- This lesson can be extended over multiple sessions, allowing for a deeper exploration of each discipline and its theories.
- Consider integrating multimedia resources (e.g., videos or podcasts) to enhance engagement and understanding of complex concepts.

Intelligence lesson plan

An intelligence lesson plan is fundamentally centered on the exploration and discovery facilitated by students themselves. While the teacher possesses knowledge and may have established answers, for students, engaging with this information represents an exercise in intelligence, prompting them to ponder concepts for the first time. The essence of the intelligence lesson plan lies in its capacity to stimulate deep and continuous thinking among students. This intellectual journey not only fosters critical thinking but also cultivates innovative problem-solving abilities.

A critical prerequisite for an effective intelligence lesson plan is that students must have assimilated the knowledge imparted in previous classes. Intelligence, in essence, is built upon a solid foundation of knowledge. A well-structured intelligence lesson plan should begin with a review of this prerequisite knowledge, ensuring that all students are equipped to engage meaningfully with new concepts. Following this review, the plan should include at least three distinct activities, each designed to encourage independent thought. Students should be prompted to reflect individually before convening in small groups to share their perspectives and collaboratively derive the most robust answers. This collaborative exchange not only enriches their understanding but also enhances their ability to articulate and defend their ideas, ultimately leading to a richer learning experience.

Intelligence Lesson Plan: The Interconnected Realms of Philosophy, Psychology, and Pedagogy

Objective:
Students will explore the interconnectedness of philosophy, psychology, and pedagogy, deepening their understanding through independent thinking and collaborative discussions.
Duration: 50 minutes

1. Review of Prerequisite Knowledge (10 minutes)
- Activity:
Begin the class with a brief review of the key concepts covered in the previous knowledge lesson. This may include definitions and foundational ideas related to philosophy, psychology, and pedagogy.
- Method:
Use a quick Q&A format where students are prompted to recall important terms and concepts, reinforcing their prior learning.

2. Individual Reflection (15 minutes)
- Activity:
Pose an open-ended question related to the interconnectedness of the three realms. For example:
"How do you believe philosophy influences teaching methods in psychology?"
- Method:
Students will write a short reflection (approximately 5-7 sentences) articulating their thoughts independently. This encourages personal engagement with the material.

3. Group Discussion (15 minutes)
- Activity:

Form small groups of 4-5 students. Each group will discuss their individual reflections, sharing their thoughts and insights on the posed question.
- Method:
Encourage students to build upon each other's ideas, challenge one another, and aim to reach a consensus or a more refined understanding of the topic.

4. Group Presentation (5 minutes)

- Activity:
Each group will appoint a spokesperson to summarize their discussion and present their collective insights to the class.
- Method:
This fosters a sense of accountability and encourages students to articulate their thoughts clearly.

5. Conclusion and Wrap-Up (5 minutes)

- Activity:
Conclude the lesson by highlighting key points that emerged from the group discussions. Pose a reflective question for students to ponder for the next class. For example:
"In what ways do you think understanding these interconnected realms can influence your future teaching practices?"
- Method:
This encourages students to think critically about the practical implications of their learning.

Note to the teacher: Out of the way!

Reflection lesson plan

A reflection lesson plan emphasizes the importance of introspection regarding vocabulary, definitions, foundational knowledge, and intellectual insights. This plan encourages students to contemplate not only the outcomes of their learning but also the intricate processes behind their intellectual thought. By reflecting on these aspects, students can hone essential learning skills, deepen their understanding, and solidify the knowledge imparted in previous lessons. Moreover, this reflective practice fosters a sense of appreciation for self-discovery as learners recognize how their intellectual processes contribute to their personal growth. This approach cultivates critical thinking and reinforces the significance of lifelong learning.

Reflection Lesson Plan: Vocabulary, Knowledge, and Intelligence Gained from Previous Lessons

Grade Level: Undergraduate
Duration: 50 minutes
Objectives:
- To reflect on the vocabulary, foundational knowledge, and intelligence developed through previous lesson plans on the interconnected realms of philosophy, psychology, and pedagogy.
- To enhance self-awareness of the learning process and consolidate understanding through reflective practice.

Lesson Components:
1. Introduction (10 minutes)
- Begin by welcoming students and briefly recapping the key vocabulary, foundational knowledge, and intelligence exercises covered in previous lessons.
- Emphasize the significance of reflection in learning, highlighting how it consolidates knowledge and fosters deeper insights.

2. Vocabulary Review (10 minutes)
 - Provide students with a list of key terms that were covered in prior lessons (e.g., epistemology, behaviorism, constructivism).
 - Ask students to spend a few minutes reviewing these terms individually and then discuss their meanings and applications in pairs.
 - After discussion, invite pairs to share one or two insights or examples with the class, reinforcing the importance of vocabulary in understanding complex ideas.

3. Knowledge Reflection (15 minutes)
 - Pose a guiding question such as, "What foundational knowledge have you acquired about the interrelationships between philosophy, psychology, and pedagogy?"
 - Give students 5 minutes to write down their responses, focusing on specific knowledge points and how they relate to the broader context of the subject matter.
 - Next, organize students into small groups to discuss their reflections, encouraging them to connect their knowledge with real-world applications or personal experiences.

4. Intelligence Reflection (10 minutes)
 - Transition to reflecting on the intelligence aspect of learning by posing the question: "How has your understanding of intelligence evolved through our exploration of these interconnected fields?"
 - Allow students 5 minutes to jot down their thoughts on how the intelligence exercises in previous lessons have influenced their cognitive processes.
 - In small groups, students discuss their reflections and share insights about how they have approached problem-solving or critical thinking differently as a result of the lessons.

5. Conclusion (5 minutes)

- Summarize the key points discussed during the lesson, reinforcing the connections between vocabulary, knowledge, and intelligence.
- Encourage students to continue reflecting on their learning journeys and how the insights gained can influence their future studies and teaching practices.
- Briefly introduce the next lesson plan, which will build on these reflections with practical applications and discussions.

Assessment:
- Evaluate student participation in discussions and the depth of their reflections on vocabulary, knowledge, and intelligence.
- Collect and review written reflections to gauge their understanding and self-awareness of the learning process.

This reflection lesson plan aims to deepen students' understanding of the interconnected realms of philosophy, psychology, and pedagogy while fostering critical thinking and self-discovery. By encouraging students to consolidate their understanding of vocabulary, knowledge, and intelligence developed through prior lessons, the plan fosters a deeper appreciation for these disciplines and their interrelationships.

Alternate strategy: Make a hybrid lesson plan with a mixture of vocabulary, knowledge, intelligence and reflection

An alternative approach to the proposed lesson plans is the creation of multiple hybrid lesson plans that integrate elements of vocabulary, knowledge, intelligence, and reflection within a single framework. Each hybrid lesson can include dedicated sections for vocabulary, knowledge, intelligence, and reflection, allowing for a more cohesive learning experience that emphasizes the interconnectedness of these components.

One advantage of hybrid lesson plans is that they provide a comprehensive structure that can cater to diverse learning styles and preferences. By integrating vocabulary acquisition with knowledge dissemination, intelligence exercises, and reflective practices, teachers can facilitate deeper cognitive engagement and promote critical thinking. This approach also allows for a more fluid transition between different types of learning, as students can see how vocabulary is applied in knowledge and intelligence activities, culminating in reflective discussions that reinforce their understanding.

However, there are potential challenges to consider. The complexity of managing multiple components within a single lesson may require more planning and organization, which can be demanding for educators. Additionally, striking the right balance among vocabulary, knowledge, intelligence, and reflection is crucial; too much emphasis on one aspect could overshadow the others, ultimately hindering the learning process. Nevertheless, when executed thoughtfully, hybrid lesson plans can enrich the educational experience, fostering holistic development in students.

Hybrid Lesson Plan: The Interconnected Realms of Philosophy, Psychology, and Pedagogy

Grade Level: Undergraduate Students
Duration: 50 minutes

Objectives:
1. To enhance vocabulary related to philosophy, psychology, and pedagogy.
2. To deepen knowledge of the interconnectedness of these fields.

3. To foster intelligence through critical thinking exercises.
4. To encourage reflection on learned concepts.

Lesson Outline:

1. Introduction (5 minutes)
- Briefly introduce the topic and objectives of the lesson.
- Explain the significance of understanding the interrelationship between philosophy, psychology, and pedagogy.

2. Vocabulary Section (10 minutes)
- Activity: Distribute a list of key vocabulary terms (e.g., epistemology, behaviorism, constructivism).
- Task: Students work in pairs to define each term and create a visual representation (e.g., concept map) of how these terms relate to each other.
- Share: Groups present their visual representations to the class.

3. Knowledge Section (10 minutes)
- Activity: Present a brief lecture on the foundational concepts of philosophy, psychology, and pedagogy, focusing on their interconnectedness.
- Task: Engage students in a discussion about how these disciplines influence one another, encouraging them to draw on the vocabulary from the previous activity.

4. Intelligence Section (15 minutes)
- Activity: Divide students into small groups.
- Task: Assign each group a scenario where they must apply concepts from philosophy, psychology, and pedagogy to devise a solution (e.g., creating an inclusive classroom environment).
- Discussion: Groups present their solutions, highlighting the thought processes involved.

5. Reflection Section (10 minutes)
 - Activity: Facilitate a reflective discussion.
 - Task: Prompt students to think about how the vocabulary, knowledge, and intelligence they have engaged with in this lesson connect to their own educational experiences.
 - Journaling: Ask students to write a brief reflection on what they learned today and how they can apply this knowledge in future learning contexts.

Assessment:
- Monitor group discussions and presentations for understanding and engagement.
- Collect reflections to evaluate individual comprehension and self-discovery.

Follow-Up:
- Prepare for the next lesson, which will build on this understanding with a focus on applying these concepts in real-world educational settings.

System Thinking Lesson Plan: Introduction to Systems Thinking

Lesson Plan: The Interconnected Realms of Philosophy, Psychology, and Pedagogy

Objective:
By the end of this lesson, students will understand the interconnections between philosophy, psychology, and pedagogy through the lens of systems thinking. They will be able to analyze how these disciplines inform and influence each other, contributing to a holistic understanding of education.

Lesson Title:

The Interconnected Realms of Philosophy, Psychology, and Pedagogy

Grade Level: Undergraduate/Postgraduate Education
Time Duration: 90 minutes

 Materials Needed:
- Whiteboard and markers
- Projector or screen for visual presentation
- Handouts or digital access to key readings (short articles or excerpts)
- Discussion prompts for group work
- Mind-mapping software or paper and pens for systems diagrams

Lesson Outline:

1. Introduction (10 minutes)
- Objective: To introduce the concept of interconnectedness among philosophy, psychology, and pedagogy.

Discussion Starter:
- Pose the question: How do you think philosophy, psychology, and pedagogy are related to one another?
- Briefly discuss initial student responses to set the stage for deeper exploration.

Teacher Input:
- Introduce the definition of systems thinking as a way of understanding how different parts of a system (in this case, philosophy, psychology, and pedagogy) work together to create an integrated whole.
- Emphasize that these three domains are not isolated but interdependent, influencing educational approaches, teacher-student relationships, and learning outcomes.

2. Exploring Each Domain (20 minutes)

- Objective: Students will explore how each domain (philosophy, psychology, and pedagogy) individually contributes to education.

a) Philosophy:
- Discuss how philosophical inquiry addresses the purpose of education, the role of the teacher, and ethical considerations in learning.
- Key ideas: Constructivism vs. traditionalism, nature of knowledge (epistemology), and ethical implications of teaching.

b) Psychology:
- Explore how psychology informs our understanding of how students learn, cognitive development, motivation, and emotional intelligence.
- Key ideas: Behaviorism, cognitive development theories (e.g., Piaget, Vygotsky), emotional intelligence.

c) Pedagogy:
- Define pedagogy as the art and science of teaching. Discuss how pedagogical practices are shaped by both philosophical and psychological insights.
- Key ideas: Teaching methods, learner-centered education, instructional design.

3. Systems Thinking Approach (10 minutes)

- Objective: Introduce students to systems thinking in education.

Key Concepts:
- Define the key elements of systems thinking: interconnectedness, feedback loops, relationships, and patterns of behavior.

become indifferent towards their learning, lacking a clear sense of direction or purpose. The absence of feedback would hinder their ability to gauge their progress, leading to a decrease in self-regulation and personal accountability. Furthermore, without assessments to drive competition and collaboration, the classroom environment may become less dynamic, diminishing the drive for students to excel and potentially resulting in a stagnation of academic growth and exploration. In such a scenario, the overall educational experience would likely suffer, as the intrinsic motivation to learn is often fueled by the challenges and rewards that assessments provide.

What should we assess?

Assessing Attributes for Socially Useful and Productive Citizens

In the contemporary educational landscape, particularly in developing nations, the aspiration of educational institutions transcends mere knowledge dissemination. The goal is to cultivate Socially Useful and Productive Citizens (SUPCs), individuals who embody a robust set of cognitive and personality attributes essential for navigating the complexities of modern society. This pursuit necessitates a thorough assessment of both cognitive skills and personality skills that contribute to the holistic development of students.

Cognitive Skills

1. Knowledge: Assessments ensure that students have grasped key concepts and information. Through examinations, quizzes, and projects, educators can measure how well students have acquired foundational knowledge, encouraging a thorough understanding necessary for advanced learning.

2. Intelligence: Exams often present novel problems that require students to demonstrate their adaptability and critical thinking. By challenging students to think on their feet, assessments cultivate their ability to apply knowledge effectively in varied contexts.

3. Self-Learning: Assignments that require research and independent study promote self-learning. When students engage in self-directed projects or study for exams, they develop a sense of responsibility for their own learning, fostering curiosity and initiative.

4. Creativity: Creative assessments, such as open-ended questions or project-based tasks, encourage students to think outside the box. By evaluating their ability to generate original ideas and solutions, educators can nurture students' innovative capacities.

5. Problem-Solving: Many assessments include problem-solving components that require students to analyze and devise solutions for complex issues. This not only sharpens their analytical skills but also prepares them for real-world challenges.

6. Critical Thinking: Through essay questions and case studies, assessments can promote critical thinking. Students learn to evaluate arguments, identify biases, and make informed decisions, skills essential for navigating today's information-rich environment.

Personality Skills

1. Integrity: Assessments that emphasize ethical considerations help students understand the importance of integrity in their work. When evaluations are based on honesty and academic integrity, students learn to value these principles in their lives.

2. Confidence: Regular assessments can build students' confidence as they experience success in their academic pursuits. The positive reinforcement gained from achieving good grades encourages them to participate actively in class discussions and take intellectual risks.

3. Motivation: Well-designed assessments can inspire intrinsic motivation. When students see assessments as opportunities to demonstrate their knowledge rather than just as hurdles, they become more committed to their learning journey.

4. Productivity: Time-limited exams cultivate productivity as students learn to manage their time effectively to complete tasks efficiently. This skill is invaluable in both academic and professional contexts.

5. Grit: Challenging assessments can teach students perseverance. When faced with difficult tasks, students learn to push through obstacles, fostering a resilient attitude towards their long-term goals.

6. Communication: Oral assessments, presentations, and group projects enhance communication skills. Students learn to articulate their thoughts clearly and collaborate effectively with peers, vital for teamwork and leadership.

7. Audacity: Open-ended assessments encourage students to express their ideas boldly, cultivating audacity. This environment promotes a culture of creativity and innovation, which is vital for personal and academic growth.

8. Team Spirit: Group assessments encourage teamwork and collaboration. Students learn to value different perspectives and

work together towards common goals, which is crucial in today's interconnected world.

9. Compliance: Assessments that require adherence to guidelines and standards help students appreciate the importance of compliance. Understanding expectations fosters a sense of responsibility.

10. Time Management: Timed assessments instill discipline in managing time effectively. Students learn to prioritize tasks, balancing their academic responsibilities with personal commitments.

11. Adaptability: Exams often present unforeseen challenges that require quick thinking and adjustment. By navigating these situations, students develop adaptability and resilience in their learning processes.

12. Consistency: Regular assessments promote consistent effort and study habits. Students who engage in continuous evaluation often demonstrate reliability and commitment to their academic responsibilities.

Assessments play a crucial role in refining knowledge and skills while instilling invaluable confidence in students regarding their abilities. They are instrumental in cultivating a broad range of cognitive and personality skills essential for holistic development. By effectively utilizing exams and evaluations, educators can significantly enhance their students' intellectual and personal growth.

Assessment types of student attribute mapping

Typical breakdown of the cognitive and personality attributes tested by different types of assessments previously listed:

1. Graded Assessments
 - Cognitive Attributes Tested:
 - Knowledge: Students are evaluated based on their understanding and retention of content.
 - Intelligence: Problem-solving abilities are tested through graded assignments and exams.
 - Critical Thinking: Graded essays or complex problem-solving tasks assess the ability to analyze and evaluate information.
 - Personality Attributes Tested:
 - Confidence: The results of a graded assessment impact self-confidence, as students must face the outcome of their efforts.
 - Motivation: The desire to achieve higher grades pushes students to invest in their learning process.
 - Time Management: Graded assessments require planning and efficient use of time to meet deadlines.

2. Ungraded Assessments (Formative)
 - Cognitive Attributes Tested:
 - Self-Learning: Ungraded assessments often encourage self-reflection, promoting autonomous learning.
 - Creativity: Students may explore innovative solutions or ideas in a low-pressure environment.
 - Problem-Solving: These assessments provide opportunities for students to practice applying knowledge to different contexts.
 - Personality Attributes Tested:
 - Grit: Continuous feedback and improvement foster perseverance.
 - Integrity: Ungraded assessments offer an opportunity for honest self-assessment without the fear of formal consequences.

- Adaptability: Formative assessments allow students to adjust their strategies based on feedback.

3. Proctored Assessments
- Cognitive Attributes Tested:
- Knowledge: Proctored exams typically assess knowledge recall under controlled conditions.
- Intelligence: The ability to apply information within a timed and restricted setting is evaluated.
- Personality Attributes Tested:
- Integrity: Proctored exams are designed to minimize dishonesty and encourage ethical behavior.
- Grit: The high-stakes nature of proctored assessments tests a student's perseverance under pressure.
- Compliance: Students must adhere to exam rules and protocols, demonstrating respect for institutional norms.

4. Unproctored Assessments
- Cognitive Attributes Tested:
- Creativity: Open-book, unproctored exams allow students to utilize resources, encouraging innovative thinking.
- Problem-Solving: In these assessments, students can access various tools to test their practical problem-solving abilities.
- Personality Attributes Tested:
- Integrity: These assessments rely heavily on the student's ethical behavior.
- Time Management: Unsupervised assessments often have flexible deadlines, requiring disciplined time allocation.
- Audacity: Students may demonstrate bold and original ideas when given freedom in an unstructured setting.

5. Independent Assessments
- Cognitive Attributes Tested:

- Knowledge: Independent work directly measures individual understanding.
- Critical Thinking: Tasks like essays or problem-solving exercises assess a student's analytical capabilities.
- Personality Attributes Tested:
- Accountability: Independent assessments require students to take full responsibility for their work.
- Self-Learning: These tasks encourage students to explore topics on their own.
- Consistency: Regular performance in independent tasks reflects dependability and commitment to personal work.

6. Grouped Assessments
- Cognitive Attributes Tested:
- Creativity: Collaborative projects often involve brainstorming and encouraging creative solutions.
- Problem-Solving: Group work challenges students to collectively tackle complex problems.
- Personality Attributes Tested:
- Team Spirit: Group assessments foster teamwork and cooperation.
- Communication: The ability to convey ideas and listen effectively is central to successful group work.
- Adaptability: Students must adjust their approaches and compromise with others in a group setting.

7. Written Assessments
- Cognitive Attributes Tested:
- Knowledge: Written tests evaluate the student's understanding of the material.
- Critical Thinking: Essays or long-answer questions test a student's ability to construct arguments.
- Communication: The ability to articulate ideas in written form is crucial.

- Personality Attributes Tested:
- Grit: Extended written assessments, especially essay-based tasks, require perseverance.
- Time Management: Written exams are typically timed, necessitating efficient organization.
- Integrity: Proper citation of sources and originality of ideas are critical in longer written tasks.

8. Oral Assessments
- Cognitive Attributes Tested:
- Communication: Oral exams or presentations test how well students can articulate their thoughts.
- Intelligence: Oral exams often require on-the-spot thinking and knowledge recall.
- Critical Thinking: In viva voce or debates, students must present well-reasoned arguments.
- Personality Attributes Tested:
- Confidence: Oral presentations and viva exams test a student's self-assurance.
- Audacity: Oral assessments often require bold expression of ideas and responses under pressure.
- Adaptability: The dynamic nature of discussions or oral exams tests the ability to adjust responses in real-time.

9. Open-Book Assessments
- Cognitive Attributes Tested:
- Knowledge Application: Open-book exams assess how students use information rather than simply recalling it.
- Problem-Solving: The focus shifts from memorization to applying concepts to real-world problems.
- Personality Attributes Tested:
- Self-Learning: Students must know where to find information and how to apply it, reinforcing independent learning.

- Integrity: Even with access to resources, students must produce original responses that uphold ethical standards.

10. Closed-Book Assessments
- Cognitive Attributes Tested:
- Knowledge Recall: Closed-book exams directly measure a student's ability to remember and retrieve information.
- Intelligence: Students must apply memorized knowledge under exam conditions.
- Personality Attributes Tested:
- Time Management: The restricted nature of closed-book exams tests students' ability to manage their time effectively.
- Grit: The intensity of these exams requires persistence, especially when recalling information under stress.

11. Objective Assessments
- Cognitive Attributes Tested:
- Knowledge: Multiple-choice or true/false questions test knowledge of specific facts or concepts.
- Intelligence: While often focused on recall, some objective assessments can test the application of knowledge.
- Personality Attributes Tested:
- Time Management: Objective assessments, especially those with many questions, require efficient time allocation.

12. Subjective Assessments
- Cognitive Attributes Tested:
- Critical Thinking: Open-ended questions or essays assess deep analysis and synthesis of ideas.
- Problem-Solving: Essays and complex case studies often require solving intricate problems.
- Creativity: Subjective assessments allow for unique responses and encourage creative expression.
- Personality Attributes Tested:

- Integrity: Subjective assessments often involve personal insights or opinions, requiring honesty in interpretation.
- Confidence: Expressing original or unconventional ideas in essays or debates tests a student's self-belief.

13. Self-Assessment
- Cognitive Attributes Tested:
- Self-Learning: Students evaluate their own learning process and progress.
- Critical Thinking: Reflecting on one's own work encourages analytical thought.
- Personality Attributes Tested:
- Integrity: Honest self-assessment requires students to critically evaluate their strengths and weaknesses.
- Accountability: Self-assessment fosters personal responsibility for one's educational journey.

14. Peer Assessment
- Cognitive Attributes Tested:
- Critical Thinking: Students must evaluate others' work, encouraging analytical comparison with their own.
- Personality Attributes Tested:
- Team Spirit: Peer assessments promote collaboration and mutual respect.
- Communication: Students must effectively convey feedback in a constructive manner.

15. Diagnostic Assessments
- Cognitive Attributes Tested:
- Knowledge: These tests help identify the student's prior understanding of a subject.
- Personality Attributes Tested:
- Adaptability: Diagnostic assessments help students adapt to the upcoming course structure.

16. Formative Assessments
- Cognitive Attributes Tested:
- Knowledge: Formative assessments track a student's ongoing understanding.
- Personality Attributes Tested:
- Consistency: These assessments emphasize regular participation and effort in learning.

17. Summative Assessments
- Cognitive Attributes Tested:
- Knowledge: Summative assessments measure accumulated knowledge.
- Personality Attributes Tested:
- Confidence: The finality of summative assessments tests students' self-assurance in their capabilities.

Challenges in administering assessments

When administering assessments, teachers may encounter several significant challenges that can affect the effectiveness of the evaluation process. Here are six major problems:

1. Time Constraints: Teachers often face limited time to prepare, administer, and grade assessments. This can lead to rushed evaluations, potentially compromising the quality and depth of the assessment. Moreover, the need to cover a broad curriculum within a fixed timeframe can create pressure to prioritize quantity over quality in assessment.

2. Student Anxiety and Performance: Assessments, particularly high-stakes ones, can induce significant anxiety among students, which may adversely affect their performance. Teachers must navigate this emotional landscape to ensure that assessments

accurately reflect student understanding rather than being influenced by stress and fear.

3. Diverse Learning Needs: In a classroom with a heterogeneous group of students, differing learning styles, abilities, and backgrounds can pose a challenge. Teachers must create assessments that are equitable and accessible, ensuring that all students can demonstrate their knowledge and skills effectively. This can be particularly challenging in subjects that require higher-order thinking or complex problem-solving.

4. Bias and Fairness: Ensuring that assessments are free from bias and fairly evaluate all students can be difficult. Teachers must be vigilant about their own biases and the potential for assessments to favor certain groups over others. Developing assessments that are culturally relevant and inclusive is essential to fostering a fair evaluation process.

5. Feedback and Improvement: Providing timely and constructive feedback is crucial for student learning, yet many teachers struggle with the workload associated with grading and giving feedback on assessments. The challenge lies in balancing the need for comprehensive feedback with the constraints of time and resources, which can hinder students' ability to learn from their mistakes and improve their performance.

6. Integrity and Academic Honesty: Ensuring integrity during assessments is a persistent challenge for educators. Teachers must contend with issues such as cheating, plagiarism, and other forms of academic dishonesty that can undermine the assessment's validity. Maintaining a fair assessment environment often requires additional measures, such as proctoring or designing assessments that minimize opportunities for dishonesty. The need to balance trust in students with the necessity for oversight can create tension

and complicate the administration of assessments. Furthermore, fostering a culture of integrity within the classroom involves continuous effort and reinforcement of ethical standards, which can be demanding for teachers.

These challenges highlight the complex nature of assessment in education and the need for thoughtful strategies to create effective evaluation processes.

Psychological approach for using assessment to enhance learning outcomes.

Effective evaluation methods are key to fostering a productive learning environment that not only measures student progress but also encourages deeper engagement and intellectual growth. Here are some detailed strategies that can be incorporated into evaluation processes to enhance learning outcomes:

1. Give Them a Winning Chance
Providing students with a "winning chance" means structuring evaluations in a way that students have the opportunity to succeed and build confidence. This can involve creating assessments that are appropriately challenging but not overwhelming, ensuring that students can experience success if they have engaged with the material. Offering multiple forms of assessment, such as projects, quizzes, and presentations, allows students with different strengths to demonstrate their knowledge and skills. The key is to strike a balance between rigor and accessibility so that all students feel they have a fair shot at doing well. This approach not only boosts morale but also reinforces the connection between effort and achievement.

2. Students Finding Out the Mistakes in the Content
Encouraging students to identify mistakes in content—whether in texts, images, logic, or other material—can be a powerful tool for deepening their understanding. This method turns students into active participants in their own learning process, fostering critical thinking and attention to detail. By challenging students to spot errors, teachers promote a more analytical approach to learning, where students must apply their knowledge to critique and improve existing materials. This activity also helps students develop a sense of ownership over their learning and can be particularly effective in subjects that require precision and logical reasoning, such as mathematics, science, or philosophy.

3. Evaluation for Motivation and Intelligence
Evaluations should be designed to assess not just knowledge but also motivation and intelligence. Grades are often seen as indicators of motivation, reflecting a student's consistency, compliance, and productivity. However, it is important to recognize that intelligence is not always aligned with high grades. Some students may display brilliance in spurts, showing deep understanding or creativity in specific areas while lacking consistency in others. Evaluation methods should account for this by including opportunities for students to demonstrate intelligence in ways that go beyond rote learning. This could involve open-ended questions, problem-solving tasks, or projects that require innovative thinking. By doing so, teachers can better identify and nurture both motivated students and those with high intellectual potential.

4. Let the Students Prepare Questions
Allowing students to prepare their own questions for exams or quizzes can be an effective way to deepen their engagement with the material. This practice requires students to think critically about what they have learned, to identify key concepts, and to

consider how these concepts can be tested. It also encourages students to reflect on the content from the perspective of an evaluator, which can deepen their understanding and reveal any gaps in their knowledge. Furthermore, by involving students in the creation of evaluation materials, teachers can foster a more collaborative learning environment where students feel more invested in their education. This method not only enhances comprehension but also encourages a more active and participatory classroom culture. I review Bloom's Taxonomy and then ask students to ask questions on a topic with increasing levels of cognition. Sometimes, I would ask them to make challenging multiple-choice questions and set the questions against each other.

Assessments play a pivotal role in driving student motivation by providing clear goals and benchmarks for achievement. When students are aware that their knowledge and skills will be evaluated, they are more likely to engage actively with the material, fostering a sense of responsibility and accountability. The feedback received from assessments serves not only to highlight areas of strength but also to identify opportunities for growth, encouraging students to strive for improvement. This cycle of setting objectives, receiving feedback, and working towards mastery cultivates a growth mindset, where students perceive challenges as opportunities for learning rather than obstacles.

Conversely, abolishing assessments could lead to a significant decline in student motivation and engagement. Without the structure and expectations that assessments provide, students may become indifferent towards their learning, lacking a clear sense of direction or purpose. The absence of feedback would hinder their ability to gauge their progress, leading to a decrease in self-regulation and personal accountability. Furthermore, without assessments to drive competition and collaboration, the classroom environment may become less dynamic, diminishing the drive for students to excel and potentially resulting in a stagnation of academic growth and exploration. In such a scenario, the overall educational experience would likely suffer, as the intrinsic motivation to learn is often fueled by the challenges and rewards that assessments provide.

Assessments can serve as powerful learning experiences, transforming the evaluation process into an integral part of the educational journey. When assessments are designed thoughtfully, they not only measure student understanding but also promote deeper learning. For instance, formative assessments, such as quizzes, discussions, or projects, encourage students to engage with the material actively and reflect on their knowledge. By receiving timely feedback, students can identify their strengths and weaknesses, allowing them to adjust their study strategies and focus on areas that need improvement. This ongoing cycle of assessment and reflection fosters a deeper understanding of the subject matter, enabling students to connect concepts and apply their knowledge in practical situations.

Furthermore, assessments can be educational by encouraging critical thinking and problem-solving skills. Well-constructed assessments challenge students to synthesize information, analyze data, and apply their knowledge to real-world scenarios. By incorporating higher-order thinking questions, educators can prompt students to engage in discussions, collaborate with peers, and explore diverse perspectives. This not only enhances their comprehension but also equips them with essential skills for future academic and professional pursuits. Ultimately, when assessments are viewed as opportunities for growth rather than mere evaluations, they can significantly enrich the learning experience, leading to a more engaged and motivated student body.

RBT based evaluation

Evaluation entails two important aspects. The increase in knowledge and the increase in the abilities of the learner in acquiring knowledge and solving problems. These are two different but entangled issues. Acquiring knowledge is about the input of new information. On the other hand, abilities are traits of personalities, such as the ability to acquire, think, communicate, analyze, etc.

The first CIA could be for RBT 1 and 2 levels.
The second CIA could be RBT 2 and 3 levels.
The third CIA could be at the RBT 3 and 4 levels.

To design evaluation levels that progress toward cumulative assessment, the syllabus should be structured accordingly.

Here is a set of eight questions on the object "pen," designed to align with the levels of Bloom's Revised Taxonomy (RBT), progressing from lower-order to higher-order cognitive skills:

1. Remembering (Knowledge)
- What are the basic parts of a pen?
- This question requires students to recall and list the components of a pen, such as the cap, barrel, ink reservoir, and nib.

2. Understanding (Comprehension)
- How does a pen function to transfer ink onto paper?
- This question asks students to explain the basic working mechanism of a pen, demonstrating an understanding of its function.

3. Applying (Application)
- Can you describe how you would use a pen to sign a document?

- This question encourages students to apply their knowledge of using a pen in a practical context, such as signing their name.

4. Analyzing (Analysis)
- Compare the writing quality of a ballpoint pen with a fountain pen. What differences do you observe?
- This question requires students to break down and compare the features and performance of different types of pens.

5. Evaluating (Evaluation)
- Which type of pen would you recommend for a professional setting and why?
- This question asks students to make a judgment about the suitability of different pens for a specific context, providing justification for their choice.

6. Creating (Synthesis)
- Design a new type of pen that combines the best features of a ballpoint pen and a fountain pen. What features would it include?
- This question requires students to use creativity and synthesis to develop a new concept by combining elements of existing pens.

7. Reflecting (Metacognition)
- How has the design and usage of pens evolved over time, and what factors have influenced these changes?
- This question asks students to reflect on the historical development of pens, considering social, technological, and cultural influences.

8. Innovating (Advanced Creation)
- Imagine a future where traditional pens are obsolete. What innovations in writing instruments or technology could replace them?

- This question challenges students to think critically and innovatively about the future of writing, pushing them to conceptualize new technologies or approaches.

These questions are structured to progressively challenge students' cognitive abilities, moving from simple recall to complex creation and innovation, in line with Bloom's Revised Taxonomy.

Assessing knowledge and intelligence

Evaluating knowledge and evaluating intelligence involves assessing different cognitive aspects:

1. Evaluation of Knowledge

Knowledge evaluation focuses on a person's ability to recall, recognize, or explain information they have learned. It typically involves assessing factual recall, understanding of concepts, and the ability to apply learned information to familiar situations.

- Characteristics:
- Relies on memorization or comprehension.
- Questions are often content-specific.
- Responses are generally based on information that has been taught or studied.

- Examples of Knowledge Evaluation Questions:
- Recall: "What is the capital of France?"
- This question assesses whether the respondent can recall specific factual information.
- Comprehension: "Explain the process of photosynthesis in plants."
- This question evaluates understanding by asking for an explanation of a concept learned in class.

- Application: "How would you use the quadratic formula to solve
the equation $\(x^2 - 4x - 5 = 0\)$?"
- This question asks the respondent to apply a learned
mathematical method to solve a problem.

 2. Evaluation of Intelligence
Intelligence evaluation focuses on a person's ability to think
critically, solve novel problems, and apply reasoning to unfamiliar
situations. It often involves measuring abstract reasoning, problem-
solving, adaptability, creativity, and other higher-order thinking
skills.

The more unfamiliar, the more intelligent the question!

- Characteristics:
- Goes beyond rote memorization.
- Involves reasoning, problem-solving, and critical thinking.
- Often requires creative or innovative thinking to solve new
problems.

- Examples of Intelligence Evaluation Questions:
- Problem-Solving: "A farmer has a 7-liter and a 4-liter container.
How can he measure exactly 5 liters of water using only these two
containers?"
- This question requires logical reasoning and problem-solving
skills to figure out a solution using limited resources.
- Critical Thinking: "Given a set of seemingly unrelated facts, can
you identify a pattern or make a prediction?"
- This question challenges the respondent to use critical thinking to
detect patterns or make inferences.
- Abstract Reasoning: "How is a tree similar to a river?"

- This question measures abstract thinking by requiring the respondent to find a conceptual connection between two seemingly different things.

 Key Differences:

- Knowledge Evaluation:
- Focus: What you know.
- Example: "List the three branches of the U.S. government."
- This question checks for recall of specific factual information.

- Intelligence Evaluation:
- Focus: How you think and solve problems.
- Example: "If you had to redesign the system of government in a country with frequent natural disasters, how would you structure it to ensure stability?"
- This question assesses the ability to apply complex reasoning to a new and hypothetical situation.

Advantages and Applications of Written Examinations

Advantages:

1. Objectivity and Standardization: Written examinations often provide a more objective measure of student performance, as answers can be graded based on standardized criteria. This minimizes biases that may arise in subjective assessments, such as oral exams.

2. Comprehensive Assessment: Written exams can cover a broader range of content in a structured format, allowing students to demonstrate their knowledge across various topics within a single

assessment. This is particularly useful in subjects requiring detailed information recall.

3. Time for Reflection: Students are given the opportunity to think through their answers and articulate their understanding without the pressure of immediate response. This can lead to more thoughtful and organized responses.

4. Anonymity: Written examinations can be administered anonymously, which may reduce anxiety and promote honesty in responses. Students may feel more comfortable expressing their true understanding of the material when they are not directly in front of an examiner.

5. Easier to Analyze: The results from written examinations can be quantitatively analyzed, allowing for a straightforward comparison of student performance over time or across different cohorts.

Applications:

- Large-Scale Assessments: Written examinations are commonly used in standardized testing environments, such as high school exit exams and university entrance tests.
- Course Evaluations: They are frequently employed in university courses to assess student understanding at the end of a semester or module.
- Certification and Licensing: Many professional fields require written examinations for certification, ensuring candidates possess the necessary knowledge to practice effectively.

Advantages and Applications of Oral Examinations

Advantages:

1. Immediate Feedback: Oral examinations allow for real-time interaction between the examiner and the student, providing immediate feedback and clarification of questions. This can enhance the learning experience and encourage deeper understanding.

2. Assessment of Communication Skills: These exams evaluate not only the content knowledge but also the student's ability to articulate their thoughts and ideas clearly. This is essential for fields where verbal communication is crucial.

3. Flexibility in Assessment: Oral exams can adapt to the student's responses, allowing examiners to probe deeper into topics of interest or address misunderstandings on the spot. This flexibility can lead to a more comprehensive evaluation of student understanding.

4. Reduction of Memorization Pressure: Since oral exams often focus on understanding rather than rote memorization, students may feel less pressured to memorize information verbatim and instead emphasize their comprehension of concepts.

5. Building Confidence: Engaging in oral examinations can help students build confidence in their speaking abilities and public presentation skills, which are valuable in both academic and professional settings.

Applications:

- Discipline-Specific Assessments: Oral examinations are often used in language courses, law schools, and other fields where verbal communication and argumentation skills are critical.
- Thesis and Dissertation Defenses: Graduate students typically defend their research in oral formats, providing an opportunity for evaluators to explore the depth of the student's knowledge and understanding.
- Seminars and Presentations: Oral assessments can be integrated into seminar formats, where students present their ideas and engage in discussions, promoting critical thinking and collaborative learning.

Both written and oral examinations offer unique advantages and applications in educational settings. While written exams excel in objectivity and comprehensive assessment, oral exams shine in evaluating communication skills and fostering interactive learning. Educators should consider the objectives of their assessments and the specific learning outcomes they wish to achieve when choosing between these two methods. Ideally, a balanced approach that incorporates both formats can provide a more holistic evaluation of student learning and capabilities.

Advantages of Providing Answers to Questions

1. Clarity and Understanding: Offering answers ensures students grasp complex ideas, reinforces key concepts and helps build a strong foundation.

2. Motivation and Engagement: Prompt answers support students' learning, encouraging active participation and a deeper interest in the subject.

3. Efficiency in Learning: Providing answers helps students avoid confusion, leading to more productive class time and fostering better comprehension.

4. Facilitation of Further Inquiry: Answers can inspire more advanced questions and discussions, promoting a culture of curiosity and exploration.

5. Building Trust: By addressing questions, teachers create a supportive environment where students feel comfortable seeking help and guidance.

Disadvantages of Providing Answers to Questions

Contrary to many commonly advocated teaching strategies, I prefer not to provide answers to students following in-class assessments. My aim is to encourage students to linger on the questions posed, prompting them to reevaluate their responses and tap into their resourcefulness to seek answers independently. This process fosters a deeper engagement with the material, allowing students to develop critical thinking skills that extend beyond merely arriving at the correct answer.

In my experience so far, students have spent more time discussing and wondering, often unsure if their answers are correct. They did become frustrated and restless, and they also complained that the answers were not provided. The fundamental belief guiding my approach is that the duration a student spends grappling with a question significantly enhances their ability to uncover solutions. This lingering engagement not only cultivates the skills necessary for independent inquiry but also nurtures a mindset geared toward problem-solving and exploration. By emphasizing the journey of discovery rather than the destination of the answer itself, I hope to equip students with lifelong skills that will serve them well beyond the confines of the classroom. This approach ultimately transforms learning into a process of empowerment and intellectual growth.

1. Dependency on Teacher: Consistently offering answers can make students dependent on the teacher, reducing their ability to think critically and independently.

2. Reduced Student Engagement: If students expect answers without effort, they may not invest time and energy in solving problems themselves.

3. Surface-Level Learning: Immediate answers can lead to memorization rather than in-depth understanding, resulting in shallow knowledge.

4. Limiting Exploration: Giving answers limits students' opportunities for discovery, reducing the likelihood of exploring diverse perspectives.

5. Inequality in Learning: Not all students learn at the same pace; providing answers may leave some behind while others advance, leading to unequal learning experiences.

Chapter 12: Tracking Progress

Tracking teaching, learning and assessment

Assessing learning outcomes and the difficulty level of exam papers using statistical analysis is a critical component of ensuring that assessments are fair, reliable, and effective in measuring student understanding. Below are some strategies and measures that can be implemented to evaluate and adjust exam difficulty and learning outcomes using the mean, standard deviation, and mode of exam results.

1. Establishing Target Metrics
- Mean Target Range (65-75%): Aim for the mean score of the exam to fall within the 65-75% range. This indicates that the exam is challenging enough but not overly difficult.
- Standard Deviation: A larger standard deviation suggests a wide range of student performance, reflecting varying levels of understanding and ensuring that the exam differentiates between different levels of student proficiency.
- Mode: Assess the mode (the most frequently occurring score) to understand where the bulk of student performance lies. If the mode is significantly lower or higher than the mean, it may indicate issues with specific questions or topics.

2. Analyzing Exam Results
- Mean Score Analysis:
- If the mean score is below 65%, consider reviewing the difficulty level of the questions. The exam might be too challenging or include content that was not adequately covered in class.
- If the mean score is above 75%, the exam may be too easy and not sufficiently challenging for the students.
- Standard Deviation Analysis:

- A high standard deviation indicates that there is a wide range of student abilities and understanding. This is desirable in ensuring that the exam fairly assesses different levels of student knowledge.
- A low standard deviation may indicate that the exam was too easy or too difficult for most students, which could point to a lack of differentiation in the assessment.
- Mode Analysis:
- If the mode is significantly higher or lower than the mean, review the questions that most students either got right or wrong. This can highlight which questions might have been too easy or too difficult.

3. Adjusting Future Exams
- Review and Revise Question Types: Analyze which types of questions (e.g., multiple-choice, essay, problem-solving) contributed to deviations from the target mean. Adjust the proportion of these question types to better align with the desired difficulty level.
- Topic Coverage: Ensure that the exam covers a representative sample of the course material. If certain topics consistently produce low scores, review how those topics are taught or consider adjusting their weight in the exam.
- Incremental Difficulty: Structure exams so that questions progress from easier to more difficult. This can help students build confidence and allow the exam to better differentiate between different levels of understanding.
- Pilot Testing: Before administering an exam, consider conducting a pilot test with a small group of students to gauge the difficulty level and make adjustments as needed.

4. Using Feedback for Continuous Improvement
- Student Feedback: Gather feedback from students about the perceived difficulty of the exam and how well they felt it reflected their understanding of the material.

- Instructor Reflection: After reviewing the statistical analysis, reflect on the teaching methods and how they might be improved to better prepare students for future assessments.
- Peer Review: Engage with colleagues to review exam results and question design. This can provide new insights and help refine the balance of difficulty in future exams.

5. Long-Term Adjustments
- Curriculum Alignment: Ensure that the exam content is closely aligned with the learning objectives of the course. Regularly review and adjust the curriculum based on exam performance data to better support student learning.
- Assessment Variety: Incorporate a variety of assessment methods (e.g., projects, presentations, practicals) alongside traditional exams to capture a more comprehensive picture of student learning.
- Data Tracking: Over multiple exam periods, track the mean, standard deviation, and mode to identify trends. Use this data to make more informed decisions about teaching strategies and exam design.

By implementing these measures, one can create a more balanced and fair assessment system that not only evaluates student performance accurately but also provides valuable feedback for continuous improvement in teaching and learning.

Self-evaluation of teaching

To accurately gauge one's effectiveness in the classroom, it is imperative to consider a variety of factors that influence both the teaching experience and student learning. These factors include class heterogeneity, the general prerequisite knowledge of the students, classroom discipline, the overall enthusiasm and engagement of the students, their compliance with classroom norms, and their trainability.

Self-evaluation in teaching is an essential practice that enables educators to reflect on their performance, identify strengths, and address areas for improvement. This introspective process involves analyzing various aspects of the teaching experience, including lesson delivery, student engagement, and assessment strategies. Self-evaluation allows teachers to critically assess how effectively they are meeting the learning objectives and how well they are addressing the diverse needs of their students. By continuously refining their teaching methods based on self-assessment, educators can enhance their effectiveness, adapt to the evolving educational environment, and ensure that they are providing the best possible learning experience for their students.

CIA Averages and End-Semester Averages

Continuous Internal Assessment (CIA) averages and end-semester (endsem) averages provide valuable insights into student performance and the effectiveness of the teaching methods employed throughout the course. CIA averages offer a snapshot of how well students are grasping the material during the semester, while endsem averages reflect their cumulative understanding and ability to apply the knowledge in a final assessment. Analyzing these averages helps teachers identify trends, such as whether students are improving over time or if there are consistent areas of difficulty. Comparing CIA and endsem averages can also reveal whether the course content and assessments are aligned with the expected learning outcomes and whether students are retaining and applying what they have learned.

Standard Deviation of Each CIA

The standard deviation of each CIA score is a critical statistical measure that indicates the variability or spread of student scores around the mean. A low standard deviation suggests that most students are performing at a similar level, while a high standard deviation indicates a wide range of abilities or performance levels within the class. Analyzing the standard deviation of CIA scores helps teachers understand the degree of class heterogeneity in terms of academic achievement and identify whether certain assessment methods are too easy, too difficult, or not well-suited to the students' abilities. By monitoring the standard deviation, teachers can adjust their teaching strategies and assessment practices to better meet the needs of their students and ensure more equitable learning outcomes.

Standard of the Question Paper

The standard of the question paper is a reflection of the level of difficulty, fairness, and relevance of the questions posed to students during assessments. A well-designed question paper should align with the learning objectives of the course and challenge students to demonstrate their understanding, critical thinking, and problem-solving abilities. The standard of the question paper is also indicative of the course's rigor and the teacher's expectations. It should be neither too easy nor too difficult but rather appropriately challenging to assess the students' true grasp of the material. Teachers should regularly review and calibrate the standard of their question papers to ensure they are fair, unbiased, and effective in measuring student learning.

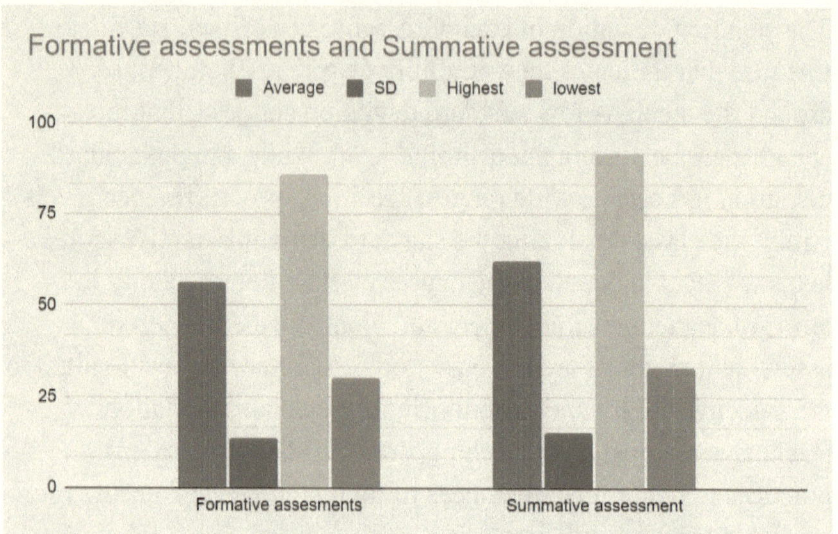

Above is a crude evaluation of myself based on student assessments. Although it is far from perfect, I occasionally used to do this as a consequence of the 'new professor syndrome'! Class heterogeneity in terms of motivation and prerequisite knowledge should be accounted for.

I begin by analyzing the highest mark achieved by the most dedicated and diligent student, ideally around 90%. If the top score is significantly lower, such as around 80% or less, it signals potential issues: either the learning objectives were not met, the question paper exceeded students' capabilities, or the evaluation criteria were excessively stringent.

Next, I assess the class average, which I expect to fall between 60% and 75%. This range typically indicates satisfactory learning outcomes while still presenting a reasonable challenge. If the average exceeds this range, it suggests that the assessment may not be rigorous enough. Conversely, if the average falls below this threshold, it raises concerns about either the effectiveness of the teaching methods or the difficulty level of the question paper.

Additionally, I consider the standard deviation of the student scores. A high standard deviation may indicate a comprehensive evaluation process that reflects a diverse student population in terms of motivation and learning styles. However, a low standard deviation suggests that the evaluation may lack rigor, as it implies a narrow range of student performance. This analysis enables us to adjust my teaching methods, question paper designs, and evaluation standards accordingly, ensuring that they align with the educational goals and effectively promote student learning. At least, this is a process of reflection on one's own teaching and learning outcomes.

Self-care of a teacher

If Rafael Nadal played tennis with me, he would likely feel frustrated. Even my coach sometimes gets frustrated playing with me because there's an expectation from an interacting partner—a mutual anticipation of skill, effort, challenge and rhythm. This creates psychological tension when one participant falls short of these expectations, disrupting the flow of engagement. In many ways, this parallels a teacher's stress in the classroom. Teachers, like skilled players, often face an inner tension stemming from their aspirations for students, and this tension escalates when students struggle to meet anticipated learning goals or standards.

Teaching involves a unique psychological stress that arises from balancing high expectations with students' varied capabilities. Teachers, deeply invested in their students' progress, often experience a tension between their desire to see each student thrive and the reality of individual learning differences. This stress intensifies as teachers strive to engage students, especially when faced with diverse learning paces, attentiveness levels, and personal challenges. Additionally, a teacher's responsibility extends beyond mere instruction; it encompasses fostering intellectual curiosity, emotional resilience, and critical thinking—outcomes not always measurable in the short term. This gap between a teacher's intentions and the immediate visible results can create a lingering emotional strain.

For a teacher, the simplest approach to managing their own mental health may be to neglect the growth of their students. However, such an attitude would be both unprofessional and unethical, undermining the fundamental responsibilities of the teaching profession and compromising the well-being and development of the students.

Teaching reluctant or untrainable students is one of the most exacting and frustrating professions.

Teachers engage in an everyday mental struggle, grappling with both themselves and society. They must resist and eliminate the biases that arise daily within their minds while navigating students' resistance and reluctance to learn. They withstand instances of dishonesty and disengagement in their work amid pressures from personal, professional, and social realms. The boundaries between these aspects often blur, complicating their roles further. Additionally, teachers must contend with perceptions of student dislike or hatred, all while maintaining a demeanor of kindness and responsibility. This environment demands that teachers continuously learn and upskill to meet these multifaceted challenges.

In the face of daunting challenges, teachers working in underprivileged conditions embody a remarkable resilience that inspires us all. Their commitment shines brightly amid crumbling infrastructure, limited resources, and the pervasive shadows of disinterest and discouragement. These educators transform bleak classrooms into sanctuaries of learning, igniting curiosity and passion in students who may have little encouragement elsewhere. With unwavering dedication, they craft innovative lessons and nurture a sense of belonging, turning obstacles into opportunities for growth. They are the unsung heroes, tirelessly championing the future of their students embodying hope and determination. Their tenacity demonstrates that true teaching transcends circumstances, proving that knowledge can flourish even in the most challenging environments. In doing so, they not only impact individual lives but also ignite a spark of change within entire communities.

Self-Care for Teachers: Psychological Well-being, Motivation, and Mental Health

Teaching is a demanding profession that can significantly impact a teacher's psychological well-being and overall mental health. To maintain effectiveness in the classroom and personal fulfillment, teachers must prioritize their self-care. This involves addressing psychological and motivational needs, managing stress, and fostering mental health. Effective self-care strategies enable teachers to sustain their energy, enthusiasm, and resilience. Here's an overview of self-care for teachers in terms of psychology, motivation, and mental health.

1. Prioritizing Psychological Well-being

Psychological well-being encompasses emotional stability, self-awareness, and a positive mindset. Teachers should focus on several key aspects to nurture their psychological health:

- Self-Awareness and Reflection: Regular self-reflection helps teachers understand their emotional states, triggers, and responses. Journaling or mindfulness practices can facilitate this process,

enabling teachers to recognize and address any negative patterns or stressors.
- Setting Boundaries: Establishing clear boundaries between work and personal life is essential. Teachers should avoid overworking and ensure they have designated times for relaxation and personal activities.
- Seeking Professional Support: Engaging with a counselor or therapist can provide valuable support for managing stress, anxiety, or burnout. Professional guidance helps teachers develop coping strategies and maintain emotional resilience.

2. Maintaining Motivation

Sustaining motivation is crucial for teachers to remain engaged and enthusiastic about their work. Strategies to enhance and maintain motivation include:

- Setting Personal Goals: Establishing personal and professional goals provides direction and a sense of accomplishment. Goals should be specific, achievable, and aligned with the teacher's values and interests.
- Celebrating Achievements: Recognize and celebrate personal and professional successes, no matter how small. Acknowledging achievements boosts morale and reinforces a positive outlook.
- Engaging in Professional Development: Pursuing opportunities for growth and learning, such as workshops, courses, or conferences, can reignite the passion for teaching and introduce new strategies to enhance the classroom experience.

3. Managing Stress

Effective stress management is vital for maintaining both mental and physical health. Teachers can employ various techniques to manage and reduce stress:

- Time Management: Efficiently managing time by prioritizing tasks and setting realistic deadlines helps prevent overwhelm. Utilizing tools like planners or digital calendars can aid in organizing workload and personal responsibilities.
- Relaxation Techniques: Incorporate relaxation techniques such as deep breathing exercises, progressive muscle relaxation, or meditation. These practices can reduce stress and promote a sense of calm.
- Physical Activity: Regular physical exercise is known to reduce stress and improve mood. Teachers should find activities they enjoy, whether it is walking, jogging, yoga, or sports, and integrate them into their routine.

4. Fostering Mental Health

Maintaining good mental health involves nurturing a balanced lifestyle and seeking support when needed. Strategies for fostering mental health include:

- Healthy Lifestyle Choices: Prioritize a balanced diet, adequate sleep, and regular exercise. These foundational elements support overall mental and physical health and contribute to sustained energy and resilience.
- Building Support Networks: Establish and maintain strong social connections with friends, family, and colleagues. Having a support network provides emotional support, practical help, and a sense of community.
- Engaging in Hobbies and Interests: Pursue activities and hobbies outside of work that bring joy and relaxation. Engaging in interests unrelated to teaching helps recharge and maintain a balanced life.

5. Developing Resilience

Resilience is the ability to adapt to and recover from challenges. Building resilience can help teachers cope with the demands of the profession and maintain their well-being:

- Cultivating a Positive Mindset: Focus on positive aspects of teaching and the impact made on students' lives. Adopting a growth mindset helps people view challenges as opportunities for learning and improvement.
- Embracing Flexibility: Be open to adapting teaching methods and approaches in response to changing circumstances. Flexibility allows teachers to manage stress and overcome obstacles more effectively.

Self-care is a critical component of a teacher's professional and personal well-being. By prioritizing psychological well-being, maintaining motivation, managing stress, fostering mental health, and developing resilience, teachers can enhance their effectiveness and satisfaction in the profession. Implementing self-care strategies not only benefits teachers but also positively impacts their students, creating a more supportive and productive learning environment. Teachers must recognize the importance of self-care and integrate these practices into their daily lives to sustain their health and enthusiasm throughout their careers.

Embracing Flexibility in Teaching: Balancing Professionalism and Self-Care

In the demanding world of education, maintaining a perfect adherence to every rule and schedule can be a significant source of stress and anxiety for teachers. While professionalism and punctuality are important, it is equally crucial to recognize that occasional deviations from the norm are not necessarily indicative of poor teaching. Embracing a balanced perspective on flexibility can help mitigate stress and promote a healthier work-life balance.

1. Understanding the Nature of Teaching Challenges

Teaching is inherently dynamic, with variables that can affect classroom management and scheduling. Factors such as unexpected personal issues, health concerns, or urgent professional responsibilities can occasionally lead to missed classes or delays. Acknowledging that these instances are part of the human experience helps maintain a realistic and compassionate approach to self-evaluation.

2. The Impact of Perfectionism on Stress

Striving for perfection can lead to increased stress and anxiety, especially in a profession as multifaceted as teaching. The pressure to adhere strictly to all rules and schedules can detract from the overall teaching experience and diminish job satisfaction. Allowing for some flexibility helps alleviate this pressure and supports a more sustainable approach to teaching.

3. Forgiving Yourself and Students

It is important for teachers to practice self-compassion and recognize that occasional lapses are normal and not necessarily indicative of poor performance. Forgiving oneself for rare deviations from the expected schedule or norms is essential for maintaining mental health and well-being. Similarly, extending this understanding to students—acknowledging that they, too, are human and may face challenges—fosters a supportive and empathetic classroom environment.

- Self-Forgiveness: Accept that perfection is not always attainable. Reflect on the broader context and the overall positive impact of your teaching rather than focusing on isolated instances of imperfection.

- Student Forgiveness: Recognize that students may also face difficulties that affect their performance. A flexible approach helps build trust and respect, enhancing the learning experience for everyone.

4. Implementing Flexible Strategies

To manage the balance between adherence to rules and self-care, consider implementing the following strategies:

- Prioritize Well-being: Regularly assess your stress levels and adjust your approach as needed. Implementing stress management techniques, such as mindfulness or relaxation exercises, can help maintain a healthy balance.
- Communicate Transparently: When deviations occur, communicate openly with students about any changes in schedule or expectations. Transparency helps manage expectations and reduces potential misunderstandings.
- Plan for Contingencies: Develop a contingency plan for unexpected events. Having a flexible plan in place can help mitigate the impact of disruptions and ensure continuity in teaching.

5. Focusing on the Bigger Picture

Ultimately, the quality of teaching is not solely determined by strict adherence to rules or perfect punctuality. The effectiveness of teaching is measured by the ability to engage and support students, foster a positive learning environment, and contribute to their overall development. Balancing flexibility with professionalism allows teachers to focus on these core aspects without being overwhelmed by minor deviations.

In teaching, a flexible approach to rule adherence and scheduling is not a sign of bad teaching but rather an acknowledgment of the profession's inherent challenges. Embracing occasional flexibility, practicing self-forgiveness, and prioritizing mental well-being contribute to a more sustainable and rewarding teaching experience. By focusing on the broader impact of their teaching and maintaining a balanced perspective, teachers can effectively manage stress and continue to provide valuable support to their students.

Coping with the psychological pressures of the teaching profession is an essential aspect of maintaining both personal well-being and professional effectiveness. Teaching is a demanding vocation that requires constant mental engagement, emotional resilience, and the ability to adapt to diverse and ever-changing classroom dynamics. The pressures can be intense, stemming from various sources such as student heterogeneity, varying motivational levels, the complexity of the subject matter, and the inherent sensitivity of being responsible for others' learning.

1. Acknowledge the Imperfections
- It is crucial to recognize that as a teacher, you are neither infallible nor expected to be. Perfection is an unrealistic goal, and every educator will face challenges that test their abilities. Understanding that there is always room for improvement allows you to approach your work with a growth mindset, embracing opportunities for learning and development rather than being weighed down by the pressure to be flawless. Your ground realities—such as the diversity of student needs, the inherent difficulty of certain subjects, and the daily challenge of engaging students—are unique and require tailored approaches.

2. Embrace the Uniqueness of Each Day
- Teaching is a dynamic profession, and no two days are ever the same. This variability can be both a source of stress and an opportunity for creativity and innovation. By accepting that each day brings new challenges and chances to try different methods, you can alleviate some of the pressure to maintain a rigid standard of performance. Flexibility and adaptability are key to thriving in a teaching environment where unpredictability is the norm.

3. Prioritize Self-Care: Engage in Sports and Arts
- The psychological demands of teaching necessitate a strong foundation of physical and mental health. Engaging in sports and the arts can be powerful outlets for stress relief and personal expression. Physical activity helps maintain a healthy body, which in turn supports a healthy mind. Sports can serve as an excellent way to release built-up tension, improve mood, and enhance overall well-being. Similarly, the arts provide a creative escape from the rigors of teaching, offering a space to explore emotions, process experiences, and find joy outside of the classroom. Whether it is painting, music, dance, or writing, incorporating an artistic pursuit into your routine can significantly reduce stress and contribute to a more balanced life.

4. Cultivate a Supportive Network
- Building a network of colleagues, mentors, and friends who understand the challenges of teaching can be invaluable. Sharing experiences, seeking advice, and simply having someone to talk to can alleviate feelings of isolation and burnout. A supportive network can provide encouragement during tough times and celebrate successes with you, making the journey less daunting and more fulfilling.

5. Practice Mindfulness and Reflection

- Mindfulness practices such as meditation, deep breathing, or even just taking a few moments each day to reflect can help you stay grounded and focused. Mindfulness encourages you to be present in the moment, reducing anxiety about future challenges and regrets about past decisions. Reflecting on your day, noting what went well and what could be improved, allows you to learn from each experience without being overly self-critical.

6. Focus on the Bigger Picture
- Teaching is about more than just delivering content; it is about shaping lives and minds. When the pressures of daily tasks become overwhelming, it is helpful to remind yourself of the larger impact you're having on your students. The knowledge that you are contributing to their long-term success and development can provide a sense of purpose that outweighs the immediate stressors.

7. Set Boundaries and Manage Time Effectively
- To prevent burnout, it is important to set clear boundaries between work and personal life. Establish a time each day when you stop working and focus on activities that bring you joy and relaxation. Effective time management is also crucial; prioritize tasks, delegate when possible, and avoid overloading yourself with responsibilities. By managing your time wisely, you can reduce stress and ensure that you have the energy to meet the demands of teaching.

8. Continuous Professional Development
- Engaging in professional development opportunities can also help manage stress by equipping you with new strategies and tools to handle classroom challenges. Learning from others, attending workshops, and participating in professional learning communities can enhance your skills and provide fresh perspectives, making you feel more confident and capable in your role.

The teaching profession is indeed demanding, but with the right strategies and mindset, you can navigate the pressures and thrive. By acknowledging the uniqueness of your situation, embracing self-care practices, building a support network, and continuously seeking growth, you can maintain both your mental well-being and professional satisfaction. Remember, the most effective teachers are those who care for themselves as well as their students, recognizing that a sound body and mind are essential to the art of teaching.

Learning is living

The evolution of students' preferences for teacher attributes reflects the progressive complexity of their educational experiences. In primary school, children are inherently drawn to kindness; it is the warmth and support of kind teachers that create a safe and nurturing environment, enabling young learners to explore new concepts without fear of failure. This foundational experience fosters a sense of belonging and encourages curiosity, making kindness an essential quality at this early stage.

As students transition to high school, their cognitive and emotional development deepens, leading them to seek a more nuanced combination of attributes in their educators. Here, students appreciate teachers who not only exhibit kindness but also possess knowledge and the ability to motivate. This shift acknowledges the increased academic demands and the need for supportive mentors who can guide them through more complex subject matter while still fostering a positive classroom atmosphere.

In university, the focus predominantly shifts towards knowledge and intelligence. Students respect educators who exhibit expertise and can challenge them intellectually. However, motivation remains crucial as students navigate the rigors of higher education.

Thus, the journey through the educational system reveals a clear trajectory: from a preference for kindness in primary school to a sophisticated appreciation for knowledge, intelligence, and motivation in university settings.

Liking a teacher emerges through kindness; fear comes through stringency; respect, however, comes through knowledge and intelligence. It is the respect that holds the most value for a teacher, not just momentarily, but throughout the entirety of their career. Respect is not freely given; it is earned, and it is continuously reinforced through the teacher's dedication to their own growth. Continuous learning is not an option but an inevitability if we wish to maintain that respect. To remain relevant and respected, we must never allow ourselves to become stagnant or obsolete, like "dead weight." A teacher who stops learning, who ceases to innovate or engage with new knowledge, risks losing their place in the evolving landscape of education. The students we face are constantly evolving, and so must we. This profession demands that we stay intellectually agile, embracing new knowledge and refining our intelligence. Only then can we continue to offer something of value, ensuring that our students not only like or fear us but also respect and look up to us as true educators. Therefore, never stop learning; it is the very foundation upon which lasting respect and true value as a teacher are built.

John Dewey's assertion, "Education is not preparation for life; education is life itself," encapsulates a profound perspective on the nature and purpose of education. Dewey contends that education transcends mere preparatory stages; rather, it constitutes the very essence of living. This perspective emphasizes that learning is not an isolated or preliminary activity but an integral and continuous process that is deeply woven into the fabric of everyday life. Unlike other animals, whose learning is often limited to immediate survival and adaptation, human education encompasses a lifelong journey of intellectual and personal development. Dewey argues that education should not be viewed merely as a means to an end but as a dynamic and ongoing experience that shapes and enriches human existence. This approach recognizes that the pursuit of knowledge, critical thinking, and problem-solving are central to human life, enabling individuals to engage meaningfully with their environment, participate actively in society, and contribute to the collective advancement of human understanding. By framing education as life itself, Dewey highlights its foundational role in cultivating a more informed, reflective, and capable individual who continually grows and evolves throughout their life.

The idea that "the moment we stop learning, we stop living" underscores the intrinsic connection between learning and the vitality of human existence. This concept suggests that the pursuit of knowledge and personal growth is not merely an academic exercise but a fundamental aspect of what it means to fully engage with life.

The principle that "the moment we stop learning, we stop living" is especially pertinent for educators, highlighting the crucial role of continuous learning in teaching effectiveness and personal fulfillment. For teachers, this concept underscores that the journey of education is not confined to the classroom but is a lifelong process essential for both personal growth and professional excellence.

1. Continuous Professional Development:
- Adaptation to New Methods: Teachers must continually update their pedagogical strategies and incorporate new teaching methods to meet the evolving needs of students. Engaging in ongoing professional development allows educators to stay abreast of the latest educational research, technological advancements, and innovative practices. When teachers cease to learn, their teaching

methods may become outdated, hindering their effectiveness and students' learning experiences.

- Skill Enhancement: Lifelong learning enables teachers to refine their skills, from classroom management to curriculum design. This continuous refinement ensures that educators can deliver high-quality instruction and respond effectively to diverse student needs. The absence of ongoing learning can lead to stagnation in teaching practices, reducing the overall impact on student achievement.

2. Engagement with Educational Trends:

- Embracing New Technologies: The field of education is constantly evolving with new technologies and digital tools. Teachers who actively engage in learning about these advancements can integrate them into their teaching, enhancing student engagement and learning outcomes. Stopping learning means missing out on these opportunities and potentially falling behind in effectively using educational technologies.

- Understanding Student Needs: Continuous learning helps teachers stay informed about changes in student demographics, learning styles, and educational psychology. This knowledge allows educators to tailor their approaches to better meet the needs of their students. Without ongoing learning, teachers may struggle to address the diverse and changing needs of their classrooms.

3. Contribution to Educational Improvement:

- Innovative Practices: Teachers who commit to lifelong learning contribute to the broader field of education by sharing new insights and innovative practices. This collaboration fosters a culture of improvement and innovation within the educational community. When learning stops, the potential for contributing to educational advancements and improving teaching practices diminishes.

- Mentorship and Leadership: Experienced teachers who continue to learn can serve as mentors and leaders within their educational institutions. They can guide colleagues, support new teachers, and lead initiatives that enhance the overall quality of education. Ceasing to learn reduces their capacity to influence and support the growth of others in the profession.

4. Personal Fulfillment and Well-being:
 - Sense of Purpose: Engaging in continuous learning provides teachers with a sense of purpose and accomplishment. The challenges and rewards associated with learning new skills and knowledge contribute to job satisfaction and personal fulfillment. When teachers stop learning, they may experience a lack of motivation and diminished enthusiasm for their profession.
 - Mental Stimulation: Lifelong learning stimulates the mind and contributes to cognitive health. For teachers, this means maintaining mental agility and creativity, which are essential for effective teaching and problem-solving. The cessation of learning can lead to cognitive stagnation and reduced mental well-being, impacting both personal and professional life.

For educators, the notion that "the moment we stop learning, we stop living" emphasizes the importance of lifelong learning in enhancing teaching effectiveness and personal growth. Continuous professional development, engagement with educational trends, contribution to educational improvement, and personal fulfillment are all interconnected aspects that reinforce the need for ongoing learning. By embracing this principle, teachers can ensure that they remain dynamic, effective, and fulfilled in their roles, ultimately fostering a more engaging and impactful learning environment for their students.

1. Continuous Growth and Adaptation:
 - Intellectual Stimulation: Learning drives intellectual stimulation and cognitive engagement, which are crucial for maintaining mental acuity. As individuals continue to acquire new information and skills, they stimulate their minds, fostering adaptability and

resilience. When learning ceases, cognitive stagnation can set in,
leading to diminished problem-solving abilities and a reduced
capacity to adapt to new challenges.
- Personal Development: Lifelong learning is integral to personal
development. It encourages self-reflection, self-improvement, and
the expansion of one's horizons. Without ongoing learning,
personal growth can plateau, leaving individuals less equipped to
navigate the complexities of life or pursue their full potential.

2. Engagement with the World:
- Curiosity and Exploration: A commitment to learning fosters
curiosity and a sense of wonder about the world. It motivates
individuals to explore new ideas, experiences, and perspectives,
keeping them engaged with the ever-evolving nature of human
knowledge and culture. When learning stops, curiosity wanes, and
individuals may become disconnected from the dynamic world
around them.
- Meaningful Interaction: Learning enhances our ability to
understand and engage with others. Through learning, individuals
develop empathy, cultural awareness, and communication skills,
which are essential for meaningful interpersonal relationships. The
cessation of learning can lead to a diminished capacity for
connection and collaboration.

3. Contribution to Society:
- Innovation and Progress: Ongoing learning drives innovation
and societal progress. Individuals who actively seek new
knowledge and skills contribute to advancements in their fields,
fostering a culture of innovation and improvement. When learning
stops, the potential for contributing to societal progress and solving
pressing global issues is also diminished.
- Role Fulfillment: Engaged learning supports individuals in
fulfilling various roles within society, from professional
responsibilities to community involvement. Lifelong learners are

better equipped to adapt to changes and take on new roles, ensuring their continued relevance and effectiveness in their contributions to society.

4. Psychological Well-being:
 - Sense of Purpose: Learning provides a sense of purpose and achievement, contributing to overall psychological well-being. The challenges and accomplishments associated with learning activities foster a sense of accomplishment and satisfaction. When learning ceases, individuals may experience a lack of purpose and diminished psychological resilience.
 - Mental Health: Engaging in learning activities has been linked to positive mental health outcomes, including reduced stress and enhanced cognitive function. The cessation of learning can lead to cognitive decline and decreased mental well-being, reinforcing the idea that learning is vital for sustaining a healthy, active life.

Conclusion

The notion that "the moment we stop learning, we stop living" reflects the profound impact that continuous learning has on various dimensions of human life. Learning fuels intellectual and personal growth, maintains engagement with the world, contributes to societal progress, and supports psychological well-being. By emphasizing the integral role of learning in sustaining a vibrant and fulfilling life, this concept underscores the necessity of embracing lifelong education as a core aspect of human existence.

Work hard and collide with your future self now, happily and enthusiastically.

Many teachers, including our own teachers and colleagues, inspire us to keep moving forward, reminding us that we are often our only limiting factor in achieving progress, which is crucial for ourselves and our current and prospective students. Work hard and collide with your future self now; that is progress. This powerful statement encapsulates growth and ambition. Envisioning our future selves—the individuals we aspire to be equipped with the skills and accomplishments we desire—sets a target. However, progress is not about passively waiting for that future to unfold; it is about actively shaping it today. It requires relentless effort, perseverance, and the decision to engage with every challenge, knowing that each step brings us closer to that envisioned self.

To collide with your future self means actively working to align your present efforts with the potential that lies ahead. Every ounce of hard work, every challenge embraced, and every moment of perseverance pulls your future closer, accelerating your growth and transforming possibilities into reality. True progress is not linear; it is the cumulative effect of countless dedicated moments. By working hard now, you not only shape immediate outcomes but also lay the foundation for a future that aligns with your highest aspirations. Approach each challenge with a positive mindset, and you will cultivate fulfillment, making every step toward your future self a joyous experience. Be your future in the present!

In our professional sphere as teachers, our growth and satisfaction is in the growth of our students. The more students are impacted, the better. Time and attention are the most priceless commodities one can pay others, especially in the educational realm. We must pay well and wisely, investing our time and attention in each student individually. The onus is on us to create an environment where students feel valued and understood. They will reciprocate the time and attention we extend to them, forging a deeper connection that enriches the learning experience.

Moreover, as educators, we must practice our way to perfection; perfection is the only mirage worth pursuing. It is the journey toward excellence that fosters growth, both for ourselves and our students. In this pursuit, we must consider the type of teacher we hope to be. Some inspire students to think critically, igniting curiosity and analytical thought. Others motivate them to work diligently, instilling a strong work ethic. Still, some focus on shaping their personalities nurturing well-rounded individuals.

As we reflect on our teaching journey, let us ask ourselves: What type of teacher are we? We must embrace our roles as guides, mentors, and inspirations. Together, let us strive to empower our students and create a lasting impact in their lives.

The best attribute to teach is intelligence.

The best teacher is one who encourages students.

The best outcome is a lasting motivation to learn and achieve more.

Be more of the great teacher you are!

until something expected happens on the other hand Nelson's Three-N-One defines wait as to stay in anticipation

Spiritual Strength

Psalm 138:3 says, "When I pray thou answerers me by giving me the strength I need" (TLB version).

"In the day when I cried thou answeredst me, and strengthenedst me with strength in my soul" (KJV version).

I remember the good old days, not many would remember it now, since everything now is instant. I was always very impatient, something I had to learn, and it has saved me a lot of heartaches.

I recall, back then when you went to an optometrist to get your eyes checked, you had to wait for another appointment—which could be a month later—to get fitted with frames, then wait another two or three weeks for the lens to be fabricated. Oh, I hated those days! I felt angry at the attendant for not giving me an earlier appointment. I would literally be so depressed; I would cry and feel terrible all day.

Later things progressed and technology improved. While living in Pennsylvania, whenever it was time for new glasses, I would travel all the way to New York on Delaney Avenue just so I could obtain it in twenty-four hours. Technology even got better; I could travel to New York and now, wait an hour for my glasses. What a relief! It doesn't really matter now, as long as I have a pair of glasses, any time, will be OK. I have finally learned, to wait.

Waiting for My Change

Sometimes circumstances in life will attempt to take away your expectancy, Psalm 62:5 explains, "For my expectancy is from him." Nothing or "no thing" will stop me from getting my change. My heart is fixed; I no longer think or feel the same even though the odds may seem different.

We have the power to determine and decide to wait. And expect to be strengthened by God our Father who knows the entire situation, the initiation, as well as the date of expiration. Wait and again I say, "Wait on the Lord" is the word of admonition to us as believers.

The psalmist said, "Come and bless the Lord all you servants of the Lord, who stand by night, in the dark situation, the storms of life, when all seem oblivious, in the house of the Lord, waiting for God, looking for a word, looking for a touch from the Master." But he instructs us to lift up your hands, those feeble hands that hang down, and *bless* the Lord and bless the Lord.

My Prayer:

Lord, help me to remain faithful to your word in those difficult times when I don't see the answer, and to lift my eye to you; and with a never ending faith, fix my heart to rely and wait on you. Till I feel my change, in Jesus's name, amen!

CHAPTER THREE

ENTER INTO MY WORLD AND SEE WHAT I FEEL

There is an old cliché that says, "Walk a mile in my shoe, and you will know what I feel." another says, "He that feels it knows it." No one knows what you see in the dark like you do. Enter into my world and see what I feel. Suffering comes in many packages. It's not always what it looks like, though it differs from person to person, yet the sting of the pain remains the same to all.

In Philippians 2, Jesus models the perfect attitude of one giving his life—a man acquainted with suffering, and yet he humbled himself and never complained.

Ever since I made the condition known to some people, there has been a multiplicity of reactions; the responses have been amazing even to me. Most times I only smile when asked about what and how much I see. I respond by saying, "I see everything, and I do; it's just how I see, how much, and how quickly I do; this makes it very difficult for me to explain. In essence, I see what I need to see, never without difficulty. What you see outwardly, I just process it inwardly."

The psalmist said the Lord is a lamp to my feet and a light unto to path. Frankly, most times I walk by faith and not by sight; He helps me maneuver and remember the familiar, being very methodical and dependent upon experiences.

Those are the days I challenge myself and refuse to give in; and God seems nearer and takes care of the minutest details for me as the Holy Spirit comforts me. Everything the devil tries to use for bad, God takes it and uses it for his glory. The Lord has impressed upon me that this gift to my life is for a *sign* and I will often make most people wonder. And if you are thinking, "then give me fi ve more if it is such a blessing," I am reminded he won't give to any of his children more than they can bear.

Suffering Is a Part of the Deal

Nelson's dictionary and Bible commentary defines suffering as agony, affliction or distress, intense pain or sorrow. Since man's fall into sin, suffering has been a human experience (Genesis 3). The book of Job deals with the problems of suffering and why God permits his children to suffer.

Nelson declares that some suffering is related to man's evil doings—as in the Garden of Eden—but some are not related but rather it looks forward and serves to shape and refine the righteous (1Peter 1:6-7; 5:10).

Suffering reflects the potential for God to manifest his power in and through us. Second Cor. 1:3-6 say, those who suffer are in a position to render comfort to others. Often times the world, or even so-called believers, make fun and are critical of those who profess to enjoy peace and serenity as God is glorifi ed. Though they await a touch or healing from God, they have accepted the challenge and allow God to be God and fulfill his plan in their lives. Even though God is not the author of sickness, he certainly permits it, and will be with you; through it, you need not fear, you can experience the closeness of God though it even while the storm rages.

Yet these junior gods tend to want to put God in a box as though he was not aware of *all* things. The bible teaches us that all things are naked and open to the eyes of God; there is absolutely nothing hidden from him.

My only desire is that of allowing God to be glorified through my suffering and in my life. In the book of 1 Peter 4:1 KJV, it tells us, "Forasmuch then as Christ hath suffered for us in the fl esh arm, yourselves likewise with the same mind," unless we have this same mentality, we cannot reign with him unless we suffer with him. The scripture teaches us that the suffering of this world is not to be compared with the glory that shall be revealed in us

After we have stood the test, we will receive the reward that is laid up for us, a crown of righteousness as the scriptures promises us.

Sometimes in my daily travel, I observe people with other challenges; my first reaction used to be to compare the odds, who was in a worse condition. Then I would begin to thank God that I wasn't that bad off; then I would hear in my spirit a sweet, gentle, and compassionate voice that whispers, "My grace is suffi cient; I am touched with the infirmities of all of my children." I know this sounds crazy, but I have learned to say "thank you, Lord" instead whenever I am overwhelmed. I run to the Rock. He is my strength and fortress, my buckler, my shield, and my high tower; in him I trust. David knew the secret, when in distress, he would often call on the Lord, his Helper. So I have also found him to be my *only* source of strength.

First Corinthians 12 tells us that we are all individuals, and he is equally concerned. We are all members of the same body; when one part hurts, the whole body hurts. We have all been made to drink into one Spirit. The same God, who deals in the lives of the well, deals with the same power in the lives of the not so well. His grace is sufficient, and his compassion fails not.

First Corinthian 12: 23-26 says that those members of the body, which we think to be less honorable, upon these we bestow more abundant honor, and our uncomely parts have more abundant comeliness.

For our comely parts have no need, but God has tempered the body together, having given more abundant honor to that part which lacked.

That there should be no schism in the body, but that members should have the same care one for another.

And whether one member suffers, all the members suffer with it; or one member be honored, all the members rejoice with it.

We as believers should not treat any with less honor and that we should bestow great honor to that part that is weak, least important, or seem odd.

The prophet Elijah prayed that the eyes of his servants would be open; that they would see what he saw.

Enter into my world and see what I feel. I have been tested by people. There were so-called friends putting things in front of me to see if I would notice it, walked beside me and touch me lightly to see if I would recognize them, watch me look for something on the floor to see if I would find it, then later would comment, "Didn't you see that thing in front of you?"

I have been left behind in the dark in parking lots—of course not willfully. Made fun of when I couldn't find my street in the dark. In riding with others in their car, I have seen people drive past my driveway, to see if I knew it, usually it was the house behind or the next one ahead. I have had to hold the arms of women to feel them squirm with embarrassment, as they helped me. I am not complaining, just sharing experiences.

This is not meant to be negative, ungrateful, to put anyone down, or criticize, but only to show how it is in the world I live in. Hats off to them; they all hang in there with me and continue to hang. I have held on to men I mistakenly took for my husband to find out he had just quickly turned aside for something.

I have screamed inside with embarrassment when I found myself talking to someone who had long left my presence. It's in these moments my heart cries out to the Lord with exasperation and a quick word of prayer, and he instantly puts a song in my heart and a smile on my lips, then I am again able to move forward.

All of these things have made me strong, I have learned how to humor myself. I have certainly learned how to laugh and forgive others and myself. These are some of the things I suffered in silence, when no one knew I had a problem. It was a secret only God and I knew about and a few special friends. There is my friend Gloria who knew how to walk with me, she would walk ahead of me and gently guide me; Heather, who was always very discreet in the way she handled me in any given setting, always mindful of my apparel and grooming; Celia was another one who also knew very well how to handle me. God has encircled my life with wonderful people who knew exactly what to do for me. My latest friend Erline is my running buddy. We go to church and the prison together, and she is such a wonderful and considerate help for me, a great comfort and encourager, and so many others I cannot count.

Last but not least my ministry partner and armor bearer Irina from Panama. She has been just superb in ministry, and she covers my flaws well whenever I am on the mission field.

Evangelist Irina Caballero has been a wonderful help to me. I have leaned to always be appreciative of my blessings and not to complain. I am constantly assured by the Spirit of the Lord as well as the old hymn to "walk on through the wind, walk on through the storm, and you'll never walk alone, walk on with God's grace in your life." So when I lie on my bed at night, and I cry out to God and share the events of the stormy day with him, I am made aware that he is my consolation. And he lets me know he knows all about it.

I have fallen (upstairs and downstairs) believe me if is such a thing possible I have; in deep pits to the point of almost been unconscious. But I still dared to get up and kept on moving. I was not going to give in to the thing that plagued my life. I am a fighter and have made up my mind; it is not over until God says it is over. This does not qualify me to step aside from the battle; there are yet many more souls to gain and victories to be won. I will beat the odds and say, like the apostle Paul said in 2 Timothy 4:7, "I have fought a good fight. I have finished my course, I have kept the faith."

People have made remarks like: "You don't seem blind," "You are not indigent," "You don't have a cane or dark glasses, no wonder people are confused," "You don't seem that old," "How many fingers do you see here?" "She is blind, she can't see," "How come your makeup is so perfect?" "Can you see an ant on the floor?" "Who cooks for you and cares for you?" Oh! The list goes on. Enter into my world and see what I feel.

At the age of twenty-four in 1972, Jesus Christ rescued my life from sin. I had experienced many challenges but the greater challenge came in 2002, after a surgical removal of a cataract from my right eye that had rapidly developed since 1996, and this culprit was rapidly robbing me of my sight.

Soon thereafter, I could no longer keep the pace that I needed in order to perform my duties skillfully and effectively as a nurse. This forced me to resign from my nursing career and apply for disability. I felt so ashamed; I found myself always apologizing for having to quit working. This was such a devastating experience; it plagued my mind for a long while, until I dealt with it. I then realized that I needed to be delivered from people and most of all from myself. Soon it became obvious to me that I was bound with vanity and false pride.

When I announced the shocking news at church, I asked the people, "Help me get delivered saints, from me and from you." It was kind of humorous, but I really meant it; and I still do. I continue to kill that flesh, I refuse to allow the condition to take away my expectation in life, or to place more demand on me than that what is necessary.

"My soul, wait thou only upon God alone, for my expectation is from him. He only is my rock and my salvation: he is my defense; I shall not be moved. In God is my salvation and my glory: the rock of my strength, and my refuge is in God. Trust in him at all times, ye people. Pour out your heart before him: God is a refuge for us" (Psalm 62:5-8 KJV).

CHAPTER FOUR

YOU SHALL BE CALLED BEULAH

You may wonder why this chapter is included in this book. It is because it occurred in a very special and memorable time in my life. I would have to say that if there was ever a time when I felt I heard the spirit of God speaking to me, it was at this particular instance. No one or nothing could change my mind. I believe that this was a divine time of visitation from the Lord. It came at a moment when I was allow ebb in my life. There was no sound or flashing light; I saw no vision. All I know is that God visited me in a sweet and personal way.

Since that day, I have experienced many other encounters; but this would be the most vivid one I can recall. That was the day I experienced the compassionate voice and touch of the *Master.*

Something changed and was renewed on the inside of me at that instant. I was healed emotionally, and there was a clean, pure, refreshed feeling on the inside of me. Again, I cannot say I heard any bells or saw any visions, but I know something happened that morning in the little town of Fort Smith, Arkansas. There was an overwhelming and supernatural sense of strength in my being. With it came a boldness that manifested itself in the sermon that morning as I expounded the word. There was such an anointing that the pastor commented, "Sis Gina! You saved your best sermon for last." It was a medley of the *Kabowd* (the weighty anointing), the presence of the Lord, and a righteous indignation against the devil that made me preach with such fervor and passion, I poured out of my spirit on the topic, "Every salutation won't cause your baby to leap."

I recall saying to the people, "I feel strong this morning!" and it was all because I experienced a supernatural touch and embrace by the Master. That day, I was *swaddled in the glory.*

I heard someone say, "God is nearer to you when you are going through the mill." I believe that with all of my heart. Jesus said, "I will never leave you, neither will I ever forsake you." He won't harm you nor reject you; he won't disappoint you nor be unfaithful to you. I take those words both literally and personally into my spirit thus causing them to produce for me whenever I need them to.

God has changed my name—as he has often done in the Bible in the old days—and he is still changing names today. It was one early Sunday morning in 1997, preparing to preach for the morning service in Arkansas. I stepped out of the house to unwind and meditate before preaching. "So I thought," to purify myself and purge my thoughts to hear what the Lord had for his people.

In a few days I was about to move to South Carolina leaving the only support system—the familiar friends and acquaintances

I had made over the previous two years; working there as a travel nurse. People who were there for me in the darkest moments of the storm. Most of all, having to leave the one I love behind, my husband, not by choice. Hear me! I needed strength, my heart was heavy you all! Can I be real?

This was a raging storm that appeared to be blowing from the four corners of the earth. The painful part of it all was that this was beyond my control.

Sometimes people would be bodacious enough to say, "Be quiet! You can't minister to others when you, yourself are going through the storm." I have my own reservations about such rhetoric. It all depends on where *you* are in your relationship with God and whether your struggle is self-infl icted through disobedience or if inflicted by others. If this were true, then no one would be laboring for the Lord because we all go through trials at some point. Maybe in a different way, but we hurt the same. It is all part of the perfecting and emptying process, to be used for his glory.

We should not allow circumstances to paralyze us and make us ineffective, rendering us not useful for working in Gods Kingdom. Understand that Jesus himself has told us, "In this world you will have troubles, trials, and tribulations. But be of good cheer I have overcome the world." (I've got you covered little children.) Also, if this were the case, I know of many prominent ministers and leaders who has had unsaved children, husbands, wives, grandchildren—some have even experienced divorce not by choice—and this has not hindered their anointing, or the flow of Gods spirit in their lives; instead it has increased the anointing and has been of great testimony and victory to the goodness, faithfulness, and keeping the power of God in their lives.

On the other hand, if one is not walking in obedience and has erred in their walk, I agree that by all means they should step aside until they have repented, reconciled, and are again walking in fellowship, and total surrender to God.

It is stated in the book of 1 Peter 4, that it is necessary for every believer to experience suffering. The Apostle Paul concluded in Romans 8:18, "For I reckon that the sufferings of this present time are not worthy to be compared with the glory which shall be revealed in us." We are also admonished to count it all Joy when you experience different trials. Second Corinthians 4:17 says, "For our light affliction, which is but for a moment, worketh for us a far more exceeding and eternal weight of glory." Lord, I thank you. For you know what you are doing.

Jesus warned Peter, "Satan has desired to sift you as wheat," we know that the only thing that remains in the strainer or sifter after, are the lumps representing *sin* in our lives. Let him (Satan) not find anything he can use against you when he comes; nothing but righteousness or faithfulness to God. That should get him on his way! Do you believe, "if you resist the devil he will flee from you"?

As I walked down the road that tepid morning, the breeze gently blowing, still thinking about my upcoming departure and what the days ahead were going to be like for me alone in a new environment. I began to take solace and refuge and focus my attention on the *Lover* of my soul. I saw myself wrapped in his sweet embrace, huddled in the cleft of the rock in the secret place of the stairs.

I desperately reached out for God's hand, (Daddy!) hearing the sweet, compassionate voice of affi rmation deep within my being, responding to my woes and fears. It was not an audible tone, but deep within my spirit I heard the song "Beulah Land, I'm longing for You." This was not a song I thought of lately or even had in my mind. My thoughts were hovering around heaven's gate, somewhere up there with Jesus. I literally heard the voice in my spirit saying, "I will clothe you with the fi nest of linen and feed you the fi nest wheat; I will feed you honey from the rock." I recall, in an audible enough voice I uttered, "Honey? I don't even like honey! It makes me sick." As an avid reader—ardent, enthusiastic—and one who loves researching scriptures, I could hardly wait to get back to my apartment to investigate this word *beulah*. I had never heard or experienced God talking to me in such a real way as this. I did not even know the word was from a passage of the Bible. I thought it was just a song I had heard. I could hardly wait to sit down that day to look it up in the Bible concordance. This was what I read in the passage from the word of God that day.

"For Zion's sake will I not hold my peace, and for Jerusalem's sake I will not rest, until the righteousness thereof go forth as brightness, and the salvation thereof as a lamp. The Gentiles shall see your righteousness, and all kings your glory. You shall be called by a new name, which the mouth of the Lord will name. You shall also be a crown of glory in the hand of the Lord, and a royal diadem in the hand of your God. You shall no longer be termed forsaken nor shall your land anymore be termed Hephzibah, and your land Beulah. For the Lord delight in you, and your land shall be married." (Isaiah 62:1-4)

Immediately I knew I was on the mind of God, that I was the apple of his eye, and he delighted in me. I had to compose myself because of the overwhelming sweet presence of the Lord in my room.

A good friend of mine, Pastor Dwayne Greene, a friend in the gospel, would often say, "We preach from the place of victory and not for victory."

That morning in Arkansas, I experienced Ephesians 3:19, "And to know the love of Christ, which passes all knowledge." I realized that God was testing my faith, I could not afford to minimize his power, presence, and promise. "He brought me to the banqueting table, and his banner over me was love" (Song of Solomon 2:4).

Thank you, my Father, for your tender loving care toward me. You have crowned me with your royal diadem and delight wildly in me, even as my soul delight in you. Amen!

CHAPTER FIVE

STANDING IN THE STRENGTH OF GOD

Each day, I am reminded of how important it is to stand not in my own strength, but in God's. I am constantly asking God how and what to do. Sometimes I feel as though he says, "Here is my child again, she must be in trouble." In the house, outside the house, in the sunlight, in the dark, in crowded areas, at people's home, everywhere and every moment I need God; and he is *always* there.

In the book of Ephesuabs 6;10-13 it says, "Finally, my brethren, be strong in the Lord, and in the power of his might. Put on the whole armor of God that ye may be able to stand against the wiles of the devil. For we wrestle not against flesh and blood, but against principalities, against powers, against rulers of the darkness of this world, against spiritual wickedness in high places."

Brethren, I believe Satan got a glimpse into my future and saw the *great things* the Father has in store for me, and has set out to wage war against me, in the most brutal way I won't even utter it. In this pursuit of my healing, I build my case before God with his word.

Romans 8:26-28 says, "Likewise the Spirit also helpeth our infirmities: for we know not what we should pray for as we ought: but the Spirit itself maketh intercession for us with groanings which cannot be uttered. And he that searcheth the hearts knoweth what is the mind of the Spirit, because he maketh intercession for the saints according to the will of God. And we know that all things work together for good to them that love God, to them who are called according to his purpose."

I refuse to give up and give in; I know what God has spoken to me and what he has taught me from his word. This book is timely and inspired by God. I was instructed by God to abstain from watching television and not to depend on too many commentaries, in order to avoid distractions, until I was finished writing. It's not that they are bad; but at the moment, I needed to remain focused and allow the spirit of God to speak to me, reveal his truths, and allow the spirit to formulate my thoughts. Some of the things I talked about in the book may seem strange to you; but it's all right, just keep an open mind and believe God; he knows what he is doing. Trust me, I am not that brainy, to even think of all these things, but I do know that as believers, we are all partakers of him, we eat of the same bread and drink from the same cup.

I train myself to read the scriptures, and then I check the commentaries to see if at least I am on course. I do not want to be guilty of keeping God in a box or to minimize what he is doing in and through me, yes me! He has purpose in everything he does.

Recently, accompanied by my friend Ida Jones who traveled with me to a worldwide convention in the beautiful state of Kentucky. Each time I had to leave the room, I am immediately threatened by the thought of crossing the beautiful, dark-colored carpet in the lobby under the dim light; it made it diffi cult for me to see my way, especially going up and down the stairs for all three meals. Every time I had to cross the lobby, I prayed until I got to the marbled tile floor.

Once upstairs I had to remain put until everyone was ready to leave. I couldn't return to my room alone if I wanted to. So again I am reminded by God, "Do not look to the left or right but to Jesus who is the author and finisher of my faith. He said he would never leave me or forsake me. With his eyes upon me, he will guide me. If I would acknowledge him, he would direct my path." Also I was swaddled; my limbs were restricted, not by the enemy, but by him so he would have to lead, guide, and direct me back to my room, and he did so.

Finally I decided I was not going to allow the enemy to paralyze me. On two occasions, I got my nerves up to attempt it alone, and I did it. Ida asked me, "How did you get back?" both times I felt proud of myself, I had a breakthrough from the oppression of the enemy on my mind, rather than a breakdown.

I reminded my self of how the Lord had impressed upon me that I was swaddled in his glory, which refers to the old Hebrew practice of swaddling the infants at birth. This practice consisted of various strips of linen wrapped around the infant tightly to restrict movement of their limbs. Then I thought of the haze I walk in daily since January 2005; this has not changed; some days are worse, sometimes making it more diffi cult for me to see. I thank God for the good days when it is not so pronounced or thick. I often describe this cloudy fog-like haziness in my vision as the "glory." It is like a shade of a pale lavender-colored curtain, evenly dispersed that I look through during the daylight, that never goes away. It's kind of a pretty shade even when the sun is not shining, but I don't like the feeling of peering through it.

Doctors were even confused, thinking I had the D. Syndrome, *D* word (diabetes). *The Devil is a liar.* They even put me on medication to find out it was nothing more than the progression of the condition of retinitis pigmentosa.

Often I would hear the Spirit of God speaking to me and encouraging me to be strong. That is when the enemy is lurking around to catch me off guard or to distract me. Then I am reminded, "Don't be strong in your own strength but in God's strength. He is at your disposal, and he is available for you!"

Be strong in the *power, strength,* and *force* of his *might*. Wow! God avails *himself* to me, not sometimes but at all time.

Once I heard someone say once, "When you put on the armor of God, you are dressed to kill." Whenever the devil sees you fully dressed, he is made aware that he is on an illegal turf when he tries to come against a blood bought child of God who understands their position. You are a threat to him then; he does not mind you talking about the armor, he just does not want you to understand what you are talking about.

My honest pursuit is to remain always armed with a positive acknowledgement of the word of God. This affi rmation I am talking about is not a menial quoting of his words when things look good, but rather in the midst of seeming defeat or storms, when the odds seem adverse. In spite of it, you cry out "I have the victory!" without apology, just a knowing in your soul that it is all right.

Walking in this season, God gives me numerous opportunities to praise him *from victory rather than for victory*. But I tell you, there are times when I miss the mark and don't hear the voice of the Father clearly; but when I recognize my shortcoming, I literally come up swinging at the devil with my praises.

I am reminded of Paul the apostle when in essence, he said, "I may be knocked down, but I am not knocked out." And I too, refuse to be knocked out. Daddy has not said so.

The scripture again tells us "For we wrestle not against flesh and blood, but against principalities, against powers, against the rulers of the darkness of this world, against spiritual wickedness, in high places" (Ephesians 6:12).

The devil and his demons play nasty; we must know his devices and that his intent is to take us out. He wants us dead, grave dead! God tells us who the enemy is, gives us the ammunition we need, and through wisdom, teaches us how to use it. Yet we play with the devil and handle our weapons carelessly, not taking time to master them.

Every soldier needs to learn how to properly use his machine gun or whatever weapon he has for battle, as he is capable of hurting himself or someone else. Why do we, as Christians, think we do not need to learn how to use our weapon effectively? Furthermore, the word says the weapons of our warfare are not carnal but mighty through God to the pulling down of the strongholds of the enemy. Yet we do not even know what weapons we have to fight against those principalities and destructive powers of darkness.

Once, while teaching the ladies at prison, I asked the Lord what were the weapons he had given me, as a believer, to fight with; and he caused me to make a list. On one side, we listed the weapons of the world or the flesh. "Though we live in the flesh, we do not war in the flesh," the Bible says. Here are some of the ones we listed:

Weapons of the Flesh

Guns, knives, bombs, anger, chemicals—such as lye, hot porridge, kerosene, acid in the face etc.—foul language, hatred, isolation, ridicule, revenge, lies, cheating, murder, so on and so on!

Spiritual Weapons:

Love, knowledge of the word, character, integrity, honesty, dependability, accountability, reliability, kindness, pleasant words, silence, self-discipline, and consistency (these really make the devil mad), and the list goes on. All of these qualities manifest his divine nature of God.

As we examined the list, it was obvious that most of the time we as believers drew from the flesh list such as anger, isolation, harsh words, vengeance, etc.—don't let me go on. This was an eye opener to myself and the ladies. And you wonder why we do not get our prayers answered or obtain the promise of victory in all places as in 2 Corinthians.

God has plainly told us, in his word, how to fi ght by putting on the whole armor of God; that we may be able to withstand or stand under in the evil days. It also warns us that *we wrestle not against flesh and blood*. It's the evil thoughts that come to bring you down, discourage you, constantly trying to talk to you even while God is talking and comforting you.

I realize now the struggle is in the flesh—shame, embarrassment, pain, defeat, ridicule, hearing too much. I tell my husband no one can blame me for much; thank God, I stay out of trouble because I don't see much. It's a good thing; it keeps me focused on God.

Many people in my situation often give up and sit in a corner, staring into space. A lady told me the other day her husband was cured. She asked how is it you still focus on people?" My response to her was, "I don't know how I can read, when I don't see my face in the mirror." When I take my glasses off to preach—which I have to do to read—I see a forest of trees! I then remind myself how blessed I am!

In retrospect as I look back over my journey I can't help but think about the many trials and test. How many storms? How many sleepless nights and tears; since I gave my life to Jesus and said I would follow his footsteps? My friend, it has been worth it all.

Standing In reverence in the Presence of Jehovah, shaking, in awe; in the stadium during this years Panama mission campaign. Witnessing the promises in the Word unfolds before my eyes. Feel the Presence of Jehovah, hear the voice of the Holy Spirit as I expounded the message with boldness; (experience him guiding me through gently); the (Parakletos), the one called to walk beside. I watched the response of the people convicted by the word. Deafness and blindness was broken off the people. It was almost, like Peter's deliverance from prison, watching them come through the first gate then the second, approach the Iron gate which opened on its own to them by God, because of their prayers and penitent heart. They chanted; and Oh! To hear them cry out: "Now we know the Lord has sent the Rain, we are Free", and they continued to deliver themselves before the altar of The Lord.

Since my return from the mission trip, I am still overwhelmed with His Presence; my Soul is still being restored. I will never forget this treasured-moment, the sufferings of this world are not to be compared with the glory that will be revealed in me, "the things God has in store for me". I can truly say, I felt the prayers of the saints throughout my entire stay enveloping me." Now! In anticipation again looking towards the Mexico crusade and what God will do, Amen!

Prayer: Father, help me to remain strong in you, and not to rely on my own strength or capabilities. For without you I can do nothing. I realize my need to always be properly dressed with your armor so that I will be able to withstand these evil days. In Jesus name, amen!

CHAPTER SIX

TEMPERED GLORY

Philipians1:6 declares, "Being confident of this one thing, that he that began a good thing is able to complete it." It means to be fully persuaded and convinced, to have no doubt on the subject.

As I awaken each morning, in my personal time with the Lord, I realize the importance of reminding the forces of evil which may be assigned to me, those forces that come to whisper and point out my weakness, and that try to keep me from walking in faith throughout the day. I make my proclamation of the promises of God, authorizing me to cancel every assignment of the devil, dispossess him of any power or ability to harm me, (rendering him to become impotent and useless, good for nothing). I remind his imps that the glory has been tempered and all of the atmosphere and all forces *must* come into alignment with the *will* of God for my life. And with this statement, I am not conjuring up any evil or plea-bargaining with them, but rather commanding them to submit to the authority vested in me through the blood. The scripture teaches us that goodness and mercy are assigned to us as ministering angels, so are the devil's angels' principalities and powers. We do not dwell on them but our focus is on God, the greater One. They that are with us are more than they that are with them. I am a *covenant child*, a daughter of the *most high* God.

Luke 13:16, Jesus asked the question: "and ought not this woman, being a daughter of Abraham, whom Satan hath bound. Lo, these eighteen years, be loosed from this bond on the sabbath day?"

I no longer take time to contend with him, I just simply remind him of the promises of God over my life.

Exodus 29:2 and 30:35 tells us that as the unleavened bread and cakes are tempered with oil, and the spices, pure and holy, are tempered for the perfume, so is the glory of God.

Tempered:

- A substance added to modify other properties.
- The degree and hardness or strength impaired.
- To work into proper consistency
- To impart strength and toughness to

Glory:

- Resplendent beauty of magnificence

- *Kabawd* properly weight used only figuratively and in good sense
- Splendor, copiousness, honor, reputation, abundance, riches, dignity

Swaddling:

Narrow strips of cloth wrapped around an infant as a blanket to restrict movement.

Swaddled in God, I have no other alternative but to be still and allow him to guide and protect me. Recognize that Satan has no power over God's children; God does not ask him permission to release them. He is the creator and he is all; he is power. Through God, every genetic and hereditary curse is broken, in the name of Jesus.

My prayer: Psalm 106:4-5, "Remember me, O Lord, with the favour that thou bearest unto thy people: O visit me with thy salvation; That I may see the good of thy chosen, that I may rejoice in the gladness of thy nation, that I may glory with thy inheritance."

Spiritual Defect Prohibited Through Christ:

Isaiah 32:3 says, "And the eyes of them that see shall not be dim, and the ears of them that hear shall hearken."

When the storms of life beset us and continually weary us out, usually they often drive us to Christ. There, we fi nd safety and are satisfied as we come to the rivers of living waters (that fl ow from deep within our beings) provided for us so that we can be spiritually refreshed daily—moment by moment.

Years ago, while visiting my sister Larett in the city of New York, I awakened early in the morning; while others slept. I began to meditate on the Lord. In my spirit, I heard the Lord say. "I am going to make you a seer." Those words were so significant to me, I, immediately went up to my sister in the bathroom, as she was cleaning the tub I said to her, "The Lord said to me earlier, that he was going to make me a seer." Her response to me was, "We all see things," and we began to share other things.

I totally disregarded the statement from the Lord. I remember coming home and looking up the word "seer", this is what it said:

A *seer* is one who sees through the eyes of God; God blesses him with vision; the veil is removed, and he sees things clearly and is able to communicate to them that hear. This spiritual defect, according to the law of Christ, is prohibited and not acceptable through Christ; one should be healed to have a clear view of divine truth. The Spirit of God opens their understanding like Christ opened the understanding of the disciples after his resurrection, showing them what he would do for all his people.

A *seer* sees clearly, so utterance to others makes it easier for them to believe and cause a distinct increase and methodical knowledge in them about the things of God; these are from the ones of whom you least expect the words to come from, how they speak intelligently to the honor of God and edify others. Their tongues are as a pen of a ready writer (Psalm 45:7).

An absolute prohibition, Isaiah 31:1 declares, "Woe! To them that go down to Egypt for help; and stay on horses, and trust in chariots, because they are many; and in horsemen, because they are very strong; but they look not unto the Holy One of Israel, neither seek the Lord!"

High praises: I thank you, my Lord, that my trust is not in men because they are strong nor in chariots because they are many. I will not go to or rely on the human flesh of the world for help; and no matter how fierce the wind blows, how gruesome the storm rages, I will remain wrapped in your arms, my Lord. You are and will be my expectancy, my hope, and my only help. In Jesus's name, amen!

HIDDEN TREASURES

Over the years, I have been totally convinced of this, that if I wanted all that God has in my life, I had to first understand to the fullest extent, what things he had already done through Calvary and the shed blood of Jesus Christ on the cross.

This has been such a pressing issue with me that before I would minister, whether in English or in Spanish, I would always quote or paraphrase these two particular scriptures to the congregation. They would be so emotionally stirring to me, I now, realize that God, in his sovereignty, was attempting to get a word of truth to me. The word I spoke to them, was also fuel for me; and more so, the revelation of the words of these two scriptures has revolutionized my life and my thinking. We experience physical as well as spiritual increase in our daily lives from the word of God, which makes us complete in him as we exercise ourselves in it. (the word).

Through readings of the Apostle Paul. I can almost hear the *rhema* word of God expressed through the pages. Every word I receive from the scriptures, I believe it; and I try to assimilate and infuse it in to my spirit as though it was God himself speaking a word in season. A tempered word just for me and relevant to my circumstance or situation. Now, as I see the visible manifestation, I walk in its victory. There are still some things I must do, according to the word of God, such as practice it, walk in it, wait on it, and take hold of it by faith. Believe it as though I already had it in my hands. Casting not away my confidence, receive it as such, as the infallible, unadulterated, pure word of God. The same word I heard coming from mortal lips is capable and have the ability to *produce* for me. First Thessalonians 2:13 declares it this way, "For this cause also thank we God without ceasing, because, when ye received the word of God which ye heard of us, ye received it not as the word of men, but as it is in truly the word of God, which effectually worketh also in you that believe." This I speak to the ears of the people, reminding them not to look on my weakness, but to remain focused on the Lord Jesus; and by so doing, they would receive what was promised unto them.

Another scripture I emphatically proclaim the word—found in the book of Philemon 1:6. Paul again was admonishing the prisoner Philemon of an eminent truth of his acknowledgement of the treasures within him, and I quote: "That the communication of thy faith may become effectual by the acknowledging of every good thing which is in you in Christ Jesus." Wow!

The hidden treasures are the word of God; Jesus himself, the hope of glory; the Peace of God; the promise of The Father His righteousness; the anointing and his anointed one. They are also: the *spirit*; the *life*; the *truth*; the *way*; the resurrected Christ, the Kinsman Redeemer; the rose of Sharon; the lily of the valley; the great I Am; the true vine; the lion of the tribe of Judah; the living water; and the list goes on. He is all in all.

When you, truly understand who you really are and the things you possess on the inside, you will be better able to identify and denounce the lies and trickery of the devil, when he tries to label you and speak about you contrary to what God has said. Things like, "We are nothing but filthy rags". I realize, I cannot be two persons at the same time, and because Jesus, the righteous one, lives on the inside of me I am in a regenerated state. I have now become the righteousness of God in Christ. His blood has availed this to me, not because of anything I have done to deserve it. There is joy in knowing that he has already done it all for me. Now, the choice is mine to lay claim to what he has said about me. I am what God says I am, and I can do what he says I can do because I am the righteousness of God. By recognizing and acknowledging this truth, my communication and sharing of the word is now more effectual, in my life and in my teaching.

The hidden treasures you posses on the inside will manifest and produce as you speak it from your lips and believe them in your heart, calling on his name and leaning on him. The songwriter sang, "What a friend we have in Jesus." That is such an awesome and comforting thought when you understand and embrace it.

Claim it, rely on it, interact with it. Make it experiential, rather than just a principle or a concept in your mind.

I believe the thing that causes the most frustration, I believe, is when the reality on the outside is greater that what is on the inside. Meaning, you talk the talk, but not walking the walk. There is no substance to the relationship and no true experience, which is sad, because everything that God has promised has already been made available to us in the spirit; we just need to access it by faith. The time is past due for us to begin to seize the gifts and treasures of God. It starts with our decision.

I often pray this prayer, "God use me as a vessel sanctified and fit for the Master's use. Take me to the potter's house and mold me, make me, fill me, Lord, then use me for your glory, Lord, make me over again, amen."

The hidden treasure on the inside, the one that sticks closer than a brother that the scripture declares, is the Lord Jesus Christ. Learn to lean on him in those desperate, dark, and dismal days when you can't see him, activate your faith by hearing or speaking the word; it will avail for you. You may ask, "Well, how can I increase my faith?" You saturate your soul with the word, whether by radio, music, watching a gospel program on television, lying in bed with a sermon in your ear, talking to a seasoned saint, attending a service, revival, conference, or just pure fellowship with the word. I believe the most valuable thing, you can do, is to find someone to witness to, even if you are experiencing a dry or difficult phase in your Christian walk. Surely, this will bring you out in time, as you are consistent, determined, diligent, and faithful about getting a hold of God. Make it a priority and watch God work on your behalf and deliver you sooner than you expected. It's Christ in you the hope of glory.

CHAPTER EIGHT

GAINING LIBERTY

One of the most amazing things I am experiencing in this season of acceptance is the liberty I have gained. Yes, there are challenging moments, but the benefit of being able to mobilize myself with my cane is gratifying.

I have learned to trust the *Spirit* more than I trust myself or even others. For example, someone would say "step down"; and without fail, my perception and theirs are never the same timing, so I have learned to take my time and feel for the edge and not allow myself to be rushed or be embarrassed that others are watching me, as I shuffle to the curb or edge of the stairs. It is certainly a humbling experience.

That is when I set my mind on the good things and realize how sensitive I am to my feelings, fears, frustrations, and my surroundings. In fact, it seems like throughout the day, I get these "rushes of my emotions" that bombard my mind; and because I am aware of them, I, instantly and mentally, am able to go through the process of elimination. Would you rather fall down the stairs? or be watched? Would you risk spilling something or allow someone to fetch the drink for you; or yet, bring your meal for you? I am in control of what change I will allow in my emotional atmosphere, that could alter my peace. There are so many choices to make; yet, with all of the struggles, I remind myself that, I can do everything God asks me to do; with the help of Christ who strengthens me with power and might.

I allow God to use every opportunity for his glory, and I draw my strength from him. In every incident, he gives me great courage and confidence to go on.

In the book of Psalms there is a passage that says, "With your help I can advance against a troop; with my God I can scale a wall." Psalm 18:28 It is God who arms me with strength and makes my way perfect. So whenever I step up by faith, it's almost as though I hear him say, "Great job, my child, take heart."

I have overcome walking into the grocery store or the bank and becoming apprehensive because everyone stares at me as though I was a freak; also to have someone say to me, "You don't need your cane just hold on to me." With boldness and without hesitation, I now reply, "I would rather hold my cane." I have had people grab me by my clothes when crossing the streets or hold my hand as though I was a child; now this gets me.

Something rises in me when this happens, something I thought I couldn't control. Thanks to the *cane*, I feel more secure.

Thanks to my instructor Dupree, he would say, "Your cane is an extension of your fingers; would you leave your fingers at home?" "No, sir!" We are always admonished by the scriptures not to fear; fear has torment. The devil would love to torment my mind keep me from advancing in the kingdom, and from pursuing and seizing the treasures for, God: but they are mine! I can have as much of God I want; and whenever I want. He will not withhold any good thing from me.

The devil's plan is for me to accept his lies and suffer defeat, but as someone has said, "Learn how to hit the Delete button"; totally eradicate his lies from your thoughts. Exodus 5:9 says, in a paraphrased manner, that the enemy intends to load your mind with worries, he wants revenge, he wants to wear you out and beat you down. But thanks be unto God who gives me the victory and causes me to triumph in every place and on every occasion, as what 2 Corinthian 2:14 is about; he knows those whose trust is in him.

Conclusion

Psalm 28:7 defines exactly what I feel, he is my strength, my shield from every danger. I trust in him and he helps me. Joy rises in my heart until I burst out with songs of praises to him."

The End

POST WORD

To my amazement, after thinking I had concluded this book, I was reminded, life experiences never do, so the book goes on. If I could entitle this chapter it would be "What others Need to Know."

Psalm 67:1-7 has become a deep thought for me to ponder upon, its message. A passion for others to know the Savior I know. Selah! Which means stop and think about this, savor this, ponder, let this be instilled in you and (marinate) in your mind.

I hear a prayer and a plea for more of the mercy and blessings of God to be upon us and for him to shine his face upon us; that *his* ways and saving health may be seen upon the earth and among the nations. When we understand that it matters not about us, but the *multitudes*; the people. They need to see God in us and praise Him. The righteous will be glad and exceedingly joyous before the Lord.

And the Lord shall bless us and cause the earth to yield such an increase that will cause the earth to fear him. The other day I heard a young man utter a very profound statement that confirmed a word the Lord had given me earlier. He said in essence, "Our lives need to be windows for others to look through; our lives should be more than just mirrors of reflection, since mirrors reflect the image, but windows expose and facilitate view of the contents."

Just a few days earlier during my time of devotion, God began to show me that I needed to enlarge the curtains of my tent. I realized that I needed a bigger window in my life. So those words were refreshing to me, to know God was speaking a word in season that my vision (window) was too small.

Know that as believers, we are the *carriers* of his power and glory as well as an extension of him on this earth. And it is not for us to hoard His blessings/(word) for ourselves alone, but to spread throughout the earth, (we all have been given a word to make a deposit in the earth). What an awesome, though!

Recently I traveled overseas to Costa Rica, and it certainly enhanced my passion and vision to see the lost saved. The Lord spoke to me in my spirit, "Remember your assignment." As I revisited my mission statement, I discovered that from the very beginning my goal and purpose was "To see the lost saved and believers walking in their calling." It was not to focus on healings, miracles, or even mass salvation; these things will come, but to remain steadfast, sensitive, and available to the *Master*. I was made aware that the same Spirit, diverse gifts, callings, and administrations (offices or functions) were granted to us as believers. Again, it's for others and not for us to keep.

The Lord began to speak to me about the time and seasons; and that these were the days of *restoration* and *reconciliation* of his people. God has promised us the rain, the former and the latter rain pouring down on the earth and on the lives of the people for a harvest. The church needs a visitation from the Lord know that everything changes with his presence. Lately, I have been praying for the glory and power of God to fall upon the church like it has never fallen before. "Lord, we need a right-now visitation on your church, a right-now revival in the church".

Prayer: Father, today the church needs you. Come now, your church needs you. Send your spirit; send your blessing to the world. Rain down on us now, in Jesus's name, amen!

While meditating on the word and on the mandate, there was an uproar on my front porch. It seemed as though a large dog from the neighborhood had illegally made his way on my porch and attacked the cat that decided to live there. Suddenly there was a scuffling, and howling that of a dog, and meowing going on. I could hear the cat mostly so I ran frantically to the window and began to tap on the glass. Then I ran to the front door to find the dog had scurried away, and the cat was hiding under my husband's van. As my grandson examined the site of the incident, he found a large ball of tan fur from the dog on the porch where the fight took place. I began to smile as the Lord was speaking to me. There was a fight, but the cat surely left her prints; the evidence of victory! She may have suffered some injuries inflicted by the dog, but she also got even; with a few grazes, she got her some fur.

You see, this way of salvation is a constant fight; and we must fight to remain saved, to maintain our integrity, poise and position if we are going to go to the next level in this fi nal hour. Satan certainly has plans for the church, but we must be willing to put up a fight and not just lie down, taking all he has to infl ict on us; after all, we have the victory, and we are more than conquerors. Do you know what that means? It means since God the creator, the Almighty is on our side, there remains not one able to stand up to us and win. So let's move on from being confessors to becoming possessors.

The lesson is that the enemy may come after us as a big bully; but don't just squeal, get you some fur and remember, *help* is on the way.

As we contend for the souls of our relatives, love ones, and friends, in the process we may suffer, be wounded, disappointments, hardships, grief, and pains, but get yourself some fur! Let the devil know whose property he is trespassing on, Just know there are *angels* on assignment coming to rescue you.

Traveling to the mission fi eld this time, has taught me to maintain my focus. Know, I am not working for God, but rather working with him. Know that I can do everything God has asked me to in Christ Jesus. Know with assurance that he goes before me. I Never get too close but maintain my distance, keeping in clear view the Captain of the host ahead.

This same principle works in my daily life. Whenever I follow others while they guide me down a stair or across the street, I often remind them as they wait for me, "I must maintain a certain distance as I follow you; I need space to keep you in view. I cannot follow too close or run into you, consequently I will be on your heels." Likewise, I don't want to run up on God, consequently I could miss his leading.

I am extending special thanks to the publishing staff at Xlibris who has all been so patient and professional with their services, their support, and encouragement. I greatly appreciate you all, and God bless you!

To contact the author:
    Evangelist Regina Thomas
    Restorative Hope Ministry Inc. and
    The Panama Mission Campaign
    Tel. 803-787-3615 803-586-6285

Email:
treginapma@aol.com
http://www.webspawner.com/users'treginapma/
http://www.webspawner.com/panamacampaign

Soon Available new book Spanish Version of Walking by Faith Swaddled in His Glory.

"Caminando Por Fe Fajado en Su Gloria"